Working the Story

Working the Story

A Guide to Reporting and News Writing for Journalists and Public Relations Professionals

Douglas Perret Starr and
Deborah Williams Dunsford

ROWMAN & LITTLEFIELD
Lanham • Boulder • New York • Toronto • Plymouth, UK

4/12/16
ww
$ 39.00

Published by Rowman & Littlefield
4501 Forbes Boulevard, Suite 200, Lanham, Maryland 20706
www.rowman.com

10 Thornbury Road, Plymouth PL6 7PP, United Kingdom

British Library Cataloguing in Publication Information Available

Library of Congress Cataloging-in-Publication Data
Starr, Douglas Perret.
  Working the story : a guide to reporting and news writing for journalists and public relations professionals / Douglas Perret Starr and Deborah Williams Dunsford.
    pages cm
  Includes bibliographical references and index.
  ISBN 978-0-8108-8910-1 (cloth : alk. paper) — ISBN 978-0-8108-8911-8 (pbk. : alk. paper) — ISBN 978-0-8108-8912-5 (electronic) 1. Journalism—Authorship. 2. Reporters and reporting. 3. Report writing. 4. Public relations—Authorship. I. Dunsford, Deborah Williams, 1956– II. Title.
  PN4775.S685 2014
  070.4'3—dc23
                                                            2013044396

Printed in the United States of America

In memory of
Carolyn Scanlon McLendon
15 July 1931–24 October 2013

Your Authority to Speak and to Report

Here is all the authority any citizen or resident of or visitor to the United States needs to speak or report on any topic. It is a constitutional right stated in and protected by The Bill of Rights, Amendment I, ratified 15 December 1791.

> Congress shall make no law respecting an establishment of religion, or prohibiting the free exercise thereof; or *abridging the freedom of speech, or of the press;* or the right of the people peaceably to assemble, and to petition the Government for a redress of grievances.

Contents

Introduction

This book is a keeper; it is both a teaching book and a reference book. As such, it will last you your entire career.

It will teach you how to be a writer—a writer of news and of public relations news releases. And it will be a source of a lot of fun, because, although writing is the hardest work that you can imagine, reporting is the most fun.

It's the most fun because no day's work is the same as any other day's work. You meet different people: professional people, politicians, government officials, generals and admirals, police officers and sheriff's deputies, firefighters, educators, blue-collar workers, ordinary people—the list is endless. You attend criminal and civil trials, meetings, banquets, celebrations of all sorts; you go on police raids and crime investigations. Wherever news happens, you are there.

And it's the hardest work that you can imagine because you have to write about what you saw and heard, and writing is the most difficult task you can undertake. Writing is so difficult that those who do write cannot imagine how anyone can love to write. The demands are too great. Writers, reporters, do not just put words together; they craft them into compelling sentences that flow rhythmically into paragraphs and stories. They not only write, they rewrite, a dozen times, sometimes more, hardly a lovable task.

But reporters do write and rewrite because they must, because they appreciate the demands of fine writing, of communicating. They write for people of average intelligence and education who read newspapers, magazines, and the Internet and who listen to radio and watch television. And reporters write under the incredible pressure of daily, hourly, and immediate deadlines.

The major requirement for writing news is *objectivity*, because reporters are just that, *reporters*, people who *report*, who tell what they saw and heard, without comment. On the job, reporters are *in* the world, but not *of* the world. Objectivity in reporting is required because the readers vary by levels of social, economic, religious, educational, political, and cultural beliefs and lifestyles, and because opinion belongs on the editorial pages.

Thus, reporting and writing news has characteristics different from writing essays and compositions in English class. The essay in English class begins at the beginning, progresses through the story more or less chronologically, and concludes; it's a sort of "once-upon-a-time . . . and-they-lived-happily-ever-after" affair.

Not so the basic news story. The basic news story tells the whole story in the first one or two sentences and provides details in descending order of importance. The ending is a period after the last, least significant detail. The basic news story has no ending, no conclusion at the end because the conclusion of the news event is the essence of the news story and is stated in the first one or two sentences.

The reporter must have sufficient knowledge to be able to secure all of the information needed for writing the story accurately, objectively, tersely, and concisely, and with attention to grammar, punctuation, spelling, word use, syntax, and sentence rhythm. The news story gets to the point, quickly, with a minimum of words and as accurately and as objectively as possible.

Given all of those requirements, this book has a double benefit. It describes and explains the workings of the news event you are reporting on—government, taxation, business, education, crime and the courts, and such groups as the legislature and the city council—and describes and explains how to gather the news and to write it in the simple but effective news story format.

True, you learn a lot of that in high school and, later, in college, but, with the pressures of living, you may have forgotten some of the details, some of the nuances of how various facets of government or business or universities or hospitals function. Moreover, you probably never were taught how to apply to government in real life what you learned about government in high school and college. Understanding what you are covering and writing accurately and objectively about it form the basis of this book.

The descriptions of those facets of life and the suggestions for gathering information and writing the news story are based in observation, study, and action. All of it was honed by an intense and happy career in reporting and writing news for The Associated Press in three states, of working in public relations in two states, in teaching both the reporting of news and the techniques of fine writing in three universities, and in a lifetime of reading.

The suggestions for grammar, punctuation, syntax, and definition and usage of words are based upon what is taught in the fifth, sixth, and seventh grades, upon what is described in *Webster's New World College Dictionary*, 4th ed., and *The Associated Press Stylebook and Briefing on Media Law*, and upon what is supported by logic.

Do not let the simplicity of the suggestions and directions mislead you; they are designed to be simple, and they work. If you follow them, you will succeed.

None of this should frighten you. If you are a true reporter or a true public relations professional, that frisson you feel at the back of your neck is not fear; it is a tingle of excitement at the prospects of what a your career proffers. The work is hard, the workdays are long, and the salary is only livable, but the intangible rewards are heady; what you are doing puts you on the cutting edge of history.

You may change your mind about loving to write, but you will never regret being a writer.

1

What News Is and Why It's Important

> The fundamental freedom of a free society is a free press—all other freedoms follow.
>
> —Christine Wells, 1993

News is the story of people. News is what is current, is what affects the most people in the strongest way, is what is most important. News is an accurate, objective report of what happened.

News is every birth and marriage and death, every activity of business and industry and government, every crime and trial and punishment, every advance in medicine and science and technology, every war and battle and peace, every hurricane and tornado and forest fire, every blizzard and flood and drought, every traffic accident, every convention, every speech; in short, news is every thing that people do or say or are involved in, everywhere, every day.

Thus, each day's collection of news is a chapter of history in the making, a first draft to be polished by historians.

With all that, news is relative; the importance of any news story lies in its time and place, in the importance of the person or the event, and in proportion to the other news stories of the day. News is of various levels of importance and interest according to the extent of influence of the people involved or to the range of effects of the news event.

A multistate flood that kills and injures hundreds of people and paralyzes business, industry, and farming for weeks is of greater interest than a flood in a small town that causes no death or injury and no disruption of business or industry or agriculture.

The death of an ordinary citizen at home is of greater interest than the death of an ordinary citizen of another state. But the death of a leader—a police chief, a mayor, a sheriff, a governor, a president—has a greater impact upon citizens of the region or state or nation and, therefore, is of greater and broader interest.

A speech by the president of the United States is of more widespread interest and of greater importance than a speech by a mayor.

The assassination of a president, a terrorist attack that destroys a building and kills thousands of people overshadows and all but eliminates any other news story for three or four days.

Nevertheless, each day's collection of news in every city and state in the world is of importance and impact upon the region and the people who live there. It is a chapter of history well worth the writing.

And the reading.

News is provided by educated, trained, and professional reporters whose stories are reviewed and approved by a crew of educated, trained, and professional editors and copyeditors to ensure accuracy, objectivity, and factual information. And news does not come from blogs, Facebook, Twitter, letters to the editor, or the like, because those are the writer's opinion, many times unsubstantiated. News is in newspapers and news magazines, on television and radio, and on a news medium's Internet Website. What this means is that you, as a reporter, will write news stories in two formats: for reading in newspapers and on the Internet and for listening on the radio or watching television.

And all of that will be news, and you want to go into the news business.

You could be a reporter. Or you could be a public relations professional. They both have similar requirements for the job. So, congratulations; either way, you've made an excellent choice, because they put you on the front line. But, both are tough jobs, demanding jobs, worthwhile jobs, so be ready to do a lot of studying and a lot of work. Fortunately, you're in the right place to begin, because here is where you will learn the basics—what is news and how to find it, and how to write clearly, concisely, tersely, objectively, and interestingly.

You're going to have to know a lot, but don't worry, your years in school so far should have given you the basics needed in either career: an awareness of how national, state, and city government work; of the history of your home state and of the United States and how it all came to be, and of the world; of geography; of science (biology, chemistry, physics, and so on); of mathematics; of, well, all those other courses you weren't sure about but enrolled in anyway. You will use it all, because in reporting, you have to know as much as possible about everything.

Here is why reporting—a free press—is so important.

Life, liberty, and the pursuit of happiness in the United States, as we know it, is in constant jeopardy, and so is the free press, which is guaranteed and protected by the First Amendment in The Bill of Rights.

Guaranteed and protected so far.

Throughout the United States, newspapers are reducing in size—smaller pages, fewer pages, less advertising, smaller news hole—and reduced staff, including fewer reporters.

The reduction of advertising results from the loss of subscribers and the demise of many businesses because of the failing economy. But advertising also dropped because the Internet carries newspaper news that is accessible easily and either free or low cost.

As a result, many newspapers have gone bankrupt; several others—among them, major newspapers—have warned that if revenue continues to drop, they, too, will declare bankruptcy. Some newspapers have given up their paper newspaper and publish online only.

Some have suggested that the federal government bail out the newspaper industry. But, if that happens, even with a promise of no federal control, the government will control not only newspapers but also every other news medium—radio, television, Internet, and whatever else the mind can invent.

There is no question; when the government puts money into any business, the government has control of that business—maybe not full control, but any control of the news media violates the First Amendment: "Congress shall make no law . . . abridging the freedom of speech, or of the press."

When dictators take over a nation, they need to have control of the people, so the first thing they do is take control of the news media to publicize their message of a better life under their leadership. Next, to solidify their control, incoming dictators take control of religion and schools. The result is that people fall in line because, short of armed rebellion, it is the only thing that they can do.

In the United States, the government already controls schools, but not religion, which also is protected by the First Amendment: "Congress shall make no law respecting an establishment of religion, or prohibiting the free exercise thereof."

But, if the government had control of speech and the press, taking control of religion would be easy.

The United States as we know it would disappear; it would no longer be a nation of life, liberty, and the pursuit of happiness. Freedom would disappear; The Bill of Rights would be meaningless because there would be no freedom of anything—speech, press, religion, and rights to a grand jury, a jury trial, assembly, petitioning the government, bearing arms, and protection from search and seizure.

All that would happen because there would be no one to keep an eye on the government and to tell the people what the government was doing and planning to do.

What it all comes down to is this: The future of the United States is up to the news media and to us. We need each other to keep the United States free and strong. So, the career you are preparing for will help ensure that the United States remains a government of the people, by the people, and for the people.

2

Your Freedoms and How They Are Protected

A free press is one of the enduring strengths of America.

—Tom Brokaw, 1984

In any country, the press protects and empowers the government, whether it be a dictatorship or a democracy. In a dictatorship, the government is one person, and that one person directs what the news media report and what people can say. In a democracy, as in the United States, the government is the people, all the people, and the U.S. Constitution gives the people a powerful tool to protect speech and dissemination of news.

You have freedoms that no other country in the world has, and you have those freedoms because of a 45-word sentence in The Bill of Rights, 10 amendments to the United States Constitution. Forty-five words! Imagine. It's the most important sentence ever written. It guarantees everyone in the United States, citizen or visitor, freedoms that people in other nations wish they had. It was written in the 1700s and ratified by the 13 Colonies in 1791, making it the law of the United States.

So, here is the First Amendment; read it and never forget it.

Congress shall make no law respecting an establishment of religion, or prohibiting the free exercise thereof; or abridging the freedom of speech, or of the press; or the right of the people peaceably to assemble, and to petition the Government for a redress of grievances.

Here is what the First Amendment guarantees you:

- It forbids the government to establish a national religion that you must adopt.
- It forbids the government to prevent you from choosing your own religion or choosing no religion at all.
- It guarantees you freedom of speech, so you can talk about the government or whatever you wish.
- It guarantees you freedom of the press, so the news media can print and broadcast news about the government and about anything else.
- And, to ensure equal protection under the law for all, it guarantees you the freedom to assemble for whatever purpose, and it guarantees you the freedom to petition the government if you have a problem.
- Most important of all, the First Amendment guarantees that you can use those freedoms without fear that the government will arrest you or punish you.

Caution—You are always responsible for what you say or do. If what you say or do causes harm to someone or damages someone's reputation, the laws of libel or forbidding invasion of privacy may require you to pay for that harm or those damages.

Nine other amendments are in The Bill of Rights, all designed to give the people the power they need to make the nation work, and to provide and protect your rights and freedoms in specific situations. You should read those 10 amendments in The Bill of Rights. Here are your rights and protections under the remaining nine amendments:

The Second Amendment does not give you the right to own a gun; it protects your right not only to own but also to carry a weapon.

In the United States, you may own a gun and keep it in your home or vehicle and carry it in public, but the only way you can carry it concealed in public is with a state license, usually after a series of lectures and demonstrations to ensure that you understand safety factors and that you know how to fire the weapon. In 1930s Germany, the Nazi government required all citizens who owned guns to register them with the government. When Hitler became führer, he confiscated all the guns because he knew who owned them and where they were housed.

The Third Amendment forbids quartering troops in your home without your permission.

In olden times, and in some countries today, when the army was sent to a town or city where there was no camp, the general simply sent the soldiers to various houses where they took over the house and forced the families to provide meals and lodging.

———

The Fourth Amendment forbids unreasonable search and seizure of you or of your home or property.

For law enforcement officers to arrest you and to search your home or property, they must have a valid reason and a warrant issued by a judge. In many countries, law enforcement officers need no reason; they simply take a citizen to jail or ransack the home.

———

The Fifth Amendment forbids putting you on trial without a Grand Jury indictment; forbids requiring you to testify against yourself; forbids putting you on trial a second time for the same offense; and forbids taking your property for public use without paying for it.

In many countries, property is confiscated, and people are put on trial at the whim of the government, many times on made-up charges. Accused people are forced to testify against themselves. If they refuse, they are tortured until they agree.

———

The Sixth Amendment guarantees that you be told of the criminal charge against you, that you have a speedy public trial by a jury, that you may confront witnesses against you, and that you have an attorney.

In many countries, prisoners awaiting trial may languish in jail for months without being told the charge, and, when they do go on trial, they have no access to a defense attorney.

———

The Seventh Amendment guarantees you a trial by jury in common-law suits.

Common law is the rules of behavior brought from England and established by judges ruling in cases. Most common-law requirements have been enacted into written law. Louisiana, the only state without common law, bases its laws upon the written Napoleonic Code. Common-law cases are tried in civil (chancery) court where the punishment is a fine or remuneration for damages. In many countries, common-law trials are conducted by a judge only, putting the defense in a difficult position.

The Eighth Amendment forbids requiring excessive bail, excessive fines, and cruel and unusual punishment.

Many countries do not permit bail, and many countries have no limits to the amount of fines or the type of punishment, including torture.

The Ninth Amendment guarantees that the Constitution shall not deny you your rights.

This protects you from the courts' denying you your rights in the Constitution. Cases under the Ninth Amendment are handled by the U.S. Supreme Court.

The Tenth Amendment guarantees that the government will not interfere with your rights and with the rights already held by the people.

This protects your civil rights.

All of those freedoms and protections depend upon freedom of speech and of the press. Without freedom of speech and of the press, liberty and democracy cannot survive. People need to know what their government is doing. So the news media, the press—newspapers in the early days—provided the information. Now, the only thing about dissemination of news that has changed is how news is disseminated, and there have been many changes and additions: radio, television, the Internet, blogs, and by thousands of people who use those media to seek an improved nation.

In the late 1920s, radio became a news medium; in the late 1940s, television; in the 1970s, the computer with the Internet and the World Wide Web.

The first computers filled a room. Eventually smaller versions came into being, desktops, then laptops, then pods and pads. Today, reporters—they are called *backpack reporters*—carry every tool they need: a cell phone, a laptop computer, a digital camera, and a voice recorder. There is no need for reporters to report to the newsroom. Because of the Internet, the reporter files the story, the photos, and the voice to the newsroom by wireless. Even the reporter's paycheck is direct-deposited to the bank.

All of those things are tools, machinery to disseminate news. But what is news? Where does news come from? How do the news media get news? Well, that's also what this book is about. It's the reporters who get the news, who go after the story, who ask the right questions, and who write what they were told and what they saw, and don't insert their opinion into the story.

So, if you are really interested in protecting and preserving life, liberty, and the pursuit of happiness in the United States, news reporting is the career you want. The United States and the people may not thank you, but they will benefit.

As has been said, "If you want to make money, choose almost any field; if you want to make a difference, choose reporting."

3

How to Gather Information

If you're concerned about how to gather information for news stories, take heart; here are some suggestions.

Gathering information for a news story is done in several ways: through interviews with one or more newsmakers, during news conferences, reading publications both on paper and online, and by observation. In seeking information for a single story, the reporter may use one or more sources of information. There is no rule for how many sources or methods of research are used. It is a judgment call by the reporter.

Covering a Beat

Covering a beat is part of news reporting. Most reporters are assigned a beat, the offices that you must cover for news daily or a few days a week. Covering a beat is not all that difficult; it just requires persistence. Here's how to make it easy on yourself.

Have a business card with your name, title, and business address, your office and personal telephone numbers, your personal email address, and your blog address.

Learn the name and title of every administrative officer and secretary, including the public relations official, on your beat. As you make your rounds on a search for news, leave with each person—officer and secretary—your business card and tell each that you are available and would welcome a call at any hour on any day. And when telephone calls come in while you're asleep, answer them and thank the caller for calling. They are not calling you; they are calling your news medium, and you answered the telephone.

Go a step further: get to know the secretary, make small talk with the secretary, smile. If it's a woman, compliment her outfit, her hairstyle, whatever; take her a flower on Secretary's Day. If it's a man, talk about something manly—sports, hunting, fishing, whatever—take him something small on Secretary's Day. If you're ill at ease with initiating conversation with a woman, ask a woman for help, but ask a woman in your own office. If politics or religion comes up, do not state your opinion; those topics are personal.

As you progress on your beat, you will learn that the secretary knows a great deal about what is going on in the office; after all, the secretary is at the Chief Executive Officer's (CEO) right hand. It won't happen at first, but, as the secretaries get to know you, they will be more forthcoming about what's going on in the company or in the agency.

A secretary will give you a tip on what to ask the CEO, so when you interview the CEO—and this is vital—do not mention the fact that the secretary gave you the tip, and, in your story, never reveal that the secretary was your source. If it gets out that the secretary was your source, you will never get any information from any secretary. Secretaries have a grapevine for spreading information on such matters.

Remember this: The CEO, not the secretary, is the authoritative source of information.

Learn to Listen

Learn to listen, because reporters, by education and training, must be great listeners, must listen more than they speak. It is a requirement of the job. It is interesting, too, to note that reporters tend not to interrupt. They get more news that way.

To gather information, you should know how to listen, how to ask questions, how to determine what questions to ask, how to handle accusations of misquoting your source, where to find information in publications and on Websites, and how to control an interview.

In addition, if you know your rights as a citizen, particularly your rights in the First Amendment, all of these information-gathering techniques will be easier. Be aware that everyone has the right to ask anyone any question, but no one is required to reply.

How to Listen

How to listen is easy to learn. Listening and hearing are not the same. Listening requires a conscious effort to pay attention to what is heard. Hearing is simply awareness of sound. The sounds penetrate your subconscious mind but not your conscious mind, because your ears are collecting sound, and your auditory nerves are carrying the messages to your brain, but your brain is not paying attention. Later, however, you may remember them.

This situation is quite common during sleep, when your ears and auditory nerves function normally but your brain is not processing the information consciously. Only when the sound becomes persistent or loud—an alarm clock or telephone—or personal—the cry of a child—does your brain take over, and you become alert and listen.

Similarly, in a class lecture or in a board meeting, you may hear the lecture or the discussion, but you may not be listening to what is being said. Until, of course, you realize that you have missed some important information.

How to Conduct an Interview

Conducting an interview is not difficult, but it is essential in reporting. All reporting is based upon observing, listening, and interviewing. Every time you visit the scene of an accident or a crime or a disaster, every time you attend a speaking situation or a meeting, you are observing and listening. Every time you talk with an accident victim, a witness to a crime, a citizen caught in a disaster, or a public official, you are interviewing. Depending upon the situation, some interviews are informal, and some are formal. The great majority of the people you will interview will be people in the public domain, people who talk to the news media frequently, people who know and understand the value of the interview for their own benefit, people who appreciate and welcome the interview. Only on very few occasions will you ever interview someone who never has been interviewed.

Thus, the task of interviewing is more frightening for the beginning reporter than it need be, probably for fear of the unknown or fear of not doing a proper job. Do not worry about either situation. The experienced interview subject will help you; the inexperienced interview subject won't recognize your deficiencies.

In reality, an interview is little more than a conversation between two people, one of whom—the reporter—has to remember in detail what was said and done. There is nothing magic about interviewing. There is no specific way to approach the task, nor any specific way to formulate questions. Each interview situation is unique; each determines its own approach. Nevertheless, some guidelines for interviewing have been formulated, and they should be observed. These guidelines can be divided into three general categories: before the interview, during the interview, and after the interview.

What to Do Before the Interview

Before you go on any interview assignment, you must prepare for it. Decide what kind of story you are going to write, what you need to know, and what and who are the best sources of information about that topic. You need to know what makes your interview subject an authoritative source of information. Most of that is available from reference works or from people who know or work with your interview subject. If you can't find information, you may have to ask the interview subject.

Develop a list of questions that cover your topic. If possible, avoid yes-or-no questions; design your questions to produce a detailed reply. However, if you do ask a yes-or-no question, follow up with a request for elaboration: "How?" "Why?" and "Would you explain that?"

You must write your questions in a notebook lest you forget some, or if interview replies lead you along other paths. A reporter's notebook (8 inches tall, 4 inches wide, and spiral bound at the top) makes an excellent place to write your questions. It opens flat to provide a firm base for writing. Although everyone has a different style of note taking, try writing your questions on the backs of the pages and the replies on the fronts.

If you have difficulty formulating questions, remember that a story about an individual or organization involves the W's, so begin with them. Ask about the Who of the story; about What the Who Did or Said and To Whom; about When and Where it was done or said; about How it was done; and, most important, Why it was done or said.

Remember to ask about the background, about what led to the present situation, and about what is coming next. And don't forget to ask what it all means to people. Ask about problems overcome and problems expected and how they were or are expected to be overcome.

If you do not understand what was said, ask for an explanation. If you do not understand it, you cannot explain it in your story.

To record the information during the interview, take with you and use your reporter's notebook containing your written questions and several pens or pencils. If you wish, take a voice recorder that will record 45 to 60 minutes. Make sure that the batteries are fresh and that you have a line cord to plug into a wall socket.

To help guard against depressing the wrong switches on the voice recorder, record music at the beginning; that way, you know that the recorder is working. That way, if, during the interview, you depress only the play switch instead of the play and the record switches, the music will alert you, and you can set the recorder properly.

For the interview, dress appropriately: for the business world, jacket and tie for men, jacket and skirt for women; for the field, casual wear, including pants for women, and appropriate footwear.

Arrive at the interview site 15 minutes early. This will enable you to review your questions and the information you have on your interview subject and prepare you for the interview. Moreover, an early arrival will make a favorable impression upon your interview subject and might gain you a few extra minutes of interview time.

Interview Site

The interview site that is most effective is where both you and your interview subject are most comfortable with each other and with the interview, and where there will be the least amount of interruption. The ultimate choice of interview site depends on your needs and those of your interview subject and on the demands of the situation. You have several options for an interview site:

- Your office or home, where you will have full power.
- Your interview subject's office or home, where your interview subject will have full power, but you will also be able to observe the interview subject at ease, in the interview subject's own environment.
- A neutral site—hotel lobby, park bench, restaurant—where neither of you will have full power. A restaurant is neutral, but you may feel obliged to eat. Do not. You are not there to eat or drink; you are there to ask questions and to take notes.

What to Do During the Interview

During the interview, it is essential that you show your appreciation immediately by greeting your interview subject pleasantly. If the interview is in an office, take your seat alongside the desk or in the lounge area of the office. Try not to sit across the desk from your interview subject; that connotes a confrontational image and puts all the power obviously onto your interview subject.

While making general conversation with your interview subject, take out your notebook and pen and your voice recorder matter-of-factly. You are in charge; you are in control of the interview situation, and in general, the interview subject will expect you to take notes. If possible, plug your voice recorder into a wall socket; if not, switch it to batteries and place it on the desk or table between you and your interview subject. Depress both play and record, and let the recorder run throughout the interview.

Note—Do not turn the recorder off and on between questions. Stop the voice recorder only if necessary, and don't forget to turn it on again.

When you are ready, and before you ask the first question, explain the reason for the interview.

If your interview subject objects to note-taking or to the voice recorder or to both, explain that they are necessary for accuracy, for you to capture the exact words for your story. Once into the interview, your interview subject—and you—will forget that the voice recorder is on, and you both will concentrate on the interview.

Do not worry about taking notes. You should have no trouble with that; you have been taking notes for years, in high school and in every college course you ever took. You need not take detailed notes on everything that is said, only enough to provide you the information you need. After the interview, you will remember quite a bit about the details of the interview. Of course, if your interview subject makes a statement that you want in detail, ask for a repeat. You have done that in class many times. Interview subjects are much the same as college professors.

Even though you are using a voice recorder, you should take pen-and-paper notes for safety; the recorder may malfunction. In addition, your notes will serve as an index to what is on the recorder. Whatever is halfway down your written notes, for example, is halfway along the recording. You won't have to listen to the entire recording to find the information you want.

During the interview, remember that you are a guest, so be courteous. An interview is not an adversary relationship or an interrogation. You are not there to argue; you are there to seek information through conversation, so be cheerful and friendly in your approach.

Never write personal opinions in your notes. Never doodle about what you really think of the interviewee. Do not, for example, write "lie" or "fake" or "this guy is a jerk." Your interviewee may want to look at your notes, or your notes may be subpoenaed in a libel suit and could show that you were hostile toward the interviewee, thereby indicating malice. But do note how the interview subject replies; facial expressions, gestures, or lengthy pauses may be worthy of inclusion in the story.

For best results, your first few questions in the interview should be general, to put both you and your interview subject at ease.

Above all, do not interrupt or badger your interview subject, but do insist upon truthful and apt replies. If you do not get a truthful reply, point out the facts and repeat the question. If the interview subject persists in the original reply, put both the reply and the fact in your story. Above all, do not call anyone a liar, especially in print. If you do not get an apt reply, point that out to your interview subject and ask for an appropriate response to the question.

In posing questions, avoid making a speech and avoid such meaningless, silly, and time-consuming preambles as "Let me ask you this"—that is why you are there—and "Let me ask you one more question"—the reply may lead to more questions.

As the interview subject responds to your questions, do not just note the responses, *listen* to them; pay attention to what is being said. The reply may provide you with information that leads to a different tack of questioning, one that is much better than any you had thought of. Besides, you can always return to your own questions; they are written in your reporter's notebook.

During the interview, do not smoke, do not eat, do not chew gum, do not drink. Keep your hands free and your mind attentive to the interview, without having to bother with cups, saucers, ashtrays, food, and the like. Above all, do not drink alcoholic beverages before or during the interview. That will only confuse your thinking, and confuse or irritate your interview subject.

After the interview is concluded, unplug your voice recorder *and switch it to batteries*, and ask your interview subject: "Is there anything else you would like to add? Is there anything I did not cover?" This provides a chance for the interview subject to expand on a favorite topic and makes the interview subject feel better toward you. Moreover, it might provide information that improves your story.

Do not turn off the voice recorder until you have left the interview site. You never know what information you may pick up almost as you leave, as an afterthought. Besides, it cannot hurt.

What Not to Ask

Some questions are just not asked in an interview. Do not ask how people "feel after learning" that their child was killed, that they lost the election, that their business failed, and so on. If people felt other than the way normal people feel after a tragedy, that would be news. If people's reaction to a tragedy is the same as anyone else's, that is not news. Do not ask about it. The response produces nothing newsworthy, and only makes the one asking the question appear unprofessional or worse. Moreover, such a tactic angers and upsets people.

Instead of asking how people feel about a tragedy, ask them what they did or plan to do about the tragedy. Responses to questions such as those will provide more meaningful information for a news story. This is particularly true when interviewing government officials. It is more fruitful to ask how victims can secure government assistance in their time of need or how to prevent reoccurrence of such tragedies.

If you cannot think of better questions than how people feel about this or that, you are in the wrong business.

What to Do After the Interview

After the interview, and as soon as possible, review and transcribe your handwritten notes and recording, adding to them as your memory brings more information to mind. Add details on gestures and facial expressions that affect word meanings. Write descriptions of the interview setting, the interview subject's dress and surroundings, whatever adds to the story.

If you find that you have neglected to ask certain questions or that your information is incomplete, telephone your interview subject and fill in the gaps. No one minds clarifying or completing information. Write the story as soon as possible, before the vividness of the interview fades.

If the interview is for a complex story involving such topics as science, medicine, or technology, before you publish it, consider taking a copy of your story to the interview subject to be read for factual accuracy. Some reporters consider this unprofessional, saying that it reflects adversely upon their competency and reliability. Some reporters think the interview subject will try to change their writing style or demand changes in the story. Sometimes that is true. But do not worry about it. You have the original; you do not have to make any suggested changes in writing style or to add or to delete information, but you do have an obligation to correct errors in fact.

After your story is published, it's a good idea to send a copy to your interview subject with a note of thanks. The practice of letting your subject review your story, if time permits, of course, and of sending a copy of the published version with a note of thanks makes a friend. You might need to interview that interview subject later concerning a difficult topic or to use that interview subject to help you gain entrée to a difficult news source.

Off the Record

You should never, in any circumstance, use the words *off the record* or *just between us*. Assume that everything said during an interview—from arrival to departure—is on the record. That is why you are there, to get information on the record, information to use in your story.

If your interview subject offers to give information off the record, explain that you cannot use off-the-record information and ask that the request be reconsidered. If your interview subject will not reconsider, ask if you can have the information for publication but not for attribution to your interview subject. If your interview subject will not permit that, you must decide whether you want the information enough to take it off the record, knowing that you are honor-bound not to use it.

> **Caution**—Once you agree to an off-the-record statement, either by word or by sign or by silence, you are honor-bound never to reveal that information. You are not only silenced, you are barred from seeking that information from another source.

If, however, without your having sought it, you do get that information from another source, you may use it. But first, you must explain the circumstances to your first interview subject, the one who put you off the record. This gives you an opportunity to assure your first interview subject that you did not violate any confidence, and it gives your first interview subject an opportunity to be the attributed source.

If, during the interview, your interview subject asks you to place off the record a statement made earlier when both of you assumed it was on the record, you are not obliged to grant that request. Once on the record, always on the record. You must explain that. Nevertheless, sometimes agreeing to put some information off the record may be of advantage to you. As a result of your agreement, your interview subject may open up on other matters. Do not be adamant about what is on and what is off the record; weigh the advantages against the disadvantages. It may be that the information your interview subject wants off the record is of little or no value to your story. Putting it off the record may do you no damage, and it almost certainly will make your interview subject beholden to you.

Misquote

Sometimes, your interview subject will cry *misquote* after reading your published story. This should not happen, but, if you are accused of misquoting your interview subject, check your notes and your recording to determine whether you did make an error. If you did make the error, you are honor bound to rectify the situation, usually through a correction or a new story.

> **Note**—If libel may be involved, act only upon the advice of your company attorney.

More often than not, however, you will not have misquoted your interview subject at all. Instead, your interview subject may find, after reading your story and reflecting upon what was said, that such a statement should not have been made. Therefore, to salvage an embarrassing situation, your interview subject cries *misquote*, seeking to shift the blame to you. In such case, ignore the whole situation. Chances are, no retraction or correction will be requested. After all, your interview subject knows it was not a misquotation. Besides, to run a retraction or correction means repeating the so-called misquoted statement, which your interview subject certainly does not want repeated. That would mean that the misquoted version would be published twice to the correct version's once. You might explain that to your interview subject.

By doing nothing, particularly by not defending yourself from an accusation of misquoting and making your interview subject appear inept, you will have made a friend, one who considers that you have done a great favor. And favors, particularly political favors, generally are repaid.

How to Develop Your Memory

You should develop a sharp memory, because, all too often in the pursuit of news, you will be in situations where observation and memory are your only aids, situations in which you are unable or unwilling—for whatever reasons—to take notes. A trained memory and acute powers of observation will offset the absence of notes. Moreover, your powers of observation will provide information about the interview subject or the surroundings that will add color and life to your story. At every opportunity, develop your skills of observation and memory, train yourself to see and hear everything and to remember what you saw and heard without the need for taking notes. Such training is the same as any other training. The more you practice, the more proficient you become.

You may have occasion only to read a letter quickly, with no time for study or taking notes; or you may have occasion only to scan a driver's license before moving on to something else. You should be able, when you have the opportunity, to reconstruct the letter and to remember the name and address of the driver. During any interview, observe the surroundings and be able to describe them without recourse to notes. In an office, what art is on the walls? What kind of furniture? Are other people present? Who are they? How are they dressed? What are they doing? Outdoors, what is the locale? Park? Street? Any street traffic? What kind? Parking lot? Woods or forest? (Not *wooded area*.) Is there a river? Any river traffic? You can go on and on. And you should.

You can practice observation in several ways, even at home. Look around the room slowly one time and, without looking again, write a description of the room, of every article of furniture and artwork in the room. Put a handful of coins on the table, study them for one minute, then cite the number of coins by denomination and what they add up to. Look at one person or several people for one minute and describe each of them: dress, color of hair, color of eyes—if you are that close—physical activity, and so on.

Each day, read parts of two books of different genres; for example, a few pages of a Western in the morning and a few pages of a spy novel in the evening. Then, try to recall in detail what you have read.

Train your listening ability by listening intently to what people are saying and reconstructing their statements without taking notes. Do the same thing at home while listening to the news on television or on radio. In casual conversation with your friends, do more listening than talking. If you must talk, do not interrupt any speaker.

Libraries and Other Sources

Although the bulk of the needed information may be gathered from a person, you may need additional information about the topic, information that is readily available in libraries and from other publications and online. You most likely will use reference works that contain important information in compiled, concise form. One of the most familiar reference works is the encyclopedia, such as *Britannica*. Many valuable reference works are available on paper and online. These include the indices to articles in periodicals (among the more useful are *Readers' Guide to Periodical Literature*, *Business Periodicals Index*, and *Social Sciences and Humanities Index*) and to articles in newspapers (*The New York Times*, *The Washington Post*, *Los Angeles Times*, *Chicago Tribune*, and *The Times* of London, are all indexed); atlases with national, state, and world maps (including National Geographic and Rand McNally editions); almanacs (perhaps the best known is *The World Almanac*); yearbooks containing facts on a variety of topics (the largest national park, the coldest location in the country, the fastest growing state); and, of course, the dictionary, preferably unabridged, but at least the collegiate edition.

Biographical information may be important to give you background on an interview subject. One place for this information is the many *Who's Who* editions. (There is even a *Who Was Who* with entries on people who are no longer living.) *Current Biography* and *Dictionary of American Biography* are among the other sources containing personal information.

Information about places, as well as people, is available in the United States Census reports, the *Statistical Abstract of the United States* and the city directory for your community. Almost every corporation has a dictionary of applicable terms. Develop a connection with the company public relations office.

These, of course, are not the only sources you might use and not the only topics you might cover. If you need help, ask the reference librarian or go to the information desk at your city, state, or public library. Here you will gain access to a wealth of information, either in hard copy or online, that will make your job easier and improve your story.

Your best sources for publications are the library and librarians. You are already familiar with your own university library and, perhaps, the public library in town. And, do not forget, you have access to any university library, public and private, while you are in school and after you graduate. After you graduate, you may not be able to check books out of school or college libraries, and few libraries of any kind will permit reference publications to be checked out, but nearly all libraries will permit you to use their documents and reference publications in the reading room and to make copies. If you do not know what you want, or where to find it, ask the librarian. Librarians are valuable sources of information.

Do not overlook the special library with its collection of publications concentrating in a specific, usually narrow, field such as agriculture, engineering, medicine, insurance, tourism, education, and law. Of necessity, such a special library is small, but its unique collection usually is complete. Special libraries include law libraries in law offices, medical libraries in hospitals, and libraries in almost every state agency. You won't be able to check books out, but you will be permitted to use the holdings in the reading room. To find these and other special libraries, ask a professional or a college professor in that field or the librarian in any library.

Every newspaper has its own library of publications and newspapers and clippings. These may be on paper or online at your workstation. This can be valuable information. It can provide background, context, or explanations.

The key to any library is the index of holdings, either a system of 3-by-5-inch cards or a computer system. If you have trouble with either, ask the librarian for help.

Another invaluable source of information is the faculty of universities. All those holding doctorates (Ph.D., Ed.D., D.Sc., and the like) are expert in their fields. Moreover, they continue to conduct research, to expand knowledge for themselves and their colleagues. Cultivate such experts. If you do not know whom to call, contact the university public information office or the office of the dean of the college; either can put you in touch with the expert you need. Because many universities require their faculty members to share their knowledge and their research findings, most faculty members are eager to cooperate with anyone seeking information in their area of expertise. It gives them a chance to provide service, one of the requirements of most universities for tenure—permanence in the job, promotion, and salary increases. Do not assume, however, that they will give you everything you need for free. Many faculty members ask to be paid for consultations. Clear up that point in advance.

Public information officers of companies, nonprofit organizations, and government agencies in the field in which you are working usually are delighted to provide information and the names of experts whom you may interview. Their job is to make their employer look good, so you must be judicious in using the information or sources they provide to ensure that bias does not creep into your stories.

News Conferences

A news conference is an interview by a group rather than by an individual. In a news conference, you are one of several reporters seeking information, seeking replies to questions. The major difference is that, though only one reporter at a time asks the question, all reporters present may use the reply.

> **Note**—In a news conference, questions and answers belong to everyone present; therefore, if you have questions about a topic that you believe is exclusive to you, save those questions for when you can schedule a private interview with the subject. Everyone is available for a private interview, even the president of the United States.

As in any situation, in a news conference, be polite. Sit up front where you can hear and where you can see facial expressions. Sometimes, in response to a question from an interviewer seated up front, the subject may speak so softly that those seated to the rear cannot hear. If you do not hear, ask for a repeat of the question and the reply.

Ask your own questions without lengthy preambles. You are not there to make speeches. As in writing, get to the point. Forget such unnecessary preambles as "Let me ask you this." Simply ask the question; that's why you're there. And never say, "Let me ask you one final question." The answer probably will lead to other questions.

Above all, listen to the reply. Sometimes, the reply will provide an opening for a question on a more newsworthy topic.

Take copious notes.

And, never mention the phrase *off the record*.

Other Sources of Information

Above all, every day, read as many newspapers and news magazines as you can. Know what your colleagues and competitors are writing about. They may have access to information that you may not have access to.

Read everything in the newspaper: page one, other hard news, editorials, columns, letters to the editor (astute public relations professionals use letters to the editor to promote their subjects), sports, living, entertainment, business, even the advertising—everything. It is all information you can use, maybe not right away, but eventually, you will find a use for the information you collect.

Citizen Journalism

Even citizen journalism may be of value. You should read appropriate blogs, short for Weblog, which is information from people who send Web messages and opinions about activities they observe or read about. These bloggers call themselves citizen journalists, because, from time to time, reporters pick up information from their blogs for their news stories. The term *citizen journalist* fits better than *citizen reporter*, because their blogs are similar to news media editorials and columns rather than to news stories.

Regardless, be careful; citizen blogs contain both factual accounts of and unsupported opinions concerning what was observed. Unsupported opinions have no place in any news story.

Basically, however, there are major differences between news reporters and citizen journalists. Reporters are educated, trained professionals who are assigned to cover and write about news events; citizen journalists are not. Reporters represent the readers/listeners who cannot attend the news event; citizen journalists do not. Reporters are trained to report what they saw and heard, omitting biases and unsupported opinions; citizen journalists are not.

Note these other differences between news reporters and citizen journalists:

- At scenes of news events, news reporters are expected and recognized by police, firefighters, paramedics, officials of government, business, and industry—the list is endless—because they have a job to do. Citizen journalists are recognized as bystanders who have no need to be present.
- Reporting is the job of the news reporter, not of the citizen journalist.
- Reporters who misuse the trust placed in them lose their jobs; citizen journalists who misuse that trust suffer no consequences.
- When a news event occurs, news reporters respond immediately, regardless of the time or the day; citizen journalists have no need to attend every news event and certainly do not attend all news events. Because the only way to cover a news event is to be there, news reporters hurry to scenes of hurricanes and tornadoes and floods, of fires,

of crimes in progress; in wars, they go on the frontline of battle; in courts, they sit through hours and days of trial testimony and write the daily account; routinely, they cover activities of government at all levels, sitting through meetings of all sorts; they dig out information about corporations and universities and associations, because it is their job to gather and write the news of the day. Citizen journalists have no such requirements.

There is another major difference between what a citizen journalist and what a news reporter posts in a blog. A citizen journalist writes a blog and puts it on the Web. A news reporter writes a blog, and, before it is published—in the newspaper, on the Web, or on radio and television—that blog, like a columnist's column, is reviewed by the city editor, the news editor, and the copyeditor, all educated, trained news professionals, to ensure absence of bias and accuracy and balance in all aspects.

Even so, news reporters should read citizen journalists' blogs, because, sometimes, they contain information pertinent to a legitimate news story.

One final point: citizen bloggers who call themselves citizen journalists base their position on the First Amendment in The Bill of Rights. They say that what they write on the Web is protected by Freedom of the Press. Can't be; bloggers are citizens, of course, but they are not journalists, and they certainly are not reporters. Even so, what they write is protected, but by Freedom of Speech, not by Freedom of the Press, because citizen journalists are not part of the Press.

4

How to Write the Basic News Story

(They taught me all I knew);
Their names are What and Why and When
And How and Where and Who.

—"The Elephant Child," by Rudyard Kipling

Writing, which combines artistry, skill, imagination, and professionalism, is the most difficult and demanding task you will ever undertake. Writing demands clarity, conciseness, terseness, and rhythm in the handling of the language. And newswriting demands objectivity in the story and, in the writing, the imagination of a dreamer, the skill of an artist, the accuracy of a mathematician, and the meter of a musician.

Writing, any kind of writing, is not easy. The entire burden of providing information to readers rests upon you, the writer. If readers do not understand your news story, the entire fault is yours; you did not make the information accurate, clear, concise, terse. And, be careful, your first reader is your editor, your CEO.

Be especially diligent in making your news story accurate, objective, and complete, all the while obeying the rules of grammar, punctuation, syntax, spelling, and word use. In addition, you must make your language flow, so that your writing does not get in the way of the information. Readers do not want to stumble over incorrectly used words or mishandled sentence structure.

Writing, as applied to news, is a misnomer. Anyone can knock out a story on the keyboard, but that is not writing, that is typing. Writing requires rewriting and revising, because that is what you do: You rewrite, you revise, as many times as you must to satisfy yourself that you cannot

25

improve the story further. There is no shame in rewriting; the shame lies in not rewriting because rewriting improves the story. Most reporters, even on deadline, rewrite their stories several times. On the way to the office, they write and rewrite the initial version of the main part of the story in their minds. At the office, they copy their story out of their minds. Old newshands call that *writing off the wall*. They type while staring at the wall, seeing the story in their mind's eye, as though "copying" the story written on the wall.

Then, they begin rewriting, revising, improving the story. Sentences are smoothed out; modifiers are relocated to their proper position; words are changed for accuracy of meaning and usage. The process is designed to produce the most information in the clearest manner and with the fewest words. And it is all done as rapidly as possible.

Writing demands a lot of the writer, but everything demanded is available to you, and you have already learned most of it. All of the demands upon the writer are there to help extract the essence of the news event, the news peg, and the reason for the news story, and to write about it in a clear, concise, terse, accurate, objective manner understandable by readers with no more than an 8th-grade reading ability.

And the greatest demand is that you never stop studying and learning your profession.

Develop an ethical sense of fairness and honesty. Be aware of the consequences that could result from the stories you write.

Develop a smooth writing style, a conversational style in which the language flows when read aloud. You can do this by reading the good writers and observing how they handle the language, and by reading aloud your own work and fixing what your ear tells you is poor.

Understand the duties and responsibilities of all levels of government and the interaction between government and business. You can do this by reading, by observing, and by asking people in those jobs.

Know the history of your city, county, and state, of the United States, and, in general, of the world. Any librarian can help you with this. Read history books and the encyclopedia.

Be able to touch-type. Eventually, you will reach amazing speeds on the keyboard if you do not have to look for the keys.

Know the rules of grammar and punctuation and syntax. Know how to use the comma, the semicolon, the colon, and the hyphen. Understand agreement between subject and predicate and between noun and pronoun. It's all in the grammar book and in dictionaries collegiate and larger. You learned most of it in the 6th grade.

Use the dictionary often. Definition and usage of words may not be what you think.

All of this may seem to be a large order, but it is essential and basic to the reporter. Others have done it. So can you. You must, if reporting, writing, is your career.

As difficult as writing is, it can be made easier if you follow a few suggestions. If these suggestions seem simple, remember, they are based not only upon the authors' education but also upon the authors' careers in news reporting and writing, in public relations writing, and in teaching reporting and writing and rewriting. These suggestions are designed to be simple, and they work. Follow them, and you will succeed.

Writing the Story

What makes easy reading is hard writing.

—Henry George

Before you can write any story, you need information, facts. Gather information from authoritative sources, people who have the knowledge and the position of trust to support what they say. In all your dealings with news sources, be polite. Say *please*, *thank you*, *sir*, and *ma'am*. Smile. People who have titles like to be addressed by their title: governor, senator, mayor, colonel, professor, doctor, Mr., Miss, Ms., Mrs. It is the professional way of gathering news.

Caution—Use staff members for tips for news stories, but never attribute any information to them; they are not authoritative sources. Only the person in charge of the office is the authoritative source to whom information may be attributed.

Take notes; ask for repeats of quotable statements; ask for clarification of information you do not understand. By the time you get out of college, taking notes and asking for clarification should be second nature to you. News sources are just like teachers; they are used to being questioned for clarification, and they are used to people taking notes.

The news story is not like the English essay, which is often told chronologically from beginning to end, a sort of "once-upon-a-time" beginning and a "they-lived-happily-ever-after" ending. For children, that approach heralds an exciting beginning to a story that, no matter what pitfalls occur, will end happily. That approach does not work with adults, because adults want to know quickly what the news is. So, the best approach is the inverted pyramid format with a summary lead. The summary lead tells the whole story in one or two terse, concise sentences and the inverted pyramid format presents details in descending order of importance. That format enables readers to know only as much of the story as they need to satisfy their curiosity.

Paragraph vs. Graf

A *paragraph* and a *graf* are different. In literature, a paragraph is a section of a narrative that contains a complete thought. In news writing, a graf is one sentence of 30 to 35 words or two sentences of a total of 30 to 35 words. There is a reason for that.

Many news stories are brief enough to be told in one literary paragraph. In a narrow newspaper column, a 100-word story would be one paragraph, 1¾ inches wide, and 3 inches deep, a formidable block of black on white for most readers. Readers want the white space of paragraph indentations.

Authors who write books and scholarly articles regard a paragraph as a punctuation mark, a symbol that indicates a complete thought or situation in the story. To achieve that, the author places in one paragraph a collection of sentences that define that thought unit, that stage in the development of the story.

That idea of a paragraph is common in every type of writing except news writing, mainly because of the simplicity of the news writing—the absence of adjectives and opinionated description—and the narrow columns in which the story is published. In news work, the paragraph is a *graf*.

In books, the printed line is 3¼ inches long in paperbacks; 4½ inches long in hardcovers. In newspapers and magazines, because column width varies, the printed line ranges from 1¼ to 1¾ inches.

For ease of reading—in books, magazines, scholarly journals, newspapers, online, wherever—printed words, sentences, and paragraphs need to be set off by white space: the first line indentation, the blank space after the period in the last sentence of each paragraph, and the white space surrounding the printed matter.

In books and scholarly journals, paragraphs can, and frequently do, run more than half-a-page deep, but, because of the width of the line and the surrounding white space of the page, such long paragraphs present little difficulty in reading.

In newspapers and online, because there is little, if any, surrounding white space, paragraphs that run more than 1 inch deep are difficult to read. For stories, on a computer screen, five lines of 6-inch-wide lines equals 1 inch in a narrow newspaper column. After each sentence or after no more than five lines of type, hit return and tab for a new sentence and a new graf. Don't be concerned if you have a graf of one word or one line of type or one short sentence; think of the additional white space that enhances reading. For online stories, after no more than five lines of type, hit return twice, once to begin a new graf and once to provide a blank space between grafs, thereby enhancing reading.

The Five Ws and the H

You already know about the five Ws and one H: the Who, What, Where, When, Why, and How of the story. But those Ws and H need to be changed in two ways:

- List their order as Who, What, Why, Where, When, and How, because that order will help you write the summary lead sentence or sentences.
- Divide What into Did What (for action stories) and Said What to Whom (for interview and speech stories). The Did What is what the Who (the person, the group, the thing) of the story did; and the Said What to Whom is a summary of what the Who said and to Whom it was said.

Much of news writing is formula writing. You can get a fine summary lead by following the revised order of the Ws and the H: Begin with the Who— the person, group, or thing you are covering; tell what the Who did in terse, concise terms; and, if appropriate, say Why the Who Did What was done. For the second sentence, follow the Where, When, and How in that order.

The following matrix will help you collect your thoughts about writing the story. Answers to the all-capitals questions—WHO, DID WHAT or SAID WHAT—must be in the lead of every story. The answer to WHY must be in the first sentence of every story about a meeting and about action by a governmental or business agency because there always is a reason for what those entities do. Answers to the capital-and-lowercased questions—to Whom, Where, When, How—should be in the first or second paragraph as appropriate.

The news event focuses on the Who and the Did What or Said What, on somebody or something doing or saying something. The Why is important because everything happens for a reason. The Where and the When of the news event are important, but secondary, because every news event occurs in a place and at a time, and the time usually is today. Most stories do not involve a How.

So, here, in detail, are the Ws and the H.

WHO

The Who of the story is the person or activity you are covering—the subject of the sentence—by name or by title. If you use the title only of a person, you must identify the person by name in the second sentence.

Do not base your lead on actions of secondary actors: people booing the speaker or a petitioner receiving or losing a petition. If such secondary actions are important, include them in the story where they belong or write them as a sidebar (hypertext on the Internet), a separate but related story.

Do not back into the story. Tell readers quickly Who did the action or said something before you tell readers Why or to Whom or Where or When or How the Who Did or Said it.

DID WHAT

The Did What of the story is what the person or thing or activity did; it is the news, the final action, the reason for the story.

SAID WHAT

The Said What of the story is a summary of the key points of what the speaker said either in an interview or in a speech. That summary is the reason for the story.

Said is the most appropriate verb for speech and interview stories because it has no hidden meanings. Other verbs—*warned, urged, called for, recommended, challenged*—may be used if appropriate.

If you write that the speaker *spoke* or *discussed* or *explained* or *spoke about* a topic, you have told readers nothing. You want a verb that tells readers not that the speaker spoke about or discussed a topic but what the speaker said about the topic. To speak is to utter words; to discuss is to present a series of arguments; to explain is to make clear what is not obvious. None of those attributive verbs tells readers anything.

To Whom

The To Whom of the story describes the setting in which the speaker made the statement: at a news conference, during an interview, in a speech at an annual convention, at a meeting, during a political campaign, and so on.

WHY

The Why of the story is the reason for what the person or thing or activity did or, if appropriate, for what the speaker said.

Where

The Where of the story is the place of the news event: city, building, private home, hotel room, school, and so on.

Note—For smooth reading, the Where of the story goes before the When.

When

The When of the story, the time element, is the day or the date (sometimes the hour as well) of the news event. The When never is so important that it should be the beginning of the news story. The news is not that "two minutes after reciting their vows, Mr. and Mrs. John Doe were killed by a drunken driver." The news is that "Mr. and Mrs. John Doe were killed by a drunken driver two minutes after reciting their vows."

How

The How of the story is not always present, but when it is, it should be placed where appropriate, in either the first or the second sentence.

After Writing the Lead

After writing the lead and before writing the rest of the story, read aloud your lead, the first one or two sentences—and listen to the flow of language. Repair any rough spots. Then, ask yourself if your lead tells the whole story. If not, rewrite before you begin writing secondary matter, the details that develop the lead.

The Body of the Story

The remaining paragraphs of the story present, in descending order of importance, the details of what the subject did or said, all properly attributed, of course.

- Paraphrase and reduce long quotations.
- Alternate paraphrases and quotations.
- Provide transitions between sentences and paragraphs for a smooth flow of information.
- If appropriate, in addition to writing what you were told, write details that you observed.

The Final Act

The final act in writing, after you finish writing the story, is to read it aloud and listen to the flow of language. Revise and correct the language as appropriate. Double-check the facts and the spelling of names.

Narrative Beginning

The narrative beginning differs from the 5-W, 1-H beginning by making the story more personal to readers, making readers relate to the news.

Not too many years ago, people subscribed to either a morning or an afternoon newspaper, sometimes to both. Radio and television news was not much competition for newspapers because the average broadcast news story is 60 to 70 words. Afternoon newspapers generally carried the same news as did the morning newspapers, but they wanted a different approach to the news story. To meet that requirement, the beginning of the afternoon version of the morning newspaper story took a futuristic approach, focusing on the next step in the news event or a new angle. At the time of afternoon newspapers, it was called second-day approach; now some refer to it as the evening edition approach, the futuristic approach, and the narrative approach.

The futuristic approach requires reporters to seek new information through follow-up interviews with the principals in the story. For example, the morning approach focused on an escape from jail, and the futuristic approach focused on the search for the escapee; the morning approach focused on a city sales tax increase, and the futuristic approach focused on what the increased revenue would be used for; the morning approach focused on the wedding of a famous person, and the futuristic approach focused on honeymoon plans; the morning approach focused on the election of a governor, and the futuristic approach focused on the new governor's initial plans for the next four years. In each case, the body of the afternoon story remained pretty much the same as that of the morning story.

At that time, all newspaper news stories began with the traditional 5-W, 1-H beginning, telling the Who, What the Who Did and Why, the Where, the When, and the How, all in 30 to 35 words. Admittedly, it was a rather stiff approach, but it was all that readers had.

Television sets began to appear in more homes, and 6 p.m. newscasts became popular. People relaxing at home after work found that watching the news on television was easier and cheaper than subscribing to a second newspaper. As the number of subscribers decreased, the afternoon newspapers began closing down. Eventually, television evening newscasts led to the elimination of most of the afternoon newspapers.

The Internet made a major change in the presentation of news, called *convergence*, causing major changes among newspapers and in reporting techniques.

Convergence describes the coexistence of the news media in a single network. Each news medium—newspaper, radio, television, news magazine—established its own Website and converged the presentation of the news in all forms—print, audio, video—and available immediately to those with electronic devices. That way, people could access the Website of any medium and read the news, listen to the news, watch a video of the news, and see photographs accompanying the news.

Those changes have four results.

The first result is that newspapers lost subscribers and advertisers and, therefore, revenue. Reduced revenue requires cost reductions, so with a continuing increase in the cost of paper and or printing, nearly all newspapers reduced the size and number of pages; some newspapers reduced the paper edition to three days a week but maintained their Websites 24/7; some newspapers used an online version only; and several newspapers went out of business.

The second result is in the presentation of the news story. Publishing the same version of a news story on the immediate Website and on the hours-old paper edition made little sense. Readers do not want to read the same story twice. The futuristic approach was moved from the afternoon newspaper to the morning newspaper. That soon fell apart, because updated versions of the original story appeared on the Website, again hours before the paper edition the next day. To keep paper subscribers, newspapers use a new approach, called the narrative approach, featurizing the beginning of the story to draw readers into the action.

The third result is that, since many newspapers own radio and television stations, their reporters write three versions of the same news story: the first in print style to be read on the Website, the second in broadcast style to be listened to on radio and television, and the third in print style in the futuristic approach, for the next day's paper edition.

The fourth result is that newspaper reporters have a new designation, *backpack reporter*, because they carry cell phones that function as digital still and video cameras, and laptop computers. Reporters no longer need return to the office to write their stories; they do it all on the scene of the story action: write stories and shoot photographs and video and transmit all of it to the office via the Internet.

Then a fifth result occurred: a change in people's reading habits. Readers no longer want the time-honored, objectively written 5-W, 1-H lead that tells the whole story in the first two sentences. They consider it too stiff, too formal, therefore less desirable. Now, readers want the news to be a story so they can empathize with the principals in the story. That's the narrative approach, an approach that featurizes the beginning of a news story and softens any harsh information that's the basis of the story.

The narrative approach invites readers into the story by using the second person to make it personal. Instead of beginning with "ten states authorized private companies to test for and issue driver's licenses," begin with "you won't stand in long lines for your driver's license beginning next month"; instead of beginning with firefighters battling a home fire, begin with a neighbor's concern as she watches the action; instead of beginning with "the City Council increased the sales tax to hire more police officers," begin with "you will pay more sales tax beginning next month, but you will have more police protection"; instead of beginning with a gasoline price increase of 35 cents, begin with its effect on your summer vacation travel.

Seek the next action of the news event:

Honeymoon trip for newlyweds—Jane and John Doe, whose wedding Tuesday attracted hundreds of friends and relatives, never thought that they would honeymoon in a Caribbean island, but they are, through the generosity of a neighbor.

Neighbor reminisces about the character of a newly dead person—Jane Roe, who died Tuesday, was a caring woman who always gave more than she received.

Begin with the past:

After two weeks of heavy losses because of bombardments, the beleaguered insurgents rallied to fight again, this time with a different battle plan.

For ease of reading both on paper and onscreen, keep these suggestions in mind as you type your story on your computer: in writing for both paper (newspapers and magazines) and onscreen, the first sentence should be no longer than 2½ lines (30 to 35 words), and no paragraph should be longer than five lines (50 words). In writing for onscreen, put a blank line between paragraphs. In a narrow newspaper column, five lines onscreen provides a graf of type no larger than 1 inch deep with white space at the indentation and after the period, the size most attractive to readers.

Here is a comparison of writing styles, 5-W, 1-H and Narrative.

5-W, 1-H—The City Council increased the sales tax from 8 percent to 9 percent effective next month to expand the police department. (21 words)

Narrative—Next month, you're going to pay more sales tax on your purchases, but you will have more police protection in residential areas around the clock.

The new tax will be 9 percent, one percentage point higher than the present tax. (40 words)

5-W, 1-H—A man, angry over his arrest for marijuana possession, used a big, noisy farm tractor to crush eight police vehicles in the parking lot behind police headquarters Tuesday. (28 words)

Narrative—Working in a quiet building with air-conditioners humming, police officers absorbed in their work didn't know what was happening in their back parking lot until a neighbor called 911.

They looked out the window and saw a man on a big, noisy farm tractor rolling over and crushing their five cruisers, two unmarked cars, and one van. (57 words)

The company magazine, too, can profit with the futuristic approach, with what is coming next. Companies have few secrets among employees. If a company signs a contract for a new product, that information is put on the company's Web page immediately, and, before the end of the day, the Web and the office grapevine have informed 85 percent of the employees. Focusing on the contract signing in the company magazine that is published months later makes dull reading.

By the time the employees and their families get the company magazine, signing the contract is old news. Employees and their families want to know what happens now. To reach those readers, the company magazine must focus on what changes and additions are being developed for producing the new product: how many and what kind of additional employees, what training will current employees need, what kind and how much different machinery, what new materials and storage facilities, what transportation equipment, and so on.

To produce such a futuristic story requires the public relations office to interview directors of the divisions involved in the changes and the additions.

In writing the story, instead of beginning with "the ABC Co. signed a $10 million contract with the U.S. Navy to produce a gizmo," begin with "the ABC Co. is hiring 45 specially trained employees and training 15 current employees to produce gizmos for the U.S. Navy under a new $20 million contract."

And don't distribute the magazine among the employees during the workday; send it to the employees' homes. That way, husbands, wives, children, and other relatives of the employees will read the story, thereby further enhancing the image of the company.

Fact Sheet

A fact sheet will help if you have difficulty determining the parts of the story you are covering. Do as public relations people do: Fill in the blanks.

- WHO—Ask yourself: "Whom (What) am I covering?" A meeting of the City Council? Write: "The City Council agreed (hired, authorized, whatever) . . ." An interview with Sen. Jane Doe? Write: "Sen. Jane Doe said (urged, called upon, denounced, whatever) . . ." Avoid the redundant "voted to agree," "voted to hire," "voted to authorize," and so on. Voting is the only way groups can do anything. The act of voting is secondary; what the vote resulted in is primary. Do not focus on secondary actors or events; they are part of the story, but not part of the lead.
- DID WHAT—Ask yourself: "What happened? What did the meeting agree upon?" "What does the senator want to happen?" Write that. This is the essence of the news story.
- WHY—Ask yourself: "What did the City Council say was the reason for the action?" "What did the senator say was the reason for what she said" (urged, called upon, denounced, whatever). Write the reason given for the action.
- SAID WHAT—Ask yourself: "What did the speaker really want the audience to do or to believe?" In general, the key information in a speech is in the conclusion. Summarize that. Avoid "in conclusion," "finally," and the like. They are unnecessary; conclusion information belongs in the lead.
- To Whom—The audience for what the speaker said: an interview, a news conference, a convention, a government meeting.
- Where—The place of the news event.
- When—The day of the week or date of the month (sometimes the hour) of the news event.
- How—The means of the news event. This is not present in all news stories. In meeting stories, the How is the vote.

The Mechanics of Writing

The mechanics of writing news—all standard in the field—apply specifically to newspapers and the Internet, and, in part, to magazines. These mechanics are time-tested and practical, and they work.

Obey the rules of grammar, punctuation, syntax, word use and spelling, subject-predicate agreement, and noun-pronoun agreement, because those rules are in common use everywhere.

Forget the English essay rule of paragraphing. It is designed for books, not newspapers and not for the Internet. The English essay paragraph comprises a topic sentence and enough sentences to complete the thought, and, in books, runs 200 or more words. But a line of type in a book measures 4¾ inches wide, twice the width of the normal newspaper and magazine line of type.

A 200-word paragraph in a book uses 16 lines of type 4¾ inches wide and 2 inches deep. In a newspaper, 200 words would use 43 lines of type 1¾ inches wide and 6 inches deep, a formidable mass of gray. On the Internet, 200 words uses 16 lines of type 2 inches deep, but the size of the screen and its near-vertical position and flickering brightness make reading arduous.

The Writing

Here is some basic writing advice:

- Write objectively; stay out of the story. Readers don't want your opinion; they want the facts.
- The summary lead sentence should tell the whole story in 30 to 35 words, no more than 3½ lines onscreen.
- Short words are easier to understand than multisyllabic words: *buy* instead of *purchase; put out the light* instead of *extinguish the illumination.*
- Simple sentences are easier to understand than compound and complex sentences.
- Strive for conversational style. Tell, rather than write, your story. Talk to your keyboard.
- Write objectively; no opinion words; avoid *only.*
- Write tight; no unnecessary words: *refer* not *refer back; is* not *is currently* and never *is presently.*
- Use words correctly; if in doubt, look up the word and read all of its meanings and usages.
- Avoid full-quotation leads; they are ineffective.
- If you ask questions in the story or begin a story with a question, be sure to answer that question.
- Use the active voice: subject, predicate, object.
- Use strong verbs, verbs of action.
- Be sparing of "to be" verbs, verbs of being. Instead of writing that someone is something, put that something within commas: Instead of "Jane Doe is a graduate of Mississippi College and volunteers as a missionary in Arizona," write "Jane Doe, a graduate of Mississippi College, volunteers as a missionary in Arizona."
- Use simple tenses: past, present, future.
- Avoid perfect tenses—*have, has*—except when appropriate; they are weak.
- Avoid progressive tense—*will be* ——*ing*—except when appropriate; it is weak: *she will teach* instead of *she will be teaching.*
- Avoid the first person—*I, me, my, mine, we, us, our, ours*—except within quotation marks; it is unprofessional.

- Elegant variation can cause confusion; repeat the person's name.
- Synonyms can cause confusion; repeat key words to reinforce under-standability: if your story is about reporters, use *reporters*, not *journal-ists*, because, although *journalist* includes reporters, it also includes various editors, photographers, sports writers, and copyeditors.
- Avoid placing quotation marks around one or two words; it changes the meaning of the word(s): two "women" were arrested; the senator identified his companion as his "wife."
- Avoid approximating round numbers that are recognized as approxi-mations: *five miles south of town* instead of *approximately five miles south of town*.
- Avoid kicker endings; they are unnecessary. Moreover, they are liable to be deleted to make the story fit the news hole, the available space on the page for the news stories. Most news readers do not read as far as the ending.

How to Attribute

Attribution in news stories is important; it provides credibility and des-ignates the source of the information. Unattributed opinion statements become the opinion of the writer or of the news medium.

Handling attribution is not difficult. The rules are simple.

State fact and attribute opinion and quoted matter. A fact is information that either is known generally or is easily verified. Facts are not attributed. Generally known facts that need no attribution are state and federal stat-utes, city ordinances, the U.S. Constitution, The Bill of Rights, the scores and winners/losers of athletic contests, products and services of corpora-tions, crime information, and so on.

Opinion, beliefs, conclusions needing attribution: statements of corpo-rate profit and loss, plans to increase or decrease the number of employees, plans to produce new or discontinue old products and services, statements of policy, campaign promises, and so on.

Quoted matter is the actual words of the person quoted and must be placed within quotation marks.

"Times have changed," she said. "Women are working now."

"I like this house," she said, "because it's so cozy."

Placement of Attribution

Properly placed attribution is essential for understandability in writing. In general, readers should not be required to read three or four sentences before learning the identity of the speaker. To avoid that, place attribution early in the first sentence of either quoted or paraphrased material.

There is no rule for placing attribution in a quoted or paraphrased sentence. Attribution may be placed at the beginning, in the middle, or at the end of the sentence. However, those three areas of power have different strengths, sometimes referred to as *primacy-recency*. This means that what is said first or last, the most powerful positions, is remembered longer than what is said in the middle.

Of the two areas of power, the most powerful area is the end. The power end of the sentence, therefore, is where you want to put the most important information. The attribution, important as it is, is the weakest information in the sentence, because previous information in the story identifies the speaker.

What this means is that, for greatest impact, attribution should be placed in the middle of the sentence rather than tacked onto the end of the sentence. Tacked-on attribution—*he said* or, worse, *said he*—weakens the most powerful part of the sentence.

Note—It is not a good idea, though it is correct, to reverse the order of attribution: *said he* or *said Smith*.

Although it is permissible to place attribution at the end of the sentence, making that a habit can result in a staccato story, each sentence reading: "statement, he said," "statement, he said," "statement, he said."

In the following sentences, see how the power shifts from the speaker to what the speaker said—in this case, the promise of no new taxes.

"Read my lips; no new taxes," President Bush said.

"Read my lips," President Bush said. "No new taxes."

Such treatment can be applied to any sentence. The following sentence loses its impact because of the tacked-on attribution. The most important information in the sentence is the reason for the delight about the contract.

"We are happy about this contract because of what it can mean to our stockholders," he said.

"We are happy about this contract," he said, "because of what it can mean to our stockholders."

Changing Speakers

Handling additional speakers is another matter. To avoid confusing readers, place attribution at or near the beginning of the new speaker's sentence. In short, when you change speakers, attribute early.

Note the confusion in the following two sentences in which the second statement, with its late attribution, seems to be from the same speaker yet contradicts the first speaker's statement.

"I feel very strongly," the vice president said, "that to salvage our company, we must sell the fabrication plant."

"The best way to resolve this issue is to retool the fabrication plant to make it more productive," the president said.

The same information, handled without confusion:

"I feel very strongly," the vice president said, "that to salvage our company, we must sell the fabrication plant."

The president disagreed: "The best way to resolve this issue is to retool the fabrication plant to make it more productive."

5

What You Need to Know about Writing News

All news writing is in English and obeys all the rules of writing, but here's where you learn how to write for the eye (to be read) and for the ear (to be heard).

In General

Here are general rules of thumb when writing:

- Write tight—no unnecessary words.
- Write objectively; stay out of the story; no adjectives; no personal opinion.
- Get to the point quickly.
- No paragraph more than 5½ lines onscreen.
- Onscreen, all copy is single spaced.
- Indent every paragraph, including the first one.
- Avoid full-quotation lead sentences. Full-quotation leads seldom work.
- Avoid question lead sentences; they must be answered.
- If you have questions in your story, be sure to answer them.
- For smooth writing, put the when, the time element, after the predicate and after the where, the place.
- Strive for conversational style. Tell, rather than write, your story.
- Write in the active voice.
- Avoid using words whose definition and usage you have not looked up.
- Be sparing with approximating numbers. Round numbers usually are recognized as approximations, and citing them as such wastes words.
- Write short words and short sentences.

- Use strong verbs.
- Use simple tenses—past, present, future—they are strong.
- Write in the past tense, because the news event and what you were told happened in the past, before you began writing your story. Moreover, interview subjects may change their minds about the plans they told you in an interview.
- Avoid weaker perfect tenses—*have, has*—unless appropriate.
- Avoid weaker progressive tense—*will be ——ing*—unless appropriate.
- Write objectively, no personal opinion words, and no first person (*I, me, my, we, us, our*) except within quotation marks.
- Avoid elegant variation; repeat names for emphasis.
- Avoid synonyms because they cause confusion; repeating key words reinforces understandability.
- Obey the rules of grammar, punctuation, syntax, precise word use and spelling, subject-predicate agreement, noun-pronoun agreement. You learned all that in the 6th grade.
- Avoid putting quotation marks around one or two words; it changes the meaning of the word(s).
- Avoid changing words or sentence structure merely for the sake of change; it may cause confusion.
- State facts; attribute opinion.
- Protect yourself; attribute only to known, authoritative sources.
- After you have written your story, read it aloud, softly, but with feeling, and listen. Your ear will recognize passages where the language is harsh, passages where the wording is disruptive, sentences where you cannot finish without taking a breath, sentences that make no sense. Unacceptable writing must be revised and simplified. If it offends your ear, your readers will turn away.
- Rewrite as many times as necessary.
- Copyedit and correct your work.

Writing Styles

Every news medium—newspaper, radio, television, magazine—has an Internet site where it posts news, sports, weather, editorials, columns, blogs, and whatever information it gathers for publication. The Web provides an electronic version of the day's news, and it publishes it immediately in print, in audio, and in video, making it available to readers now. That means that reporters must write their news stories in this order:

- A first version for the Web page, because the deadline is now.
- A second version for radio and television upcoming newscasts.
- A third version for tomorrow's newspaper, whose deadline is hours away.

Just as television and radio evening newscasts killed the afternoon newspaper, so is Internet news killing—at least, stifling—paper news. Putting the news on the Web page means that readers with cell phones or computers can read about news events minutes after they happen. By the time tomorrow's newspaper arrives, most readers already know the news event; they have read it on the Web page, heard it on the radio driving home from work, and watched it on television at the six o'clock or the ten o'clock news.

To counter that, reporters must learn a new technique, the second-day, or follow-up, story. The Web gets the first-day story; tomorrow's newspaper gets the follow-up story.

The first-day version is the same version that newspapers have published for years. For example, the first-day version is that the city council raised the sales tax from 8 to 9 percent to provide funds to hire additional police officers.

The follow-up version begins with interviews with appropriate city officials and the police chief about what the additional revenue will mean to the city and to citizens. The story could begin with city plans for advertising for applicants for police work, or that the city is trying to provide more police presence to curb the crime rate and make the city safer, or whatever news your interviews turn up.

That same follow-up approach—interviews with appropriate company officials—must be used by public relations professionals writing in the company magazine about the contract. The day the multimillion-dollar contract is signed, the company grapevine will tell 85 percent of the employees about it. To write about the signing in the company magazine, which is not published for several months, is to provide ancient information. What employees want to know is what the company is doing about that contract: Are more employees needed? How many? What kind? Is new machinery needed? How many? What kind? Has it been ordered? When is it expected? Training to use the new machinery? What about building expansion? Vehicles to transport the new product? Materials to manufacture the new product? The list is as endless as your imagination. And, of course, the public relations office can distribute the company magazine story to appropriate trade journals.

For the Internet (Writing for the Eye)

Use the summary lead to tell the whole story in the first sentence, to explain quickly the *Who* and the *Did What* or the *Said What* and *to Whom*, and *Why* the *Who Did* or *Said* that. In the second sentence, tell *Where* and *When* the news event took place. If there was a *How*, explain that in either the first or the second sentence. Note as well the following:

- The lead should be one sentence of 30 to 35 words, no more than 3½ lines onscreen.
- Stories about group action and government action must explain *why* in the first sentence.
- Put secondary details (*where, when, to whom, how*) in the second or third sentence.
- No kicker endings. Too many readers do not read the whole story.
- Use *said* unless another attributive verb, which you looked up, is appropriate.
- Attribute in the first sentence.
- Put attribution at the natural break in the sentence.
- When changing speakers, attribute early to avoid confusion.
- For ease of reading, put a blank line between paragraphs and use subheads to tell readers what comes next.

For Radio and Television (Writing for the Ear)

When writing for the ear, adopt the following rules of thumb:

- Indent every paragraph, including the first one, and write one sentence per paragraph.
- Write the broadcast story the way you would *tell* it to a friend.
- Write a beginning sentence of 10 to 15 words that captures the essence of the story.
- Put details in the second sentence.
- Avoid synonyms. Repetition of words and consistency in sentence structure is vital because listeners have only one chance at understanding the information.
- Put titles and appositives before the names.
- Put attribution before the statement.
- Quotation marks have no place in broadcast. If a full quotation is necessary, precede it with *in these words.*
- Numbers tend to confuse listeners. Round off large numbers without saying that they are approximations.
- Sentence fragments are permitted.

For Newspapers (Writing for the Eye)

Use the summary lead to tell the whole story in the first sentence, to explain quickly the *Who* and the *Did What* or the *Said What* and *to Whom*, and *Why* the *Who Did* or *Said* that. In the second sentence, tell *Where* and *When* the news event took place. If there was a *How,* explain that in either the first or the second sentence. Note also

- The lead should be one sentence of 30 to 35 words, no more than 3½ lines onscreen.
- No graf longer than 50 words, 5½ lines onscreen.
- Stories about group action and government action must explain why in the first sentence.
- Put secondary details (*where, when, to whom, how*) in the second or third sentence.
- No kicker endings. Too many readers do not read the whole story.
- Use *said* unless another attributive verb, which you looked up, is appropriate.
- Attribute in the first sentence of the graf.
- Put attribution at the natural break in the sentence.
- When changing speakers, attribute early to avoid confusion.

For Public Relations (Writing for the Various News Media)

There is no special format for public relations writing; writing is writing. In public relations, design the news release according to the requirements of the intended medium: in Internet format for the Internet, in newspaper format for newspapers, in broadcast format for radio and television, and in magazine format for magazines. See specific rules above.

Most newspapers prefer news releases of no more than three grafs. You should be able to tell your story in fewer than 100 words. If your story is worth 500 words, tell the news medium about it and let the newspaper assign a reporter to do the story.

Above all, never send a newspaper version to a radio or television station or a broadcast version to a newspaper; it will not be rewritten; it will be discarded. And your professional standard will be in question.

6

Ethics, Objectivity, and Reporter Rights

As in any activity, ethics plays a major role in reporting; and you have rights as a reporter; this explains it simply.

Reporters, like any other citizen of the United States, have the constitutional right—guaranteed by the First Amendment—to pin on a political campaign button, sign a petition, put a campaign sign in the yard, or march in a demonstration.

But unlike other citizens of the United States, reporters who pin on a campaign button, sign a petition, put a campaign sign in the yard, or march in a demonstration announce a bias that has several highly undesirable results:

- Such actions violate the codes of ethics of newspapers, television stations, radio stations, Internet news media, professional associations, and other reporters.
- Such actions usurp the editor's right to voice opinion.
- Such actions endanger the credibility of all reporters.
- Such actions jeopardize reporters' jobs.

Legally, of course, becoming a reporter does not require surrender of any rights of citizenship. But citizenship rights—legal rights—is not the issue. The issue is ethics—whether it is right, ethically, morally, for reporters to advertise bias.

Certainly, everyone has biases—some more than others, and some stronger than others—and those biases either are known or may be discerned by deduction or conjecture.

Reporters' rights of citizenship are not to be taken lightly, and they are not. The issue has been studied and reviewed and argued for years.

The codes of ethics of at least four major news organizations speak against reporters' advertising their political or other biases. And no distinction is made between reporters who work the political beat and those who do not, or even whether the reporters are on the job or at home or at play.

The codes are applicable to reporters in all news media: newspaper, radio, television, magazine, the Internet.

Here are the applicable parts of the four codes of ethics:

- From the *American Society of Newspaper Editors*
  Journalists should "neither accept anything nor pursue any activity that might compromise or seem to compromise their integrity." "Good faith with the reader is the foundation of good journalism."
- From the *Associated Press Media Editors Association*
  "Even the appearance of obligation or conflict of interest should be avoided." "Involvement in such things as politics, . . . that could cause a conflict of interest, or the appearance of such conflict, should be avoided."
- From the *Society of Professional Journalists*
  "Political involvement, . . . should be avoided if it compromises the integrity of journalists. Journalists . . . should conduct their personal lives in a manner which protects them from conflict of interest, real or apparent."
- From the *Radio Television Digital News Association*
  "Broadcast journalists shall govern their personal lives and such non-professional associations as may impinge on their professional activities in a manner that will protect them from conflict of interest, real or apparent."

The point is simple: Like Caesar's wife, reporters must be above suspicion. Reporters are different from all other citizens. Reporters report what they saw and heard; they are not participants, they are observers; they are in the world, but not of the world.

Reporters who act, who wear a campaign button, sign a petition, put a campaign sign in the yard, or march in a demonstration announce their bias, tell their news audience that they favor one side before all others.

The news audience cannot but assume that what such reporters report must be biased and is, therefore, unreliable.

That may not be the case, however, since many reporters are professional enough not to let their biases show up in their reporting. But the news audience, who cannot know the extent of the reporters' professionalism, will assume bias in the story. The reporters' objectivity, their credibility, will have been damaged. They will no longer be above suspicion. Because their effectiveness is compromised, their jobs could be jeopardized.

Some reporters argue that their editors or news directors do not object to their activities, especially on their own time. No matter. No editor has the right to violate the credibility or trust of editors or news directors in general. No editor or news director may give a reporter permission to violate the code of ethics. To do so would jeopardize the rights of all editors, all news directors, all reporters, all news media, all people.

The next argument, of course, is that legally, morally, and actually, reporters do express their opinions in the opinion columns or analyses that they write.

True, but an opinion column and an analysis are different from a campaign button, a petition, a campaign sign, or a demonstration. An opinion column, an analysis, is presented as an opinion piece, and, written properly, presents both sides of the issue and develops opinions and conclusions through logical presentation of facts.

A campaign button, a petition, a campaign sign, a demonstration—all present a one-sided opinion without presenting argument or facts in support. Each is but an assertion, without stated foundation.

The only time reporters can, and should, participate in government is in the privacy of the voting booth. Reporters, like any citizen of the United States, do not surrender the constitutional privilege of voting—although some journalistic purists avoid even that.

Voting, however, is a different type of expression of opinion. Votes are cast in secret. The news audience may know that the reporters voted, but the news audience cannot know for whom or for what they voted. Nor may the reporters disclose the direction of their votes, because that would announce their bias.

Reporters must guard closely their objectivity, preserve their integrity, and stand above suspicion.

Loss of objectivity in the news media, loss of trust by the people, could prove too great a price for the reporter, for the nation, to pay.

In the aftermath of the terrorist declaration of holy war against the United States by a modern-day kamikaze attack on September 11, 2001, United States flags popped up all over the country like dandelions after a rain as people rallied around flag and country.

Flags flew from stores, houses, mailboxes, and automobiles and trucks; newspapers published full-page flags for display; television newscasts displayed flags in the background; and reporters, newscasters, and politicians and officeholders sported flag pins on their clothing and on their homes.

Then came the question of whether wearing a flag pin destroys reporter credibility as objective and accurate observers and writers by flaunting bias toward the United States. Opinion remains divided; some reporters wear a flag pin; some don't; some editors forbid reporters to wear a flag pin; some don't.

Wearing a flag pin, however, is different from wearing a symbol of political leanings or of social causes. The flag pin shows bias, of course, but it shows everybody's bias, bias not to a political or a social cause but to the nation itself.

Wearing a flag pin does no damage to reporter credibility. It is but a statement of nationality. Reporters who wear a flag pin, like anyone else in the United States, are saying simply, "I am an American and proud of it." They are saying that they live by the First Amendment of freedom of speech and of the press and all the other guarantees of life in the United States. That's all.

American reporters are Americans first and are viewed as such, whether they wear a flag pin or not.

One more thing: Never forget that you are a reporter. As such, your duty is to report only what you see and hear. Thus, when you are on the job, do not applaud. If anyone questions you, your response is, "I am a reporter; I do not take sides."

7

How to Write for the Internet

Writing for the Web is merely a change in the medium, from paper to the screen, so, despite all the talk, writing does not change.

Now that the personal computer—the PC and the Macintosh—is in nearly every office and every home, it has replaced the typewriter and the pen as the tool for writing, and the Internet has taken its place alongside newspapers, news magazines, radio, and television, as a medium of mass communication. The traditional news media use the Internet as an additional outlet for their news; and reporters use the Internet as a research tool.

A major result is that the Internet allows the various news media—print and broadcast—to do more than file news stories onto their Websites in their own format. Though each news medium retains its separate identity as a print, audio, or video medium, on the Internet, each news medium presents its news in every format: text, graphics, sound, and video. The Web allows a melding, a converging, of news formats, to the advantage of the news consumer.

Equally important, the Internet allows immediate distribution of and immediate access to news, a major breakthrough from the traditional. The newspaper at a breakfast table was published last night and carries stories of news events that occurred up to 24 hours earlier. The news magazine, published weekly, carries stories of news events that occurred up to seven days earlier. Radio and television stations, though they may break into any program at any time with news, generally wait until the scheduled news program on the hour, so their news stories may have been written less than 60 minutes earlier.

The conventional news media vary widely in their presentation of news: Radio and television lack detail, largely because of time constraints; newspapers publish yesterday's news, but in great detail; and news magazines publish the week's news, but put it all into perspective with analyses. But the Internet stands alone. It carries stories of news events that occurred a few minutes before they were written and in as much detail as is available.

Regardless of the news medium, the task of the reporter remains the same: to gather the news and to write the story. And because of the Web and the convergence of the news media, reporters must be familiar with the formats of all media and be fluent in writing for both print and broadcast. However, print reporters, more accustomed to writing the news, may not have the stage presence to deliver their news orally on radio or television. Stage presence requires a quality of voice and a rhythm of speech that let the words slip into the listener's ear without effort, and, on television, an appearance pleasing to viewers.

Some news media have a Webmaster, a staff member assigned to file news stories on the Web pages; some use their reporters to file news stories on the Web page. Regardless of who files the stories on the Web, writing for the Web remains the same as writing for any print medium, because whatever is written has to be read and understood.

The same procedure is followed before any story can be published or aired or filed on the Web. The story must be written, corrected, rewritten, and copyedited. In most situations, the story written for print or broadcast is sufficient for the Web. If the writing works for print or for broadcast, it works for the Web. It's all the same English.

That means that there is no need to learn a different writing style to write for the Web. The newswriting techniques taught in journalism school and practiced professionally in newspapers or news magazines or radio or television are well suited to the Web. Web reading on the small computer screen, however, is difficult, so to make it easy for readers, adopt this 5–0, 5–0 rule:

- Five lines of copy—one blank line, five lines of copy—one blank line.
- No paragraph longer than five lines.
- No line longer than 5 inches onscreen, which equals 1 inch of copy in a 2-inch-wide column.
- A blank line between paragraphs. The blank line indicates the end of one paragraph and the beginning of another, so there is no need to indent paragraphs.
- For lengthy stories, it is a good idea to insert subheads, an old newspaper technique to break up the copy, to provide white space, and to alert readers to what is coming next.

If You Have an Option

The Web poses problems that paper media do not. The computer screen is vertical or nearly so, an unnatural place for ease of reading; and the images on the computer screen flicker, causing eyestrain. To help Web readers, the following suggestions are recommended.

Use a sans-serif font, either Geneva or Verdana, both of which were designed for reading onscreen. Serif fonts are easy to read on paper but are difficult onscreen because of the serifs; condensed fonts are difficult to read; and small fonts and ALL-CAPITALS (all-caps) have no place onscreen. Capital-and-Lower Case (c/lc) fonts are easier to read because the space for each letter is tailored for that letter. For printing, Times New Roman uses the least amount of ink. Below are samples of various standard fonts in caps-and-lower case and in all-caps. All of the sentence examples are in the same type height, so note the difference in line length. Here are some examples:

A typewriter font in which all letters, capitals and lower-cased, occupy the same space.

```
Courier          Freedom of speech and of the press.
COURIER          FREEDOM OF SPEECH AND OF THE PRESS.
```

Sans-serif fonts designed for the computer screen in which each letter occupies a space tailored to that letter.

Verdana   Freedom of speech and of the press.
Geneva   Freedom of speech and of the press.

Some fonts are somewhat difficult to read on the computer screen because they are condensed.

Helvetica   Freedom of speech and of the press.
Arial   Freedom of speech and of the press.

Serif fonts, some easier to read on paper than others, but all are difficult to read on the computer screen because they are so small.

Century Schoolbook   Freedom of speech and of the press.
Times New Roman   Freedom of speech and of the press.
Palatino   Freedom of speech and of the press.
Baskerville   Freedom of speech and of the press.
Garamond   Freedom of speech and of the press.
Times   Freedom of speech and of the press.
Bell   Freedom of speech and of the press.

All-capital versions of the fonts are difficult to read because each letter is the same height.

Sans-serif fonts:

Arial	FREEDOM OF SPEECH AND OF THE PRESS.
Verdana	FREEDOM OF SPEECH AND OF THE PRESS.
Helvetica	FREEDOM OF SPEECH AND OF THE PRESS.
Geneva	FREEDOM OF SPEECH AND OF THE PRESS.

Serif fonts:

Century Schoolbook	FREEDOM OF SPEECH AND OF THE PRESS.
Times New Roman	FREEDOM OF SPEECH AND OF THE PRESS.
Palatino	FREEDOM OF SPEECH AND OF THE PRESS.
Baskerville	FREEDOM OF SPEECH AND OF THE PRESS.
Garamond	FREEDOM OF SPEECH AND OF THE PRESS.
Times	FREEDOM OF SPEECH AND OF THE PRESS.

Sidebars and Hypertexts

If the main story is supported by stories of related interest (called sidebars in newspapers, hypertext or hyperlinks on the Internet), the Webmaster inserts buttons so readers may click on them to call up the related stories.

The sidebar and the hyperlink are used because incorporating their information in the main story would make the main story overly long or unduly complicated, or because the topic is tangential to, but does not fit precisely with, the topic of the main story.

The format for writing the sidebar and the hyperlink is the same as for writing any news story. Do not forget to include, up high, a reference to the main story.

8

How to Write for Broadcast: Radio and Television

Writing for the ear—radio and television—differs from writing for the eye—paper and onscreen—but it's not all that difficult.

Writing news in broadcast style—for the ear—differs from writing news in print style—for the eye—in that broadcast style news writing is conversation on paper. Broadcast news writing, unlike print news writing, uses redundancies and repetition, and sentence construction barred from print news writing, because the newscaster is talking to the audience.

The goal of broadcast news writing is understandability at first listening. A print news story can be read as many times as is necessary for understandability. In broadcast, there is no second chance at understanding. The news broadcaster does not repeat stories verbatim, so there is no second listening.

Some rules of writing are the same, though. As in a print news story, a broadcast news story must be long enough to cover the topic and short enough to be interesting. Print news stories average 250 words; broadcast news stories average 60 words because of time constraints. Such conciseness demands that words and details be selected with extreme care.

Until you become adept at writing in broadcast style, it may be easier for you to write the essence of your story in one sentence; then use that as a guide for writing the broadcast version. When you write your story, remember that broadcast writing is talk writing, conversational writing. Strive for that approach. Imagine that you are talking, not writing, talking to a friend, telling your friend the news. Talk to the keyboard.

The essence of broadcast writing is that it be clear on first listening because listeners who do not understand the first sentence of a newscast will try to make sense of it and will miss the second sentence. The third sentence will be confusing, so listeners will lose the entire news story.

Here are some suggestions for making broadcast news copy readily understandable:

- Most broadcast newscasters prefer copy written in ALL CAPITALS.
- Strive for the present tense, but don't force it. The simple past tense is acceptable, frequently desirable. Using the present tense for an obviously past action jars listeners. And the present perfect tense—*has, have*—is a copout; you can write better than that.
- Write the broadcast story in 60 to 70 words, three sentences.
- To make it easy for the broadcast newscaster to read from cue cards, write one sentence per paragraph.
- Indent every paragraph, including the first one, five spaces.
- Omit unnecessary words and details.
- Use short words and short sentences.
- Use sentence fragments for emphasis.
- Use slang, if it fits the sentence and the story.
- Use concrete words, not abstract or vague words.
- Use second-person personal pronouns: *you, your, yours.*
- Avoid first-person pronouns: *I, me, my, mine, myself, we, us, our, ours, ourselves.*
- Keep sentences parallel.
- In a list, repeat auxiliary verbs: *have, had.*
- In a list, repeat prepositions.
- In a list, repeat the *to* in infinitives.
- In a list, use the articles: *a, an, the.*
- Write in the active voice: subject, predicate, object.
- Avoid synonyms; repeating key words reinforces comprehension. Moreover, no two words mean exactly the same thing.
- Generalize statistics.
- Round off numbers. Listeners cannot assimilate detailed large numbers. Therefore, adding such qualifiers as *approximately, about, some, nearly, more than* is unnecessary; it only adds useless words.
- After you have written your story, read it aloud and listen to the flow of language. If you have to read a sentence twice to understand it, your listeners will not be able to understand it. Recast and simplify.

In the examples that follow, note the necessary repetition of key words throughout the broadcast stories:

Newspaper Lead (35 words)

The Clinton City Council hired Hugh Robb, city manager of Tallahassee, Fla., for the past 10 years, as city manager today, replacing Mary Emory, who resigned last month to enter private law practice in Jackson.

Broadcast Story (44 words)

THE CITY OF CLINTON HAS A NEW CITY MANAGER.
THE NEW CLINTON CITY MANAGER IS HUGH ROBB, WHO SPENT THE PAST TEN YEARS AS CITY MANAGER OF TALLAHASSEE, FLORIDA.
ROBB REPLACES MARY EMORY, WHO RESIGNED LAST MONTH TO ENTER PRIVATE LAW PRACTICE IN JACKSON.

Newspaper Lead (27 words)

The tax attorney firm of Cole and Emory began collecting delinquent property taxes in the Hinds County school district today under a contract with the school board.

Broadcast Story (47 words)

IF YOU HAVE NOT PAID YOUR HINDS COUNTY SCHOOL TAXES RECENTLY, BE WARNED.
THE HINDS COUNTY SCHOOL DISTRICT IS AFTER YOU WITH A PROFESSIONAL TAX COLLECTOR.
LAST MONTH, THE HINDS COUNTY SCHOOL BOARD HIRED THE TAX ATTORNEY FIRM OF COLE AND EMORY TO COLLECT DELINQUENT SCHOOL TAXES.

Newspaper Story (102 words)

The best high school students in the United States ranked Texas A&M University sixth in this year's list of institutions of higher education they prefer to attend.

The ranking was made by high school students listed in *Who's Who Among High School Students* because of their academic and extracurricular excellence.

The top five universities are Harvard, Duke, Stanford, University of California–Los Angeles, and University of North Carolina–Chapel Hill.

The publisher of *Who's Who Among High School Students* asked its 100,000 members to indicate which college or university they planned to attend. Their preferences were compiled to form the nationwide ranking.

Broadcast Story (69 words)

THE BEST HIGH SCHOOL STUDENTS IN THE UNITED STATES CONSIDER TEXAS A-&-M THE SIXTH BEST UNIVERSITY IN THE COUNTRY.

TEXAS A-&-M UNIVERSITY'S TOP RANKING CAME IN A SURVEY OF 100-THOUSAND MEMBERS OF *WHO'S WHO AMONG HIGH SCHOOL STUDENTS* WHO WERE ASKED WHAT UNIVERSITIES THEY PLANNED TO ATTEND.

THE TOP FIVE UNIVERSITIES ARE HARVARD, DUKE, STANFORD, UNIVERSITY OF CALIFORNIA AT LOS ANGELES, AND UNIVERSITY OF NORTH CAROLINA AT CHAPEL HILL.

Broadcast Writing Style

Here are the basic style requirements for broadcast writing to help the newscaster read the story and the listener understand the story.

- Abbreviate only *Mr., Mrs., Ms., Dr.*
- Spell out all other titles.
- For ease of understanding, put all titles and appositives (a word or group of words that identifies another word or group of words) before the names, because it puts the name immediately before the verb. For accuracy use *a, an, the,* as appropriate, before appositives:

AN 18-YEAR-OLD BIOLOGY MAJOR, CAITLIN PRICE, WON.

A SENIOR JOURNALISM MAJOR, LIAM JAMES, IS THE NEW.

THE PRESIDENT OF LOUISIANA STATE UNIVERSITY, KEVIN LEE, DELIVERED.

THE PROVOST AND VICE PRESIDENT FOR ACADEMIC AFFAIRS, DR. PATRICIA COLE, ARGUED IN.

PRESIDENT BARACK OBAMA WARNED.

MAYOR GREGORY SCOTT RESIGNED.

If letter abbreviations are to be used—and use abbreviations sparingly—handle abbreviations this way:

For abbreviations that are read as individual letters, separate them with hyphens:

F-B-I, N-A-A-C-P, U-N, P-H-D, G-I, A-P, U-S-D-A, U-S, A-M, P-M,

A-T-&-T.

For abbreviations that are pronounced as words, place them within quotation marks:

"NASA," "HUD," "NASCAR," "UNICEF," "NATO," "NASDAQ."

If numbers are to be used—and use numbers sparingly—handle numbers this way:

Spell out numbers from one to eleven.
Use figures from 12 to 999.

Use a combination of figures and words for 1,000 and up, and hyphenate:

FIVE-MILLION, 330-THOUSAND, 12-HUNDRED-DOLLARS.

Round off large numbers unless the exact number is significant:

THE UNIVERSITY OF MISSISSIPPI HAS 25-THOUSAND STUDENTS [not 24,885].

Write numbers the way they are spoken, and round them up or down:

THE BUDGET IS 62-AND-ONE-HALF-MILLION-DOLLARS [not $62,462,385]. Better: THE BUDGET IS 62-MILLION-DOLLARS.

If you use percentages, do not use the % sign; spell out *PERCENT*. And round off numbers; instead of 54 PERCENT and 48 PERCENT use *HALF*.

Spell out first to eleventh—JULY FOURTH, JUNE SECOND—use a combination of figures and letters for 12TH and above—32ND ANNUAL CONVENTION, 23RD, NOVEMBER 15TH.

Hyphenate years: 19-98, 20-OH-THREE, or TWO-THOUSAND-THREE, 18-90s, 20-12.

For ages, list the age before the name and hyphenate it:

A 21-YEAR-OLD STUDENT, A 46-YEAR-OLD PROFESSOR.

Use quotation marks sparingly. Instead, introduce direct quotations with *IN THESE WORDS, SAID IT THIS WAY*.

Use some contractions freely: THEY'RE, IT'S, WON'T.

Avoid *n't* contractions because they may be confusing, and the pronunciation emphasis is not on the *n't*: Write *are not* instead of *aren't*, *did not* instead of *didn't*. *Won't* is acceptable because there is no *willn't*.

Provide pronouncers for difficult names. Put the pronouncer immediately after the difficult name, within parentheses, and use an apostrophe to indicate the emphasized syllable: MOBLEY (MOBE'-LEE,) HAJASH (HASH) [or (RHYMES WITH CASH)], KNOBLOCK (NO'-BLOCK), KNUTE (KUH-NUTE'), VYVLECKA (VIV-LETCH'-KUH).

Follow traditional punctuation. However, take a close look at semicolons. You probably will be able to make two simple sentences from a compound sentence with a semicolon. And shorter sentences are more understandable.

Place all attribution before the statement, never after, and never in the middle of the statement:

SABATINI SAID HE WAS BORN WITH THE GIFT OF LAUGHTER AND A SENSE THAT THE WORLD WAS MAD.

SABATINI SAID, IN THESE WORDS, I WAS BORN WITH THE GIFT OF LAUGHTER AND A SENSE THAT THE WORLD IS MAD.

9

How and Why to Edit Copy

> The copyeditor is the last person in the writing chain, the one who corrects errors—spelling, grammar, punctuation, and so on, and, most important, fact—so the writer does not look like a dummy.

Regardless of how many times you rewrite your work, there always exists a chance of error—of commission or of omission—because you are too close to your own creation. Much of what you read in your own story exists in your mind rather than in the writing. You tend to read into the story information that is not there. Thus, someone else should read your copy to ensure that it says what you intended it to say.

Don't complain when the copyeditor finds errors in your copy; the copyeditor is the last person in the chain of writing for publication who can keep you from looking dumb in print.

But, first, let's look at terms and people in the chain of publishing.

Writer—That's you. You have gathered all of the information and written your story. You submit it to your City Editor.

City Editor—Reads your story for accuracy and completeness. If errors are found, the City Editor returns the story to you for repair. When your story is ready, the City Editor submits it to the News Editor.

News Editor—Reads your story and decides where best to put it in the newspaper and what kind of headline it should have, and submits it to the Copy Desk for final reading and the headline.

Copyeditor—Reads and corrects errors in spelling, grammar, punctuation, syntax, and fact, and, if necessary, moves paragraphs to more appropriate places in the story. The copyeditor writes the headline and submits the story to the Slot Copyeditor.

Slot Copyeditor—Checks every story and headline to ensure that they are correct and that they meet the headline requirement of the News Editor, and sends your story to the backshop for publication.

Proofreaders—This is done by two people, one to read aloud your copyedited draft; the other, to follow and correct the typeset version, called the *proof*, and so on. The proofreaders approve your story and it is published.

You should know that these terms, *copyedit, edit,* and *proofread*, have different meanings and usages. *Webster's New World College Dictionary*, 4th ed., © 2005, provides these definitions:

copyedit—To edit and correct the grammar, punctuation, etc. of articles or manuscripts, as in a newspaper office or publishing house.

edit—To revise and make ready for publication a writer's work by selection, arrangement, and annotation.

proofread—To read and mark corrections on printers' proofs, etc. to ensure that the typeset version is identical to the writer's final draft. But, if the writer's final draft contains errors, check with the writer; maybe the errors were deliberate. The proofreader reads to ensure that the typeset copy follows exactly the original version, and the proofreader marks the errors for others to correct.

It is extremely difficult to copyedit your own work. The best way to copyedit your own work is to set it aside for a few days, letting the details of the work slip away from your active memory. Even so, you will miss a lot.

To edit copy properly, you must read it at least three times. Read it the first time to correct errors in spelling, grammar, punctuation, and syntax. Read it a second time for sense, for accuracy in fact, and for completeness of information. Read it a third time to pick up the errors you missed in the first two readings. The story—the whole story and each sentence—must make sense. Information must be accurate, true, and complete.

The best way to edit your own copy—though it may not always be possible—is to follow the advice of Quintilian, a teacher and critic of literature who lived from C.E. 35 to 100. He advised this method: "There can be no doubt that the best method of correction is to put aside what we have written for a certain time so that when we return to it after an interval, it will have the air of novelty and of being another's handiwork."

So copyedit.

- Compile a list of the errors you commit most frequently. For example, you may habitually misspell certain words—"alot" instead of "a lot,"

Forth Worth instead of *Fort Worth*, *Flroida* instead of *Florida*—or omit the second comma in appositions, or substitute it's for its. Once you know your errors, they should be fairly easy to find and correct. So, follow these steps for editing your own copy, whether on a computer screen or on paper.

- Read the story three times, once aloud for general impact and twice for detail. It is the copyeditor's job to improve the story if possible, to let it alone if not.
- Do not hesitate to delete words, sentences, and paragraphs, if that improves the story or if they are unnecessary or in poor taste.
- Do not hesitate to substitute words, if that improves the story.
- Do not hesitate to change the structure of sentences and paragraphs, if that improves the story.
- Read your copy one time for each error you know you commit, correcting each, and other errors, as you find them.
- Double-check the spelling of names and double-check numbers.

Editing copy onscreen differs from editing copy on paper in that onscreen, you type the corrections directly, and on paper, you use copyediting marks to notify the typesetter of the errors. In general, however, you will edit copy onscreen rather than on paper. If you are reading hard copy, paper copy, use the correct copyediting marks, not the proofreading marks. Copyediting corrections are made with a dark pencil—never a ballpoint pen—above the line of type being corrected. Proofreading marks are made with a light blue pencil in the left and right margins of the column of type on a proof sheet.

Every publication—every daily and some weekly newspapers, magazines of all kinds, newsletters, books—has a stylebook or style sheet to help ensure uniformity in the mechanics of writing. Publishers consider it unprofessional to use different abbreviations, capitalizations, uses of numerals, punctuations, spellings, and so on. In this sense, style has little, if anything, to do with the prose style of the reporter. For most daily newspapers and some weekly newspapers and magazines, the common style guide is *The Associated Press Stylebook and Briefing on Media Law*, a copy of which should be on your desk and open.

Copyediting Marks

Copyediting marks tell the typesetter what you want done to the copy. Thus, your editing and marking of the copy must be clear.

- Make your marks with a No. 1 or No. 2 pencil.
- Read *The Stylebook* entry.
- Use copyediting marks.

- Do not use the delete mark; that is a proofreader's mark. Instead, strike out the unwanted material.
- Correct the spelling error only; do not rewrite the whole word.
- Do not double the correction with the mark and what it means.
- Do not insert quotation marks arbitrarily; you heard nothing.
- Make all corrections (except marks for commas and capitals) above the line.

Figure 9.1 shows copyediting marks in correct usage.

Copyediting Marks

This ℱ is a Proofreader's Mark. DO NOT USE IT.

The Jackson City Council raised the sales	INDENT FOR PARAGRAPH
tax Tuesday. The increase is from 8.25	NEW PARAGRAPH
percent to 9 percent.	
The additional revenue will be used	NO PARAGRAPH
for teacher pay raises.	
The plan unprecedented was written	TRANSPOSE
for at least sixty-five years	USE NUMERALS
there were 8 in the group	SPELL IT OUT
Clinton, Mississippi is the hometown	ABBREVIATE
An Okla man was arrested	DO NOT ABBREVIATE
president royce opened the meeting	UPPERCASE (CAPITALIZE)
as a Result, this will be	LOWERCASE
he said he co uld raise the money	DELETE SPACE AND CLOSE UP
El Paso, Texxas, is west of Dallas	DELETE LETTER AND CLOSE UP
ElPaso, Texas, is west of Dallas	INSERT SPACE
The ruling a fine example (is)	INSERT WORD
the this source declined comment	DELETE WORD AND CLOSE UP
El Paso, Texas is west of Dallas	INSERT COMMA
He said he couldnt do it	INSERT APOSTROPHE
He shouted, Wait!	INSERT QUOTATION MARKS
The robber fled	INSERT PERIOD
12 year old girl	INSERT HYPHEN
The plan unprecedented in Biloxi calls	INSERT DASHES

This is a delete mark (vertical) — Texas

This is a lowercase mark (slant) — Texas

ONLY ONE SPACE after period, comma, colon, semicolon.

Figure 9.1. Copy showing copyediting marks in correct usage.

How to Avoid Common Style Errors

You are expected to have memorized and to use all of these most common style requirements as listed in *The Associated Press Stylebook and Briefing on Media Law.*

Place only one space after the period, not two as in using a typewriter. As a reporter, you are setting type, not typing a letter.

Numbers

- Look up every number you plan to use to determine whether to use numerals or words. If a large number must be spelled out, as in broadcast, do not use *and.* The *and* indicates a decimal point.

The twenty-eighth of December one thousand nine hundred forty-nine, one hundred sixty-two dollars, one hundred sixty-two dollars and fifty cents.

Telephone numbers no longer require parentheses around the area code; they use the hyphen.

123-456-7890.

- Put a comma in numbers of more than three digits.

100, 1,000, 10,000, 100,000.

But $6 million, 3.7 million.

- Use numerals for the following:

Addresses: 9 Royal Road, 10 Downing St., 4215 Chestnut Ave., 300 Marshall Foch Blvd.

Ages: 1, 5, 18, 65, 2 months.

Dates: Jan. 1, July 2, Aug. 3, Nov. 15, but do not use st, nd, rd, th.

Dimensions: 2 by 4, 8½ by 11 inches, 2-by-4 board, 8½-by-11-inch sheet, 150 pounds, 2 pounds, 2-pound weight, 6-foot-tall man, 6-footer

Highways: Interstate 35, U.S. Highway 1.

Money: No pennies or zeroes except where important, as in tickets: $2.50 for adults, $1.25 for children. $12, $125,500, $22.5 million, $12,486, $1.75.

Percentages: Do not use ¢ or % because some publications do not have those symbols in their software. 2 percent, 1.5 percent.

Scores and Votes: 7–6, 21–14, 3–2, 6–5 vote, 3–2 vote.

Temperatures: 2 degrees, 105 degrees, zero degrees.

Time. Use lower-cased letters for a.m. and p.m.: 1 a.m., 4:30 p.m., and no zeroes for zero minutes. Use *noon* and *midnight*. Do not use *12 noon* and *12 midnight* or the confusing *12 a.m.* and *12 p.m.*

Quotation Marks and Other Punctuation Marks

- All periods and all commas go inside all close quotation marks.
- All colons and all semicolons go outside all close quotation marks.
- Question marks and exclamation points go inside or outside close quotation marks, depending upon the meaning of the sentence.

He said, "Wait."

"Wait," he said.

The title of the book is "Help."

She said, "He replied, 'Wait.' "

She has not read *Roots*, but he has read *War and Peace*.

- Avoid putting quotation marks around one or two words; it tends to change the meaning of the word(s):

Two "women" were arrested.

The prostitute said she was a "good mother."

The senator and his "friend," a television anchorwoman, were killed in the accident.

The businessman introduced the woman as his "wife."

- For internal attribution, put quotation marks around only what was said, not around the attribution.

"He was born with the gift of laughter," she said, "and a sense that the world was mad."

- Use only one attribution per quotation, regardless of how many sentences or paragraphs the quotation is.

Apostrophe

- The apostrophe is a single close quotation mark (') that indicates the absence of a letter: doesn't, rock 'n' roll, 'tis, Class of '12 (although it's better to use the year: Class of 2012).

  Form the apostrophe on the Macintosh: Shift Option]; on the PC: Ctrl ' '.

Titles

- Put long titles after the name, lower-cased, and with commas before and after.

Rick Perry, governor of Texas, said.

William McClain, lieutenant general of infantry, said.

Put short titles before the name, upper-cased, and abbreviated as appropriate.

Gov. Hugh Perry of Texas

Lt. Gen. William McClain

Lt. Gov. Jane Doe

Professor Douglas Starr

Mrs. Patricia Cole

Abbreviations

- Do not abbreviate or capitalize *professor*.
- Abbreviate street, avenue, boulevard in addresses.

4215 Chestnut St., 1066 Napoleon Ave., 1215 Marshal Foch Blvd.

- Abbreviate state with city. And separate the state with two commas.

Shreveport, La., (not LA) is near Texas.

- Abbreviate month in date.

Nov. 15, June 12, July 4, Dec. 28.

- Spell out months when used alone.

November, December, January.

- Spell out the following words, even in addresses.

Road, drive, lane, trail, alley, circle.

- Spell out the following words when used alone.

Street, avenue, boulevard, state, month.

- Abbreviate United States as adjective.

U.S. Coast Guard, U.S. Supreme Court.

- Spell out United States as noun.

The United States comprises 50 states (never *is comprised of*):

- Use these standard abbreviations of states.

Ala., Ariz., Ark., Calif., Colo., Conn., D.C., Del., Fla., Ga., Ill., Ind., Kan., Ky., La., Md., Mass., Mich., Minn., Miss., Mo., Mont., N.C., Neb., Nev., N.H., N.J., N.M., N.Y., N.D., Okla., Ore., Pa., R.I., S.C., S.D., Tenn., W. Va., Vt., Va., Wash., Wis., Wyo.

- Do not abbreviate Alaska, Hawaii, Idaho, Iowa, Maine, Ohio, Texas, Utah.
- The two-letter abbreviations, all-capitals, no periods, no spaces, are abbreviations of the U.S. Postal Service. Use them only in complete postal addresses.

AK, AL, AZ, AR, CA, CO, CT, DC, DE, FL, GA, HI, IA, ID, IL, IN, KS, KY, LA, MA, MD, ME, MI, MN, MS, MO, MT, NC, NE, NV, NH, NJ, NM, NY, ND, OH, OK, OR, PA, RI, SC, SD, TN, TX, UT, VT, VA, WA, WV, WI, WY

Other

- Capitalize all proper nouns.
- Put a space before the open parenthesis and after the close parenthesis.

The Department of Housing and Urban Development (HUD) listed housing available in College Station.

- Use the colon (:) to introduce a full quotation and to introduce a list. Use the semicolon (;) to separate thought units.
- Use two commas with appositives.

Dr. Jonathan Price, president of Texas A&M University, said today.

- When long titles are placed before the name, as in broadcast, begin with an article: *the, a, an*:

The president of Louisiana State University, Dr. Liam James, said today.

An associate professor of biology, Miss Caitlin Alexander, said today.

- Use the comma before the conjunction (and, but, for) in compound sentences.
- The pronoun for people and animals that have names is *who*; for things and animals without names, *that*.

Those are the shovels *that* are broken.

She fed her cat, Percy, *who* is ill.

They are the students *who* were evicted.

They fed the animals *that* were suffering.

- The dash (—) separates thought units and tangential phrases. Look up the dash in *The AP Stylebook* before you use it. The dash (em dash) is the width of the capital M. Typing two hyphens does not make an em dash. On the Macintosh, hold down Shift Option and press hyphen (—). On the PC, hold down Ctrl fn Alt and press semicolon (;).
- The hyphen (-) joins words with no space on either side.

10-year-old girl, 6-foot-tall man.

- Compound adjectives before the noun are hyphenated and singular.

2-year-old girl, first-quarter touchdown, 5-foot, 6-inch-tall man, full-time job.

- Compound adjectives after the noun are not hyphenated and are plural, as appropriate.

The girl is 2 years old.

He works full time.

The touchdown came in the first quarter.

She is 5 feet, 6 inches tall.

Note—The plural of foot is feet. It is incorrect to write: The man is 5 foot tall. Try it with inches. It would be silly to write: The man is 5 foot, 6 inch tall.

- No hyphen after "ly" adverbs: easily remembered rule, widely known woman, highly regarded official.
- Suspensive hyphenation requires two hyphens and a space after each hyphen but the last.

First-, second-, and third-grade pupils are released at 2 p.m.

She received a 10- to 20-year prison sentence.

- It is incorrect to write "second-and third-grade pupils," "10-to 20-year sentence." The reason is that "second" and "third" each modifies "grade," and "10" and "20" each modifies "year." It is the same as saying "second-grade and third grade" and "10-year and 20-year. "Besides "second-and" and "10-to" are not words.
- The names of the degrees are Bachelor of Arts, Master of Science, and so on. That "of" means that it's a title, so there is no possessive or plural in the title. But, generically, they are bachelor's degree, master's degree, doctor's degree, doctoral degree, doctorate. "Bachelor of Arts degree" is redundant because a Bachelor of Arts is a degree. For plurals, it is Bachelors of Arts, Masters of Arts. "Doctorate degree" is redundant because a doctorate is a degree.
- There is no *i* in *doctoral*.

10

How to Cover Speeches

Covering a speech is the easiest task a reporter has; it has one speaker and one or two topics, is in one place and has one audience, and, most of the time, reporters have a copy of the speech to work with.

A speech is nothing more than an explanation of a person's thoughts.

Most speeches are delivered to organized groups—business associations, civic groups, church groups, unions, guilds, and so on—and are on topics of specific or general interest to the audience. Speeches by candidates for public office are delivered to organized groups and, from the *stump* (the place where a political speech is delivered) to whoever gathers at the site. In any event, speeches are advertised well in advance of delivery to help ensure attendance.

Covering a speech is the easiest assignment of all, particularly because:

- Reporters usually know all of the details well in advance: the name and background of the speaker, details about the audience and the place of the speech, and the reason for the speech.
- Copies of the speech are delivered to reporters either in advance of or during the speaking event, enabling reporters to follow the speaker's delivery.
- The speech usually is about one or two topics and no more than 20–30 minutes long; and
- The speaking situation is in one place.

Most speeches follow this three-part format: beginning, middle, end. The beginning of the speech sets the stage for the speech, tells its purpose; the middle details explanations and support for the speaker's ideas; and the end presents the conclusion, the position of the speaker on the topic.

Two types of speech have more than two topics and last longer than 20 minutes, but they don't happen very often: the president's annual "State of the Union" speech and the governor's annual "State of the State" speech, and every politician's speech opening the campaign for election or reelection. Fortunately, each of those speeches is a one-time speech, with no need to be repeated.

In the hour-long "State of the Union" and the "State of the State" speeches, the president and the governor describe and explain their multiple successes and the problems they dealt with last year. Topics include just about anything that could happen to the nation or to a state: education, the budget, the economy, business, medical care, the war, natural disasters.

The hour-long opening speech of every political candidate's campaign describes the issues that they will face if elected and how they will handle those issues. Thereafter, during the 60-day campaign as they cross the state seeking votes in various cities and towns, they don't repeat that speech. Chances are that every newspaper in the state has carried that speech story, and the voters know where their candidates stand on all those issues. To keep their image alive as they visit town after town, the candidates focus on one, sometimes two, topics from the speech and reduce their speeches to 20 minutes each.

Because of the multiple topics, writing the news story of those long speeches is tricky. You must lead with the most important one or two topics in each speech and include the secondary topics in the body of the speech. Don't forget, of course, to include the number of times the audience applauded, thereby forcing the speaker to postpone continuing until after the applause dies down.

The key to writing stories about speeches is to summarize the speech or to present one or two key points in the lead sentence. The following matrix will help you determine your lead for a speech story. Answers to the all-capital questions—WHO, SAID WHAT—must be in the lead of every speech story. Answers to the caps-and-lower-case questions—to Whom, Why, Where, When, How—may be placed in the first paragraph but not later than the second paragraph.

WHO

The Who of the story is essential in stories about speeches. This is the person delivering the speech. If the person is widely known (someone in the news regularly), begin with the name and title (Mayor Jonathan Price). If the person is not widely known, begin with a description of the speaker (an assistant professor of biology) and place the speaker's name in the second paragraph.

SAID WHAT

The Said What of the story is essential in stories about speeches. The Said What is either a summary of the speech or a description of one or two key points of the speech. The summary usually is at the end of the speech, in the conclusion section, and is usually preceded by *in conclusion* or *finally* or *therefore* or *to sum up* or the like. It is the time in the speech when the speaker tells the audience briefly the reason for the speech and what the audience should know or should consider doing.

To Whom

The To Whom of the story is the speaking event—the audience and the reason for the speech—and usually is placed in the second paragraph. Include the name of the group, the reason for the speaking event (annual banquet, political campaign, civic club luncheon, and so on), and the number of people present. Be sure to mention anyone of importance, such as elected officials, and whether and how frequently the speaker was interrupted by applause.

The size of the audience is available through several means. In an outdoor event, the most reliable source is a police official, because the police are used to handling crowds and can estimate size fairly accurately. In a paid-for event—an auditorium, a hotel dining room—ask the proprietor or manager for the *gate,* the number of paid admissions or meals served. In a small event, count the number of attendees yourself. If a gate is unavailable and you know the number of seats in an auditorium, estimate the number of attendees by sight.

Why

The Why of the story is the reason for the speech and the speaking event. Usually, this is built into the description of the To Whom.

Where

The Where of the story is the place of the speech: city, building, room number, and so on. Sometimes, it is built-in: New Orleans Rotary Club.

When

The When of the story is the day or date, and sometimes the hour, of the speaking event. It is never *recently,* which is vague and meaningless.

How

The How of the story is not always present in stories about speeches. When it is present, however, it must be included.

So What

After you have written your lead, read it aloud and listen to the flow of language. Ask yourself if what you have written tells the whole story of the speech, if what you have written summarizes the speech or presents one or two key points. If not, rewrite the lead. If your verb is *spoke about*, rewrite the lead because *spoke about* tells readers nothing more than the topic of the speech. Those are called *speaker-spoke* leads because they tell readers only that someone spoke. Your task is to tell readers what the speaker said, not that the speaker said something or what the speaker spoke about.

The Story

The key points in a speech story are the speaker and what the speaker said, a summary of the speech.

The lead should follow this format, if the speaker is in the public domain:

Dallas Mayor Jonathan Price [Who and built-in Where] urged members of the Chamber of Commerce [To Whom] to support the city's plan to increase property taxes [Said What] to provide more recreational parks [Why].

The mayor was the keynote speaker at the annual Chamber of Commerce awards banquet that attracted 125 members and their spouses and guests.

Or your lead should follow this format, if the speaker is not in the public domain:

The president of the DPS Co. [Who] urged members of the Dallas Chamber of Commerce [to Whom and built-in Where] to support the city's plan to increase property taxes [Said What] to provide more recreational parks [Why].

President Andrew Hampden was the keynote speaker the annual CofC awards banquet that attracted 125 members and their spouses and guests.

Thereafter, alternate paragraphs of information with paraphrased statements and quotations. Select only quotable, meaningful, quotations. If you can paraphrase a quotation better, the quotation is not quotable.

Notes

If a question-and-answer session follows the speech, use the information in your story, but identify that information as being from the question-and-answer session and not as being part of the speech itself.

In writing about a political campaign speech, include the name, title, and political affiliation of the person introducing the speaker because it indicates the political strength of the speaker in that community. In other speeches, identifying the introducer is your decision.

It is proper to use partial quotations in the lead. But do not begin a speech story with a full quotation. Quotations lifted from a speech do not lend themselves to lead material because they do not summarize the speech. In addition, using a complete quotation as the lead requires a second sentence that usually begins, "That is the position of the president of the DPS Co. who spoke to _____." Such an approach is poor writing and should be avoided.

Do not end a speech story with *in conclusion* or *finally* or *concluded* or *in closing*, and so on. Information in the conclusion of a speech usually belongs in the lead and should not be repeated at the end of the story.

Titles of speeches and themes of conventions and speeches are meaningless to readers and a waste of words. Omit them from the story. Some speeches are titled "As I See It" and "The View from the Capitol," both of which tell readers nothing. Convention themes frequently are titled "Frontierland" and "New Beginnings," equally meaningless.

Said is the most applicable and appropriate verb of attribution; use it frequently. It has no hidden meanings, and it hides in the story. Otherwise, the verb of attribution must reflect the speaker's meaning: *warned, urged, cautioned, called for, suggested,* and so on. *Stated* and *added* generally have no place in a speech story.

Before using any verb of attribution other than *said*, check the dictionary definition for meanings and usage. Do not trust your memory or your normal use of the verb. For example: *Refute* requires solid evidence; people may *deny* anything, even the truth; only officials really *state* anything, and only occasionally; and, because most speeches are prepared well in advance, seldom is anything ever *added* to a speech.

Avoid such verbs of attribution as *discussed, explained, addressed,* and *spoke* because they tell readers nothing, at all.

At the close of any speech, you may approach the speaker for additional information. If you use the additional information in your story, be sure to explain that it was not part of the speech.

11

How to Cover Meetings

This explains how groups function, how groups do what they do, the rules that groups must follow, and what to look for when groups meet.

All groups, from a three-member committee to the 435-member United States House of Representatives, operate the same way, under the same rules of order, and each group represents a larger body. All groups have the same charge: to do for the larger group what the larger group—because of its size—cannot do for itself. For example, the Congress represents the nation; the state legislature represents the state; the city council represents the city; the board of directors represents the corporation; the board of deacons represents the church.

Groups are made up of elected or appointed officials (state legislature, city council), corporate boards of directors (usually based upon their positions in the corporation), association boards of governors, church boards of deacons, and the like. Groups have committees, and committees have subcommittees. Each group (the main or parent group, the committee, the subcommittee) represents and acts for and in behalf of the next higher group. The subcommittee reports to the committee; the committee reports to the main or parent group.

All groups do three things and three things only: They meet, they discuss items on the agenda, and they vote on those items. A group cannot vote unless it meets, and whatever the group votes for becomes effective immediately or at a date specified. The vote is the voice of the group, not of the members. Members speak for themselves during discussion, but each member votes as part of the group.

The vote is the way the group speaks; it is the How of the story. The vehicle of speech for the group is what it votes on: *resolution, ordinance, bill, statute, proposal,* whatever—all merely pieces of paper. To learn what the group vote said, you must read the resolution, ordinance, bill, statute, proposal, whatever, and write your story on what that piece of paper says.

Before you can cover any group, you must know three things: the group's function, the reason for the group and what it is legally allowed to do; the rules of order that all groups follow; and the group's action, what goes on during the meeting.

Group Function

Groups come in three main types: final action, recommendation, and legislative. Be careful, though, some groups—such as the national Conference of Catholic Bishops, Southern Baptist Convention, church boards of deacons, sorority and fraternity executive groups, and some corporate boards of directors and association boards of governors—are private, and you may cover them only by permission. Otherwise, you may violate their right of privacy.

- **Final action groups** are those whose decisions are effective immediately. They include city councils, county commissioners, corporate boards of directors, association boards of governors, and church boards of deacons. The final action of such groups can be overturned only by later action by the group or by the main body of citizens whom they represent, or by the civil (chancery) courts.
- **Recommendation groups** include committees, subcommittees, the faculty senate of most universities and colleges, and, in some states, city planning and zoning commissions. The final action of such groups is only to recommend action to a higher authority, the group of final action. The subcommittee recommends to the committee; the committee recommends to the group of final action; the planning and zoning commission recommends to the city council; the faculty senate recommends to the president of the university or college.
- **Legislative groups** have a different charge. In general, they are groups of recommendation, but they can be groups of final action. Both the U.S. Congress and the legislatures in 49 states consist of two houses: a House of Representatives and a Senate. The Nebraska Legislature consists of a Senate only. The Congress and the legislature in all 50 states function much the same way: To become law, whatever bill is approved in one house must be approved by the other house (except in Nebraska) in exactly the same language and be signed by the president or by the governor or let become law without a signature.

The Congress and legislatures become groups of final action by overriding the veto of a bill by the president or by the governor, thereby implementing the action of the Congress or the legislature.

Note—Most city, county, state, and national government meetings are open to the public. However, some items taken up in government are, by law, private, and are discussed only in *executive session*. When a group goes into executive session, either the meeting room is cleared of all but members and group officials or members and group officials move to a private room. The final action, however, the vote on matters discussed in executive session, must be taken in public.

In writing your story, consider:

- It is wordy and unnecessary to tell readers that the group met, because groups do not exist until they meet. Thus, when you write "The Springfield City Council," you have told readers that it was a meeting, that the members sat as a group. Until a group meets, its members have no more power, except that of influence, than any other citizen.
- It is wordy and unnecessary to tell readers that the group voted, because all groups vote at least once: to adjourn. For a more powerful lead sentence, pick a verb that tells what the group did, the group's final and most important action, such as: *increased* (instead of *voted to increase*) a tax, *ordered* (instead of *voted to order*) something done, *established* (instead of *voted to establish*) something, *abolished* (instead of *voted to abolish*) something.
- It is wordy and unnecessary to tell readers that the group discussed or explained anything; that's what groups do. Telling readers that the group *discussed* an agenda item does not tell readers what the group *did* about that agenda item. Moreover, a discussion involves information on both sides of the issue, and an explanation requires detailed information, which, in either case, you will have later in the story.
- It is necessary, however, to remember that groups represent and act in the best interest of the whole community. Groups take into consideration what witnesses and petitioners request or suggest, but they do not act because of what witnesses and petitioners request or suggest. Thus, do not focus your meeting story on whether the request of a few people was approved or denied. Information from such people may be in support of, but, in general, it is not the primary reason for, the group vote. If it is the primary reason for the group vote, and you can document that, you have a much better story, because the group may be biased or have a conflict of interest.

Parliamentary Procedure

By law, every group must follow the rules of order that govern meetings. Those rules—guidelines, really—are called *parliamentary procedure* and *parliamentary law*. They are not tricks to circumvent action by some members. It is a set of procedures that enables groups to conduct business. To cover meetings properly, you should be generally familiar with parliamentary procedure. No group—public, private, church, student, whatever—is above following parliamentary procedure. Actions of any group are subject to review in civil (chancery) court, and the court has the legal right to overturn actions that violate the group's constitution, even actions of church groups.

The rules of parliamentary procedure are described in two books:

- Darwin Patnode, *Robert's Rules of Order: Modern Edition*, revised, Uhrichsville, OH: Barbour & Company, Inc., 1996.

"Robert," who only seems to own the Rules of Order, was Henry Martyn Robert, a colonel in the U.S. Army during the Civil War. In 1862, troubled by the absence of order during church meetings, he codified the rules of parliamentary procedure that are used today.

- Alice Sturgis, *The Standard Code of Parliamentary Procedure*, 4th ed., Revised and Updated, New York: McGraw-Hill Book Company, 2001.

Sturgis defined parliamentary law as "the procedural safeguard that protects the individual and the group in their exercise of the rights of free speech, free assembly, and the freedom to unite in organizations for the achievement of common aims. These rights, too, are meaningless, and the timeless freedoms they define can be lost, if parliamentary procedure is not observed."

Group Action

Groups always accomplish at least one of the following:

- Pass an agenda item.
- Kill or reject an agenda item.
- Refer an agenda item to a committee.
- Postpone or delay an agenda item. Never use the term *table*, because *table* has two meanings: to postpone an agenda item indefinitely, which kills the agenda item; and to postpone an agenda item to a date.
- Receive or collect information from a staff member or from an outsider. Never write *heard* or *listened to* because you don't know if anyone

heard or listened to the information. Most information is presented to a group both orally and in writing, so members can read it later. In your story, be sure to state the source and purpose of the information and what action the group took.

- Recommend a course of action on an agenda item.
- Take under consideration an agenda item or a proposal.
- Take no action on an agenda item. Remember, *took no action* is an action.

How Groups Function

The group considers proposals presented by members—only members can introduce items for consideration—but, because the group usually cannot consider every item presented, it establishes committees, both standing and special, and assigns members to them. Each committee is assigned a specific area of study: taxation, the budget, highways and bridges, public health, education, agriculture, insurance, public safety, law enforcement, the courts, and so on.

The committees do the detailed study of the proposal, inviting testimony from witnesses and experts and lobbyists, and recommending that the parent group approve or disapprove the proposals. The final decision on whether to approve or disapprove the proposal rests with the parent group, and there is no requirement that the parent group follow the committee recommendation.

Items presented for consideration take the form of resolutions or ordinances or laws or amendments or other pieces of paper. In themselves, those pieces of paper are merely the vehicles for putting into effect what the group wants to do. The key information is not the piece of paper itself but what the piece of paper would put into effect.

The Congress and the states pass laws; cities pass ordinances. All groups adopt (not pass) resolutions, documents complimenting or honoring people or groups for their accomplishments and actions for society.

Any group—the Senate, the House of Representatives, the church board of deacons, whatever—can do anything it wishes. However, because the same parliamentary rules of order apply to all groups, if what the group does is illegal or violates parliamentary procedure, a civil (chancery) court may void that action.

In general, groups consist of an odd number of members to help guarantee a majority vote because a tie vote loses.

Large groups (more than eleven members) tend to operate more formally than do small groups (three to eleven members).

A *quorum* is the least number of members of a group needed to transact business. The most usual quorum is a simple majority of the members, one more than half. But the bylaws of the group may fix the quorum at more or fewer members.

Proposals under discussion may be changed by *amendments*, which must be voted on before the final vote on the proposal itself.

All actions in groups begin with a motion by a member, a request that an action be taken. The member, after being recognized by the presiding officer, announces, "I move that" a bill be called up for consideration, the debate be closed, the meeting adjourned, and so on.

All motions require a second, an agreement by another member. A second does not announce support for the motion; it merely announces support for consideration of the motion. A motion to adjourn is the only motion that may not be debated before the vote.

Many groups have a parliamentarian, a person hired to work for the presiding officer and to offer advice, opinions, and explanations about parliamentary procedure.

Proposals proffered by witnesses cannot be considered immediately, but are submitted to a committee or a knowledgeable group for study and recommendations.

Every action a group takes—even if it takes no action—is a positive action, is the will of the majority, and each member and the parent organization accepts and abides by the decision.

Groups cannot *fail* to do anything, because groups operate on majority rule. If an agenda item does not pass, the group did not *fail to pass* the item, the group *defeated* or *killed* or *refused to pass* the item, always a positive action. Thus the United States Senate cannot fail to override the president's veto, but it can and frequently does refuse to override the president's veto.

Although whatever action a group takes is binding, it cannot be binding forever; the group can change or negate the action on a later date. A law or action approved by one Congress, one legislature, one city council, one board of directors, and so on, can be amended or repealed by a later Congress, a later legislature, a later city council, a later board of directors, and so on.

Do not write that a witness or petitioner *told the members*, but either that the witness or petitioner *said* or *told the group*. It is the group, not the individual member, that votes, acts, receives information, and so on. The members vote individually, of course, but their voting is a group action.

During meetings, you should not interrupt members—in fact, some groups forbid such action—but before and after any meeting, you may approach any member of the group or such group officials as the secretary and the attorney for additional information.

Occasionally, the mayor will present a citation or award to a person, a group, a school, a team, a whatever action worth reporting. In the presentation, the people present will applaud. Reporters do not applaud. Reporters are there to report the action, not to participate in the action.

Covering Meetings

In covering a meeting, don't forget the Ws: Who, Did What, and Why. You are not writing minutes; you are telling readers everything that the group did, beginning with its most important action. The vote is the How, how the group did what it did, the parliamentary procedure the group followed in doing what it did, in accomplishing its action.

The Who is the name of the group: Springfield City Council, Southern Baptist Convention, the ABC Corp. Board of Directors, the Committee on Equal Rights, and so on.

The Did What is the final action of the group, not the action of witnesses or petitioners. If you mention the vote, put it up high in the story.

The vote count itself usually is important enough to be reported, though not always in the lead sentence. Sometimes, it is important to name the members who voted *aye*, who voted *no*, who abstained from voting, and who were absent and why. It is not always important to name the member(s) who introduced the proposal, but if it is important to the story, include the name(s). But, regardless of who introduced the proposal, once the group adopts it, it is the action of the group.

The Why of the story is essential, because group action is always done for a reason. If the city council increased the sales tax, find out why and tell readers what the city plans to do with the additional revenue. If the organization accepted associate members, find out why and tell readers the reason.

Above all, write tight; get to the point; avoid redundancies.

The group considers proposals presented by members—only members can introduce items for consideration—but, because the group usually cannot consider every item presented, it establishes committees, both standing and special, and assigns members to them. Each committee is assigned a specific area of study: taxation, the budget, highways and bridges, public health, education, agriculture, insurance, public safety, law enforcement, the courts, and so on.

The committees do the detailed study of the proposal, inviting testimony from witnesses and experts and lobbyists, and recommending that the parent group approve or disapprove the proposals. The final decision on whether to approve or disapprove the proposal rests with the parent group, and there is no requirement that the parent group follow the committee recommendation.

Items presented for consideration take the form of resolutions or ordinances or laws or amendments or other pieces of paper. In themselves, those pieces of paper are merely the vehicles for putting into effect what the group wants to do. The key information is not the piece of paper itself but what the piece of paper would put into effect.

Every group meeting makes available an agenda or calendar, a list of items to be considered, and you should have a copy for reference during the meeting. The agenda items are taken up one at a time in the order listed.

In covering a meeting, you may—in fact, you should—ignore such actions as who opened the meeting, who led the Pledge of Allegiance, who led the opening and closing prayers, the approval of the minutes of the previous meeting, and other housekeeping actions, all of which are part of the minutes of the meeting as prepared by the group secretary.

Be alert not only to the vote but also to the wording of the proposal being voted on because a positive vote on a negatively stated motion defeats the motion. And, remember, a tie vote loses.

On the other hand, in writing about action of the Senate and House of Representatives, and any other group of recommendation, your lead should include the vote because the action is only a recommendation to the other house or to the president or to the governor. Thus, your lead should say, "The House of Representatives voted 86–25 to abolish the death penalty and sent the bill to the Senate," or something similar.

If the vote count is important, the form changes: The group "voted 5–4 to admit associate members," or, "added associate members on a 5–4 vote," or, "increased the sales tax on a unanimous vote."

The following matrix will help you determine your lead for a meeting story. Answers to the all-capitals questions—WHO, DID WHAT, WHY—must be in the lead of every meeting story. Answers to the c/lc questions—Where, When, How—may be placed in the first or second sentence or paragraph.

WHO

The Who of the story is essential in stories about meetings. This is the group itself, the name of the group. You are not covering the members of the group, the witnesses, the petitioners, or anyone else; you are covering the group itself. Begin your story with the name of the group.

Report in the body of the story what members of the group did or said if their actions or statements are newsworthy.

DID WHAT

The Did What of the story is essential in stories about meetings. The Did What is the final action of the group. It is not the action of the witnesses or the petitioners. If you mention the vote, put it up high in the story.

WHY

The Why of the story is essential in stories about meetings and about government because their action is always done for a reason. The reason is important and must be included in the lead. If the city council increases the sales tax, find out and tell readers what the city council intends to do with the additional revenue. If a group admits associate members, find out and tell readers why the group thinks associate members are necessary or desirable.

> **Note**—During meetings, you should not interrupt members—in fact, some groups forbid such action—but before and after any meeting, you may approach any member of the group for additional information. The group secretary is a prime source of information, but do not quote any secretary by name without permission.

Where

The Where of the story is the place of the meeting: city, building, room number, and so on. Sometimes, it is built in: Springfield City Council.

When

The When of the story is the day or the date, and sometimes the hour, of the meeting. It is never recently, which is vague and meaningless.

How

The How of the story is not always present in stories about meetings. When it is present, however, it must be included.

So What

After you have written your lead, read it aloud and listen to the flow of language. Ask yourself if what you have written tells the whole story of what the group did, and if it gets to the point. If not, rewrite the lead.

The Story

Your lead should follow this format:

The Springfield School Board [Who with built-in Where] increased property taxes by two cents [Did What] Tuesday [When] to enlarge the high school football stadium [Why].

The second paragraph should fill in the major details in support of the lead sentence, including the amount of revenue expected, the cost per $1,000 of property value, and the date the increase becomes effective.

Subsequent paragraphs should provide newsworthy quotations from members of the school board and from citizens and school officials who spoke before the school board, and appropriate actions during the meeting.

Use this format to list group action of lesser importance:

In other action (or business), the City Council:

- Ordered a traffic signal installed at the intersection of Woodward Avenue and Briarcrest Road in an effort to reduce traffic accidents.

- Set June 12 for the election to elect a municipal court judge to fill the vacancy left by the death of Ray Wilhelm. Wilhelm, who had served as a judge for 32 years, was instrumental in helping change state law to require that municipal judges hold a law degree.

- Honored Caitlin Alexander, 12, for her courageous efforts in saving the lives of her mother, Holly Alexander, and infant brother, Liam, after a candle ignited curtains in his bedroom.

- Declared October Children's Good Health Month for free inoculations for flu.

Note—Each line of each bulleted paragraph wraps to the left margin. But, use your own bullets or numbers, not the bullet or number icon on the ribbon at the top of the document.

The subject of each bulleted item is "City Council" in the first line of the story.

Each bulleted item is indented and begins with a capitalized past tense verb and ends with a period, instead of with the grammatical semicolon. This is done so that, if the last bulleted item is deleted, the previous bulleted paragraph need not be reset to replace a semicolon with a period at the end of the line.

12

How to Cover Education

> Covering education is not as difficult as you might think, and it can be
> profitable and, well, educational.

Education probably is the least covered of any government endeavor. That
may seem strange in light of the fact that, by law, until age eighteen, every
child is required to attend school, and more and more people of all age
groups are voluntarily attending colleges and universities, either in class
or online.

Covering education, like covering any other human endeavor, is not so
much difficult as it is demanding. You must know your topic; you must
make your rounds; you must observe, you must know your sources, you
must ask questions, you must listen to the answers, and you must write
your stories.

All schools are either public—established by the people, funded by tax
revenue, and controlled by a school board—or private—established by a
religion or a private group of citizens and funded by private means.

Although private schools at any level are just that, private, they must
abide by state laws concerning education in general, including required
courses for and certification of teachers. It's the requirements of those laws
that give the reporter the right to cover private as well as public schools and
colleges and universities.

Schools are set up, in general, in three stages: elementary school (grades
kindergarten to 6), junior high school (grades 7, 8, 9), and senior high
school (grades 10, 11, 12); Colleges are two-year community colleges (that
proffer basic classroom courses) and vocational colleges (that proffer on-

the-job courses in welding, cabinet making, plumbing, and so on), both of which confer associate's degrees; four-year colleges and universities that confer bachelor's degrees in multiple areas of study; and universities that proffer years of graduate work and confer master's and doctor's degrees in multiple areas of study and in research.

Public schools are established by cities, by counties, or by districts, and are supervised by school boards, groups of citizens headed by a superintendent, that meet regularly and have the authority to hire and fire teachers and administrators, to provide salary increases, to enlarge schools, to fund programs, and to help with the decision on what books will be in the school libraries.

> **Note**—Students do not *graduate* high school, college, or university. It's the other way around: The high school, college, university graduates the student. However, it is acceptable to say that the student *graduated from* high school, college, university. High schools award diplomas; colleges and universities award degrees.

Nearly every public school has a Parent Teacher Association (PTA) that provides a relationship between parents, teachers, and students; assists teachers; raises funds for supplemental educational materials; supports school and family social interaction; and provides a forum for sharing information on issues that impact children.

Your task in covering education is to cover the whole operation, including groups that function within the schools. The best way to cover any school is to visit the school frequently and to ask questions.

More important, though, is to cover the governing body of the schools, the school board and superintendent. Get to know the superintendent and the key staff members. More important, get to know the secretary of each key staff member; if you treat them properly, the secretary at any level can provide you more information than you can imagine. Just don't mention the secretary's name in your story or in your follow-up interviews.

Visit each school in your area on a regular basis and get to know the principal and vice principals and their secretaries, and the office staff. Give each principal and key staff member and secretary your business card and invite each to contact you with whatever information they have, at any hour, day or night, on any day, workday, or weekend or holiday. Emphasize that you will feel free to contact them on the same basis for whatever information you want from them. And don't hesitate to do so when the need arises.

Community colleges are set up by counties or by districts to provide the first two years of college courses for two purposes: to enable students to save money by living at home rather than in a dormitory in another city, and to relieve universities of the expense of providing faculty and space to teach those two years of courses. Community colleges confer associate's degrees.

Universities, set up by states or by religions or private groups, are more expensive because they provide four years of study and dormitories, laundry equipment, cafeterias, medical facilities, barbers, chapels, and so on, because students are in another city and cannot always go home for such needs.

A university is a collection of colleges—liberal arts, science, engineering, business, education, agriculture, and so on. A college is a collection of departments—the College of Engineering has departments of civil, of electrical, of mechanical, of nuclear, of petroleum, of computer science, and so on. Some departments are a collection of study fields—the Department of Communication has speech, journalism, broadcasting, public relations, advertising, and so on. All of that information is available either in a university or college handbook or online at the university or college Website. That handbook and Website list the name and teaching area of every administrator, faculty member, and staff member on campus.

In covering schools, colleges, and universities, do not disrupt classes; wait until class ends before approaching the teacher or a student. In covering the administrative side, remember that people at that level are continually in meetings or in discussions with colleagues or with visitors. You may have to schedule an appointment.

Remember how colleges and universities are set up:

Universities are governed by a president and vice presidents of Academic Affairs, Student Affairs, Operations, Facilities, Finance, Legal, Research, Public Relations, and so on, depending upon the size of the university, and universities consist of colleges that teach various programs of study.

Colleges—Liberal Arts, Education, Architecture, Business, Engineering, Science, and so on—are governed by a dean, an associate dean, and several assistant deans because each college consists of several departments: College of Science has Biology, Chemistry, Mathematics, Physics, Statistics. Some departments have schools to teach specific programs.

The president and various vice presidents will give you information about the entire university, increase and decrease in the budget or in donations, the number of students, the number of incoming students and graduates, plans for increasing or reducing faculty and staff—all good story ideas. Deans will give you the same information about the college, and department heads will give you the same information about the department.

Department heads will go further, giving you information about what faculty members are doing, what research they have conducted or are conducting. You want to meet with research faculty and ask them about their research and what it means, who it will benefit. Nearly every one of them is worth a story.

State universities are regulated by a state board, so be sure to add that agency to your beat and to attend board meetings.

Coverage of school, college, university activities will be rather routine—budgets, hiring/firing personnel, evaluation of teachers and schools—but there is a part of coverage of college and university that is more interesting and exciting: research conducted by faculty members and graduate students.

Most universities require their professors to *publish or perish*, conduct research and publish the findings in a scholarly journal available to all faculty members in the field and to anyone interested in reading it. Research and publication are essential in teaching because they provide teachers the latest information in their field, thereby enhancing the information they pass on to their students and to teachers nationally.

But university research is not confined to the university. Much of the findings in university research is useful to professionals.

Covering Research

The major fun part of covering education is covering faculty members' research projects at universities and colleges. Promotion, tenure, and salary increase are based on the amount of research and service done by the faculty member and the quality of the faculty member's teaching. The requirements work this way:

Faculty members with a doctorate are hired as assistant professor, the lowest rank and pay scale. They have six years to qualify for promotion to associate professor with tenure. To qualify, faculty members must do research and publish the findings in scholarly journals and provide service to the department, to the college, to the university, to the city, and to various organizations.

> **Note**—In universities and colleges, tenure means a permanent appointment, but it does not mean that a tenured faculty member cannot be fired.

After three years, the efforts are evaluated and the assistant professors are advised on what they need to do to continue.

After six years, those who complete the requirements are promoted to associate professor with tenure, and a salary increase commensurate with the rank. After that, they have five years to qualify, with more research, publication, service, and teaching quality, for promotion to professor and a salary increase commensurate with the rank. No one is promoted to *full* professor; there is no such rank, just as there is no *full governor* or *full president.*

Research projects serve three main purposes:

1. Published in a scholarly journal or not, they help faculty members gain promotion, tenure, and salary raises.
2. Published in a scholarly journal, they provide faculty members in the same discipline in other colleges and universities new information to teach, thereby enhancing education.
3. Published in a scholarly journal, they provide information for professionals in the field to use to improve their business techniques. The catch is that most professionals never read scholarly journal reports about research projects.

What that means is a feature story tells about the research findings and their application in the field. Getting faculty members to talk about their research findings and their application is fairly easy. Any mention of the findings in any publication—newspaper, magazine, Internet—is helpful to the faculty member.

You have two options to write about research: You can interview the faculty member or you can read the scholarly journal article.

Interviewing the faculty member is easy. On campus, ask a department head who in the department is conducting research and schedule an appointment with that faculty member. Without doubt, the faculty member would be delighted to be interviewed and have a story about the research published in a newspaper or a magazine or on the Internet.

If you have to read a scholarly journal to learn about research projects, it's only a bit more difficult, and you still should interview the faculty member.

Why and How to Read Scholarly Journals

Scholarly studies are too complete for anyone but faculty members, providing a discussion of what the study is about, a review of literature of previous studies along the same lines, a detailed account of the methodology used in completing the study, a discussion of findings, a conclusion, and a list of references and people cited in the article, and all done in stuffy writing. Dull stuff, indeed, yet it's no worse than reading an appellate court decision. You just have to know what articles to read and how to read them.

The best part of those scholarly research reports is that they provide current information on activities relevant to newspaper, radio, and television reporters and to advertising and public relations executives. For example, advertising executives could benefit from a study on the effect of humor in advertising, and managing editors could benefit from a study on what news stories men and women read, how much of the stories they read, and how they react to them.

So far, professionals have profited little from scholarly research studies, because they don't read them. But, news, advertising, and public relations practitioners should sift through the appropriate journals to help them become more proficient in their jobs.

Each year, 7,000 scholarly journals are published nationwide, each one containing six to eight articles, altogether too many for the average reporter or account executive to sift through regularly. But, professionals may take heart; scholarly journals are published quarterly, not monthly, and you don't need to read all of them, or even all of one article.

But you do need to read them. Here are some scholarly journals that everyone in the mass media should find helpful:

- **Mass Media Journals:** *Journalism and Mass Communication Quarterly, Communication Theory, Journal of Communication, Communication Research, Critical Studies of Mass Media, Journal of Communication Inquiry, Journal of Applied Communication Research.*

Journals specific to the fields of news media:

- **Newspaper:** *Newspaper Research Journal.*
- **Broadcast:** *Journal of Broadcasting, The Journal of Radio Studies.*
- **Public Relations:** *Public Relations Quarterly, Public Relations Review, Public Relations Research, Public Opinion Quarterly.*
- **Advertising:** *Journal of Advertising Research, International Journal of Advertising, Journal of Advertising.*
- **Marketing:** *Journal of Marketing, Journal of Marketing Research.*

However, reading even one publication of a scholarly research problem leaves most professionals bleary-eyed with minutiae so necessary to academicians: details about the methodology of the research project, references to applicable previous studies, and a bibliography of studies and people cited, none of which may be appropriate to the professional.

The solution is fairly simple. Professionals should go online or to a university library and find the journal(s) appropriate to their work. The name of the journal usually indicates the professional market. Don't forget, the librarian is a marvelous aide.

Search Engines

- Google Scholar; Alternative Press Index; Academic Search Premier/Elite (EBSCO); MasterFILE Premier (EBSCO); Wilson OmniFile Full Text, Mega Edition.
- ABI/INFORM Global: for worldwide business and management issues in 1,300 journals.
- Cambridge Scientific Abstracts: for business, organization, management communication, writing, mass communication, journalism, public opinion, television/film studies, and media studies.
- ComAbstracts: for abstracts of studies in communication, speech, composition, journalism, mass media, and social sciences.
- Dialog/DataStar: for case studies of company profiles, management and marketing techniques, and customer relations.
- LexisNexis Academic: for articles from newspapers, magazines, newswires, and television and radio transcripts.

One of the advantages of most of those search engines is that they provide an alert service. Once you click on the alert button and complete the information form, the search engine will alert you when new information is filed on that search engine. Another advantage is that you can email to yourself the entry called up.

If you go to a university library to read the journal books, you have another advantage: Every ten years, journals publish an Index of Titles of the previous ten years. With two Indexes, you can go through 20 years of journals in half an hour. Ask a librarian.

Reading a Journal Article

But all of that just produces the scholarly research report in all its dull glory. That's only if you read the journal articles in full. Professionals really don't need to do that.

The best part of the journal article is the part that explains what it means. So, here's how to find that information, easily and quickly.

Call up the appropriate journal. Read the titles in the Table of Contents. Scholarly journal titles are not like newspaper headlines; they are full sentences that describe in some detail what the research study is about.

If the title tells you that the article may be of value to you, turn to the article and read the Abstract. Scholarly journal Abstracts, 250 to 300 words, describe the research study in clear detail: what the project studied and what conclusions were drawn.

If the abstract whets your interest, skip the review of literature of previous studies and the methodology; they are there for other academics who may want to replicate that study. Instead, go directly to the Results and Conclusions section at the end of the article. That's where you will find how you can apply the results of that study to your work. Chances are, that section will be 500 words at most. The writing style may be stuffy and pedantic, but the information will be invaluable.

So, there you have it, a four-part operation:

- Find the appropriate journal(s).
- Read the article titles.
- If an article title attracts you, read the article's Abstract.
- If the article's Abstract attracts you, read the article's Results and Conclusion.
- And profit by what you have learned.

Before writing a story, though, reporters should interview the research author for additional information.

13

How to Cover Universities

Universities provide so much newsworthy information that it's a wonder that they are not covered more thoroughly.

Universities probably are the least covered of any human endeavor, and they have so much to offer: They teach people to prepare for life and for careers, and the faculty members conduct research that results in ways to improve every facet of life for everyone. Research is conducted in every field: medicine, government, science, technology, engineering, architecture, agriculture, art, music, and so on; the list is almost endless. Teaching itself depends upon research. Without research and publication of the findings, there would be little new to teach, and life and careers would a lot less interesting and a lot more difficult.

Because research is so important to teaching and to universities, most universities require their faculty to conduct research and publish the findings, usually in scholarly journals, and as frequently as possible.

All universities—public, private, large, small—function the same way; they have the same organization; and they operate like any corporation. The only difference is that the product of the university, unlike that of a manufacturing corporation, is the graduate, the educated student, who has a broader view of life.

Public universities are state agencies; they are run by the state. Their administrators and faculty and staff are paid by the state. Most private universities are run by a religion—Baylor, Baptist; Notre Dame, Catholic—and some are run by private enterprise—Stanford University.

Nevertheless, their corporate structure remains the same. The top administrative officers are the president and vice presidents for Academic Affairs,

Note—In a sense, a university is a city; indeed, some universities have a greater population (students, faculty, staff) than some cities, even than some counties. Moreover, the general population of the university (the students) ranges in age from 18 to 25 years and has generally the same degree of education, ranging from high school to three years of college. Adding graduate students and the faculty elevates the education level of a university to an extremely high plane.

for Administration, for Development, for Finance, for Student Affairs, for Legal, and so on. Each vice president has several assistants, each charged with specific duties. Each office is essential to keeping the university operating: deciding what courses to teach; deciding what buildings to erect, to refurbish, to raze; daily upkeep of the buildings and grounds, and securing the money to pay for the whole thing.

Public universities are governed by a board of regents or board of governors, usually appointed by the governor, whose duties are to authorize construction or remodeling of buildings, to add or delete degree programs, to promote and grant tenure to members of the faculty, to hire presidents, and so on. Private universities under the auspices of religious organizations are governed by a board usually appointed by the religion's officials.

Public universities and colleges are supported by the state and by contributions from private groups and from individuals. Private universities and colleges are supported by private groups and by individuals. The fiscal records of public universities and colleges are public record; the fiscal records of private universities and colleges are not.

Most universities have a provost, a chief officer who is second to the president, a sort of executive vice president. In fact, the provost usually serves as vice president for Academic Affairs.

Universities provide a system of government for their colleges: Agriculture, Business Administration, Communication, Education, Engineering, Liberal Arts, Science, Medicine, Theater, Veterinary Medicine, and so on.

Colleges are headed by a dean and associate deans and encompass departments and schools: Anthropology, Biology, Chemistry, Communication (or Journalism or Mass Communication), Economics, English, History, Psychology, Physics, Sociology, Government, various disciplines of Business Administration (Finance, Marketing, Management, and so on), various disciplines of engineering (Chemical, Civil, Electrical, Mechanical, Nuclear, Petroleum, and so on), various disciplines of Agriculture (Animal Science, Forest Science, Horticulture, Plant Pathology, Poultry, Soils and Crops, and so on).

Schools, headed by a director, are smaller than colleges and greater than departments and are limited to one field of study.

Departments are headed by a head or a chairman/chairwoman (never "chairperson," a vague term) and encompass divisions and programs of study: History is divided into United States History, World History, Ancient History, and so on; Communication is divided into Rhetoric and Public Address, Communication Theory, Mass Communication, Journalism, Advertising, Broadcast, and so on; English as a Second Language; Speech Pathology; and so on.

In addition, universities have centers and offices for various programs that cross college jurisdictions.

In summary, the administrators run the university; the deans run the colleges; the chairmen/chairwomen and directors run the schools and the departments, all making certain that the functions are fulfilled, that the faculty teach their courses and conduct their research and publish their findings. The administrative staff (the secretaries and clerks and other office workers) assists the administrators and the faculty, ensuring that supplies are available and that everyone is paid and on time. And the operations staff ensures that equipment and classrooms are available, in working order, and clean; maintains the grounds; and provides parking facilities.

Universities generally require their faculty members to hold a doctorate, the highest degree proffered at any university, signifying completion of formal education, a research project, and a commitment to research. Research is necessary because it provides additional information that can be disseminated to other colleges for use in teaching and research.

Faculty members have these duties: to teach, to perform service (to department, college, university, to city, to state, to nation, and so on), and to conduct research and to publish the findings in scholarly journals.

Note—Scholarly journals are *refereed*, meaning that, for a research manuscript to be accepted for publication, it must have been reviewed and recommended by at least three reviewers in the same discipline as the research. The reviewers frequently suggest improvements. It is a blind review, meaning that the author's name is removed from the manuscript so the reviewers do not know who conducted the research and wrote the paper.

The ranks of faculty member vary by university, but, in general, they are four, and all of them are on either a 9-month or 10½-month contract. Administrators are on a 12-month contract.

Instructor or Lecturer: The lowest teaching rank. Some universities use the title *instructor*, some use *lecturer*. Some universities use this rank for temporary or part-time teaching faculty. In general, instructors and lecturers are required to be excellent teachers and to perform service to the department, the college, and the university, but they are not required to conduct research and publish the findings.

Some universities have lecturer ranks: associate lecturer, lecturer, senior lecturer, and distinguished lecturer.

Assistant Professor: The lowest faculty rank and the first on *tenure* track. In general, incoming assistant professors have six years to qualify for tenure and promotion to associate professor, the next rank. After their third year, they are reviewed and advised. Failure to qualify results is dismissal. Qualification requires excellence in teaching, extensive service, and, most important, a sufficient number of publications in scholarly and professional journals.

> **Note**—Tenure signifies excellence, but it is more than that. It is job protection, a guarantee that the tenured faculty member will not be discharged without cause, without proof of undesirability for stated reason(s), or inability to teach or to produce publishable research, or wrongdoing.

Associate Professor: The middle tenure-track faculty rank and the one at which most faculty members retire. Requirements continue for excellence in teaching, for service, and for research and publication. Generally, the time limit for advancement is five years.

Professor: The highest faculty rank. There is no rank of *full* professor. Promotion to professor requires continued excellence in teaching, service, and research and publication, and at least five years as associate professor. Requirements continue for excellence in teaching, for service, and for research and publication.

Other professorial ranks are available:

Distinguished Professor: A special faculty rank to honor professors who have achieved national or international recognition. Many are on a 12-month contract.

Chair: Corporations and individuals frequently establish chairs in departments by providing invested funds whose interest pays the salary of the faculty member chosen for the honor of holding chair rank.

Professor Emeritus: An honor bestowed upon retirement after long or distinguished service. It permits, but does not require, continued service to the department and the college, and sometimes continues to provide an office. Some professors emeritus continue their research long after they retire.

Visiting Professor/Visiting Associate Professor/Visiting Assistant Professor/Visiting Distinguished Lecturer/Visiting Lecturer: Faculty members hired for a fixed period (one or two years) for a specific purpose, usually to teach a specific course or two.

Most universities use graduate students, those seeking master's and doctor's degrees, as teaching and research assistants. This provides the graduate student both an income and experience in teaching and in research. The salary is fixed and the hours are restricted to 20 a week because graduate students need time to attend their own courses.

Most faculty members are on a 9-month contract, teaching one or two, sometimes three, courses from September to May. This permits them to devote considerable time to research and writing. Some faculty members are on a 10½-month contract, meaning that they teach from September to May and half of the summer session. Few faculty members are on 12-month contracts. All contracts provide paid sick leave, but only 12-month contracts provide paid vacation.

The pay scales for each faculty rank have a minimum and maximum. The maximum of the lower rank is greater than the minimum of the higher rank. Thus, an associate professor with many years in the department could earn a higher salary than a professor with fewer years.

Community (Junior) Colleges

Most states have community (junior) colleges, two-year programs providing courses at the freshman-sophomore levels only. These colleges are supported by a single county or by groups of counties to provide the first two years of college education close to home. Community (junior) colleges are relatively inexpensive because they provide no dormitory space, and students can live at home and attend school as day students, much as do high school students. Community (junior) colleges award associate's degrees: Associate of Arts, Associate of Science, or specific degrees, according to the program.

Most important, community (junior) colleges relieve the burden on universities by teaching the first two years of courses required by all university degree programs. As a result, universities need fewer faculty members to teach the freshman-sophomore courses and can concentrate on the junior-senior and graduate courses and the demands of research and publication.

University Degree Programs

Most universities provide a full-service education, awarding bachelor's, master's, and doctor's degrees in nearly all disciplines. A few universities are restricted to the junior-senior level and the master's and doctor's programs.

The names of the usual degrees are Bachelor of Arts (B.A.), Bachelor of Science (B.S.), Bachelor of Business Administration (B.B.A.), Master of Arts (M.A.), Master of Science (M.S.), Master of Journalism (M.J.), Master of Business Administration (M.B.A.), Master of Public Administration (M.P.A.), Doctor of Philosophy (Ph.D.), Doctor of Education (Ed.D.), Doctor of Arts (D.A.), Doctor of Science (Sc.D.), Doctor of Medicine (M.D.), Doctor of Veterinary Medicine (D.V.M.), Doctor of Dentistry (D.D.S.), Juris Doctor (J.D.)

Note—The names of the degrees are neither plural nor possessive, never Bachelors of Science or Master's of Science. The degrees may be referred to in general as bachelor's degree, master's degree, and doctor's degree or doctoral degree or doctorate. But the title of the degree has the preposition "of." Look at any diploma; no *s* or *'s*.

Note—Colleges award degrees; high schools award diplomas.

Note—Students do not graduate college or high school. It's the other way around: The school graduates the student. However, it is acceptable to say that the student graduated from college or from high school.

There is little difference among bachelor's degrees and among master's degrees. Nearly all bachelor's degrees, notably the B.A., the B.S., and the B.B.A., require four years of study, and all have the same rank. The B.A. requires a foreign language; the B.S. substitutes courses for language; and the B.B.A. is business-based. The same is true of the master's degrees; the M.A. and the M.S. require 36 hours of coursework (32 hours if the student writes a thesis). The M.B.A., which is business-based, requires several years of professional experience for admission to the program and 52 hours of course work. The Master of Fine Art (M.F.A.) is a terminal degree in Fine Art, equivalent to the doctorate for promotion and tenure purposes.

The doctor's degrees are ranked. The Ph.D. is the highest degree because it is a research degree applicable to all fields of study: Journalism, Chemistry, Mechanical Engineering, Computer Science, Agriculture, Philosophy, and so on. Those who hold the Ph.D. are experts in their field.

The other doctor's degrees are specific to the discipline: the M.D. to physicians; the D.D.S. to dentists; the J.D. to lawyers; the Sc.D. to the sciences, the D.V.M. to veterinarians, the Ed.D. to teachers and principals, and so on.

Universities confer honorary degrees upon people whose accomplishments are noteworthy or who have contributed significantly to the university awarding the degree. Such degrees are Doctor of Letters (Litt.D.) and Doctor of Laws (LL.D.). Honorary degrees usually are conferred during commencement, before which the honoree makes a speech. An honorary degree does not require that the recipient even attended, much less graduated from, a college or university.

Note—There is no honorary Ph.D.; the only way to get one of those is to earn it.

The double requirement of research and service makes members of the faculty—particularly those with the Ph.D.—a prime source for information about almost every facet of life. Serving as a source for information about their research qualifies them in both research and service. As a result, research professors are eager to serve as a news source for reporters.

Reporters, therefore, should cultivate research faculty members, visiting them regularly for information about their research. In addition, reporters should cultivate department secretaries as a source for information because their job gives secretaries access to a broad range of information. Most secretaries are willing to talk to reporters about what research their professors are conducting.

> **Note**—Do not attribute information to a secretary without permission, and do not reveal the secretary as your source of information. Secretaries provide excellent tip service, but their CEOs are the only authoritative source of information.

In addition, get to know the president and vice presidents, the deans and department heads and other administrators. On a regular basis, make the rounds, in person or by telephone, of each one. Distribute your business card and invite each to contact you with whatever information they have, at any hour, day or night, on any day, workday or weekend or holiday. Emphasize that you will feel free to contact them on the same basis for whatever information you want from them. And don't hesitate to do so when the need arises.

Writing the University Story

The following matrix will help you determine your lead for a university story. Answers to the all-capitals questions—WHO, DID WHAT, WHY—must be in the lead of every university story. Answers to the capital-and-lower-case questions—Where, When, How—may be placed in the first or second paragraph.

Covering some activities of a university—meetings of groups, preparation of budgets, public lectures and speeches, theater, exhibitions of works of art, and so on—is similar to covering any governmental agency or corporation. Covering research may be more difficult because of the technical nature of the researcher's work.

WHO

The Who of the story is essential in stories about research. This is the researcher, by name if widely known or by title if not. In any case, this research is the source of the story. All of the information about the research is attributed to the researcher.

DID WHAT

The Did What of the story, essential in stories about research, is the results of the research, what the researcher learned and what conclusions were reached.

WHY

Research stories have both a *Why* and a *WHY*. The Why is the reason for the research; the WHY is the potential benefit to people. In general, the reason for the research, the Why, is that the researcher had a question and wanted an answer. The WHY is more important because the researcher's goal was so people could live better or be better educated or be better informed about life.

Where

The Where of the story is the place of the research, the university and the researcher's academic department.

When

The When of the story is the day or date, and sometimes the hour, of the interview about the research. It is never recently, which is vague and meaningless.

How

The How of the research is always important and of interest. It describes how long the research took and the details of the work of the researcher, including the difficulties the researcher overcame to arrive at the results.

The Body of the Story

The remaining paragraphs of the story present, in descending order of importance, the details of the research.

14

How to Cover Government, Taxes, and Political Campaigns

> Government is the heart of the United States. You're going to have a lot of
> fun covering government and taxes and political campaigns.

Government exists to do for the people what the people cannot do for themselves.

Examples are all around. The government provides for education, fire protection, law enforcement, the courts, health inspections, trash and garbage collections, sewage systems, potable water, highways and bridges, welfare, military defense. The list is almost endless.

To make it all work, the governmental establishes and staffs departments to oversee each governmental activity, and collects taxes from citizens to pay the costs.

Federal laws regulating all of those departments and levying taxes are made by Congress and approved by the president; similar state laws are made by state legislatures and approved by the governors.

Laws are designed to protect the citizens. Health inspections ensure that barbershops and beauty parlors and restaurants provide sanitary service. Firefighters not only extinguish fires but also provide information on fire safety. Paramedics and their ambulances respond to your home and to traffic accidents for medical concerns. The sheriff and the police provide protection against crime, arrest criminals, and provide information for individual protection against criminal acts. The courts prosecute and imprison criminals. The education department certifies teachers, chooses textbooks, builds schools, and provides education for students. The health department ensures that every faucet produces potable water and that sewers carry away effluent. Trash and garbage and recyclable materials are hauled away. Highways and bridges connect every city and town. Farm roads connect farms and ranches to town. Indigent, aged, and ailing people are provided money, food, and medical care through the welfare system. The military preserves the peace and protects against international attack and defends the country in time of war.

To pay for all those services, citizens pay taxes—taxes on property (home and automobile, called *ad valorem* because the tax is in proportion to the value), utilities (gasoline, electricity, water, sewage, natural gas, telephone), sales (of goods, but not always food and medicine), rental of hotel/motel rooms, inheritance, entertainment (movies, plays, concerts, cable systems). All that tax revenue is allocated to the various departments of government according to need. At the national level and in most states, a tax is levied on annual income. And, of course, there is Social Security, another tax.

Tax Revenue

Before you can become a complete citizen or a professional reporter, you must know what services and protection the government provides and how they are paid for, and how the duties of some agencies of government affect other agencies. It's simple: The people pay the government, through taxes, to do what they cannot do for themselves. A tax is a percentage based upon a fixed amount, and the money the tax produces is revenue. Thus, taxes are collected, but revenue, not taxes, is sent to the appropriate governmental agencies.

Here are examples of some of the protections and services provided by the governments:

Nation: Military defense (Air Force, Army, Coast Guard, Marine Corps, Navy); law enforcement and courts; immigration; purity of food, drugs, and medicine; highways and bridges; protection of rights of authors and inventors; retirement.

State: Military defense (National Guard); police protection; law enforcement and courts; health and medical; highways and bridges; welfare; education.

County: Records of birth, marriage, death, sale of property; health and medical; education; sheriff, law enforcement, courts.

City: Fire protection; police, law enforcement, and courts; medical and hospital; streets; utilities; education.

To provide all that protection and those services, government needs money. To get money, the government taxes its citizens. Here are the major taxes that the ordinary citizen pays and what the revenue is used for.

Nation: Income tax for general operation of the government; Social Security tax as a supplement to retirement; excise tax on such items as telephone and television; gasoline tax for highway construction, maintenance, and repair; alcohol tax and tobacco tax for enforcement of alcohol and tobacco laws.

State: Income tax (in most states) for general operation of the government; sales tax—the major source of revenue for the state—for general operation of the government; gasoline tax for highway construction, maintenance, and repair; alcohol tax and tobacco tax for enforcement of alcohol and tobacco laws.

County: Property tax—the major source of revenue for the county—on land, buildings, homes, vehicles for general operation of the government.

City: Sales tax—the major sources of revenue for the city—for general operation of the government; hotel/motel tax for attracting conventions; tobacco tax; utility tax for maintenance and repair of utilities; gasoline tax for street construction, maintenance, and repair.

School Districts: Property tax—the major sources of revenue for schools—for general operation of schools.

The sales tax, collected on the sale of just about everything—most states exempt food and medicine—is paid by everyone, regardless of income. Because it indicates how much people spend, sales tax revenue is an excellent indicator of the state of the economy.

In business, those who collect the sales tax are paid a fee for their work and are responsible for sending the revenue to the government tax collector.

Every month, businesses of all sorts and sizes send to the state comptroller's office the revenue from the taxes collected. The comptroller distributes to each governmental agency the amount of revenue due in accordance with the tax levied.

Revenue from gasoline taxes, which are levied by the nation, the state, and the city, is used for maintenance, repair, and construction of the federal and state highway systems: roads, bridges, culverts, fencing, mowing, city streets.

Revenue from taxes on hotel and motel rooms is used to attract conventions to the city. Conventions are a major source of revenue for the host city because every member of the convention spends upwards of $100 a day, a boost to the economy of the city. That adds up to a lot of tax revenue from hotel/motel rooms; general sales, including restaurants (because convention-goers eat out); and gasoline.

Revenue from property taxes, collected by the county tax collector, is distributed to the financial offices of the county, the city, and the school district.

To be a good citizen and an effective reporter, you need to know how the government functions and the role of its departments and how they interact. It is both simple and complicated, but it is more simple than complicated.

Three Branches of Government

You know from your study of civics in high school that the government, federal and state, is designed with checks and balances among three branches to prevent unwarranted concentration and abuse of power. The three branches are Legislative, which makes laws; Executive, which enforces laws; and Judicial, which interprets laws. All three branches are equal.

Legislative

At both the federal and state levels, the Legislative branch comprises a Senate, presided over by the president of the Senate (the vice president at the federal level and, usually, the lieutenant governor at the state level, neither of whom has a vote except in case of a tie), and a House of Representatives, presided over by the speaker of the House of Representatives, elected by the membership and third in line to succeed a fallen president or governor. At the federal level, the legislative branch is called Congress; at the state level, it is called *legislature.* Members of the federal House of Representatives are called representatives, abbreviated *Rep.,* or congressmen and congresswomen (there is no abbreviation *Cong.*). Members of state houses of representatives are called representatives and referred to as legislators or lawmakers. Members of the Senate at both the federal and state levels are called senator, abbreviated *Sen.*

Although only a representative may introduce a bill into the House and only a senator may introduce a bill into the Senate, private citizens and private organizations do have influence on the legislators because the legislators represent the people. From time to time, civic groups and private citizens request that a representative or senator introduce a bill for consideration.

The day-to-day work of studying the thousands of bills introduced in the House and Senate is assigned to the committees. This takes the burden off the whole House and the whole Senate.

The committee votes on recommending approval or rejection, and the bill is sent to the House or the Senate, as appropriate, for consideration and final action. In the House and in the Senate, no one but members may argue on a bill. Committee approval of a bill is not a guarantee, but it almost always results in approval by the House or the Senate.

Committee meetings usually are open to the public, so when bills come up for consideration in committee, anyone may testify for or against them, describing the need for and benefits of the bills. This is where the *lobbyists* come in.

A lobbyist is a person who represents a special interest group or private enterprise and tries to influence the introduction of or voting on legislative and other governmental matters. Some lobbyists are government employees who describe the potential effects of the proposal on the government agency involved, usually the cost of enforcing the terms of the proposal. As in any occupation, lobbyists generally are honorable people, seeking the best for their employers' interests.

Note—The term *lobbyist* came from the early-days practice of meeting with congressmen in the lobby of the U.S. Capitol.

After a bill passes both houses, it is *engrossed* (written in final form) and signed by the speaker of the House of Representatives and by the president of the Senate and sent to the governor or to the president to be signed into law, to be vetoed, or to become law after ten days if the governor or president declines to sign it into law or to veto it.

For a bill to become law, it must be approved in both houses and signed or let become law without a signature by the president or the governor. Thus, each house only recommends a bill to the other house, and, together, the two houses only recommend a bill to the president or to the governor.

What that means is that the lead for a story about passage of a bill by one house reads something like this.

The House of Representatives passed 68–35 and sent to the Senate Tuesday a bill to increase the state gasoline tax from 6 cents to 7.5 cents per gallon to help offset the increased cost of highway construction, maintenance, and repair.

Once an approved bill gets to the other house, it follows the same path to approval or rejection: introduction, assignment to committee, committee study and recommendation, and consideration by the whole house. You cover and report on those actions every step of the way.

To save time, some bills are introduced in both houses at the same time, enabling the appropriate committees to begin their study immediately and propose their recommendations. Differences in the two versions of a bill are ironed out in a Compromise Committee comprising members of both houses.

Each house considers bills, resolutions, joint resolutions, and concurrent resolutions. Bills become laws, and resolutions are recommendations or honors or citations for public service. Each carries the name(s) of the member(s) introducing it and is titled and numbered in the sequence introduced: House Bill 1, HB 2, House Resolution 1, HR 2, House Joint Resolution 1, HJR 2, House Concurrent Resolution 1, HCR 2. The Senate follows the same system: SB 1, SR 1, SJR 1, SCR 1. Resolutions are the property of the originating house; Joint Resolutions and Concurrent Resolutions involve both houses.

> **Note**—Each day, an agenda committee in each house determines the order that bills and resolutions will be considered in that house. A bill that rose to the top of yesterday's agenda may be below a series of bills considered more important on today's agenda. That agenda committee's sessions may be behind closed doors in the office of the House speaker and of the Senate president.

Executive

At the federal level, the executive branch is headed by the president; at the state level, by the governor. The president has a vice president, who serves as president of the Senate. Most states have a lieutenant governor, who serves as president of the state Senate. Neither has a vote except in case of a tie. And, of course, the vice president and the lieutenant governors stand ready to assume the higher office in time of need.

The main function of the vice president is to replace the president in case of death or inability to perform the duties of office. If the vice president is unable to serve as president, the speaker of the House of Representatives is third in line, and the president pro tempore of the Senate is fourth. After that, the secretaries of the various Cabinet agencies are in line. The same is true at the state level.

The U.S. Cabinet consists of the following secretaries and their major duties, listed in order of presidential succession after the vice president, the speaker of the House of Representatives, and the president pro tempore of the Senate.

Agriculture (USDA): Improves and maintains farm income and develops and expands markets abroad for agricultural products; helps to curb and to cure poverty, hunger, and malnutrition; enhances the environment and maintains production capacity by helping landowners protect the soil, water, forests, and other natural resources; researches findings that directly or indirectly benefit all Americans; safeguards and ensures standards of quality in the daily food supply.

Commerce: Encourages, serves, and promotes the nation's international trade, economic growth, and technological advancement; provides a variety of programs through the competitive free enterprise system; offers assistance and information to increase America's competitiveness in the world economy; administers programs to prevent unfair foreign trade competition; provides social and economic statistics and analyses for business and government planners; provides research and support for the increased use of scientific, engineering, and technological development; works to improve understanding and benefits of Earth's physical environment and oceanic resources; grants patents and registers trademarks; develops policies and conducts research on telecommunications; provides assistance to promote domestic economic development; and assists in the growth of minority businesses.

Defense (DOD): Provides the military forces needed to deter war and to wage war to protect the security of the nation. Under the president, who is commander in chief, the secretary of defense exercises authority, direction, and control over the department, which includes the separately organized military departments of Army, Navy—which includes the Marine Corps, and the Coast Guard in time of war—and Air Force, the Joint Chiefs of Staff providing military advice, the combatant commands, and defense agencies.

Education: Establishes policy for, administers, and coordinates most federal assistance to education.

Energy (DOE): Fosters a secure and reliable energy system that is environmentally and economically sustainable; is responsible as a steward of the nation's nuclear weapons; cleans up the department's facilities; leads in the physical sciences and advances the biological, environmental, and computational sciences; and provides premier scientific instruments for the nation's research enterprise.

Health and Human Services (HHS): Serves all people requiring health services.

Homeland Security (DHS): Protects the nation against terrorist attacks. Component agencies analyze threats and intelligence, guard the nation's borders and airports, protect the critical infrastructure, and coordinate the response of the nation for emergencies. Besides providing a better-coordinated defense of the homeland, DHS protects the rights of citizens and enhances public services, such as natural disaster assistance and citizenship services, by dedicating offices to those missions.

Housing and Urban Development (HUD): Responsible for programs concerned with the nation's housing needs, fair housing opportunities, and improvement and development of the nation's communities.

Interior: Protects and provides access to the natural and cultural heritage; manages public lands and minerals, national parks, national wildlife refuges, and western water resources; and upholds federal trust responsibilities to American Indian tribes and commitments to island communities; is responsible for migratory wildlife conservation; historic preservation; endangered species protection; surface-mined lands protection and restoration; mapping; and geological, hydrological, and biological science.

Justice: Headed by the Attorney General (AG) who serves as counsel for citizens; houses the Federal Bureau of Investigation (FBI), ensures healthy competition of business and enforces drug, immigration, and naturalization laws.

Labor: Fosters, promotes, and develops the welfare of the wage earners to improve their working conditions and to advance their opportunities for profitable employment; guarantees workers' rights to safe and healthful working conditions, a minimum hourly wage and overtime pay; provides freedom from employment discrimination; provides unemployment insurance and workers' compensation; protects workers' pension rights; provides for job training programs; helps workers find jobs; and keeps track of changes in employment, prices, and other national economic measurements.

State: Advises the president on foreign policy; promotes the long-range security of the United States; negotiates treaties and agreements with foreign nations; speaks for the United States in the United Nations and other international organizations in which the United States participates; and represents the United States at international conferences.

Transportation (DOT): Establishes the nation's overall transportation policy. Under it are eleven administrations whose jurisdictions are highway planning, development, and construction; motor carrier safety; urban mass transit; railroads; aviation; and the safety of waterways, ports, highways, and oil and gas pipelines.

Treasury: Recommends economic, financial, tax, and fiscal policies; serves as financial agent for the U.S. government; and supervises manufacturing coins and currency.

Veterans Affairs (VA): Operates programs for veterans and their families: pensions, education and rehabilitation, home loan guaranty, burial, and medical care.

Judicial

At the federal level, the judicial branch consists of every federal court; at the state level, of every state court. At the federal level, the U.S. Supreme Court is headed by the Chief Justice of the United States; at the state level, by the Chief Justice of the Supreme Court. Other members at both levels are associate justices. Both the federal government and the state governments have trial courts to prosecute criminals and imprison them and civil (at the state level, sometimes *chancery*) courts to settle disputes between citizens, and appellate courts to handle appeals from trial courts.

How Government Works

Although the government is responsible for just about everything that goes on in society, for the hands-on work, the government relies upon private enterprise. In fact, it is illegal for the government to compete with private enterprise. That would be unfair because the government can, and usually does, pay less for labor and materials than does private enterprise.

The process works this way: In most states, the legislature meets every other year and plans for the ensuing two-year period called the fiscal biennium. Although the legislature enacts laws affecting almost every part of life, two of its most important duties are to levy taxes and to appropriate the revenue to governmental agencies. Most taxes are already levied, so about all the legislature can do is to increase or to decrease the percentage, which is done from time to time as the need arises or as the cost of living and doing business rises or falls.

Six months or so before the legislature convenes, the various state agencies prepare their budgets, listing how much money they think they will need during the next biennium, and state fiscal experts guess at how much money the state will collect in tax revenue during the next biennium. Although it is a guess, it is an educated guess, based upon experience, the economic situation and the outlook, and the stock market, so it is fairly accurate.

The information is sent to the legislature, which sends the information to the Appropriations Committee to match the estimated revenue (the state income) to the requests of the various departments and agencies that list projects and estimated costs.

By the end of the legislative session, each state agency will have received pretty close to the amount of money it requested. That amount of money should last the department or agency throughout the two years.

In general, the departments and agencies are left to handle their duties as they see fit. However, the state auditor reviews the financial records of every state department and agency to ensure that they follow procedure.

For example, state appropriations are made for general and for specific use: Some money is put into the general fund for whatever is needed; some is dedicated for salaries for personnel and some for equipment and supplies, and neither can be spent for the other purpose. Thus, it is a misdemeanor to use personnel money for equipment, and vice versa.

Most of the state departments and agencies are administrative only, that is, they decide what work is to be done, and they hire private corporations to do the job. Except for minor tasks, departments and agencies do not build or do major repair work. A good example of how this system works is the state Department of Transportation.

The DOT is charged with the maintenance, repair, and construction of highways and bridges. To perform this function, DOT highway engineers make on-site inspections of highways and bridges throughout the state and report deficiencies to the DOT, which reports to the legislature.

DOT road crews handle minor routine maintenance and repair of highways and bridges, but larger jobs—widening of highways and construction of highways and bridges—are done by private highway construction companies hired by the DOT for specific jobs.

The process is routine and nationwide: The DOT advertises the details of the highway needing work—length, width, number of lanes, width and type of median, width and type of shoulders, type of surface and subsurface, and so on—and calls for *sealed bids* from private highway construction firms.

At the designated time and in open meeting, the DOT opens the bids and selects the lowest and best bid and awards a *contract* to that chosen bidder.

> **Note**—It is a contract, not a bid, that is awarded. Though you see the phrase on meeting agendas, it is not only incorrect, it is also impossible to *award a bid*.

Under the contract, the construction company is required to complete the job within a stated number of days. If completion is delayed—except for storm, flood, snow, ice, earthquake, and so on—the contractor pays a fine of as much as $10,000 for each day beyond the deadline. Some contracts include a bonus if the job is completed ahead of schedule. Thus, not only is it profitable for the construction company to complete the job as rapidly as possible, but also, the sooner the job is completed, the sooner the construction company can seek other jobs. Construction companies do not like to sit idle; there is no profit in sitting idle.

And, of course, highways, like everything else, are built according to *modern safety standards*, the safety standards in effect at the time of construction. Safety standards change as new technology is developed, but highways are built as safe as is known at the time of construction.

The same is true of any construction: buildings of any kind and size, bridges, stadiums, parks, dams, lakes, even such weapons of war as guns and ammunition, ships, tanks, and airplanes. In all contracted work, the construction company works as rapidly as possible and according to modern safety standards. To do otherwise would be costly to the company in loss of time and money and in lawsuits for damages arising from faulty construction.

State Government Agencies

State governments consist of agencies dedicated to specific areas of public good, each headed by a person whose title is secretary, commissioner, superintendent, or the like. The main agencies and their leaders are these:

Agriculture: Usually headed by a commissioner; helps farmers and ranchers.

Attorney General: Researches the laws for recommendations to the legislature and serves as the attorney for the state and state agencies and for the counties in legal matters. In some states, legal opinions issued by the attorney general have the force of law.

Commerce: Secretary; sometimes Commerce and Industry; regulates commerce and industry.

Comptroller (pronounced con-TROLL-er): Collects the tax revenue from business and industry and sends it to the treasurer for deposit into banks. Some deposits are placed into interest-bearing accounts, and some into checking accounts from which state *warrants* (checks) are paid for services, goods, and salaries of state employees.

Education: Superintendent; oversees public education.

Insurance Commissioner: Regulates the insurance business. Not all states have an insurance commissioner as a Cabinet member.

State: Secretary; publishes the laws enacted by the legislature and charters corporations. Every corporation on the secretary of state rolls is obliged to pay corporate taxes and to send to the comptroller the sales taxes collected. Therefore, it is a good idea to check the rolls of both the comptroller and the secretary of state to determine if corporations are not paying taxes or submitting tax collections.

Treasurer: Receives the tax revenue from the comptroller and deposits it into banks throughout the state. Some deposits collect interest, so tax revenue in those accounts should be deposited every day, including Friday, because *interest* is paid daily, including Saturday and Sunday. Holding revenue until Monday may cost the state hundreds of thousands of dollars in interest. Tax revenue designated for payment of salaries and expenses are placed into non-interest-bearing accounts.

Cities

Cities are both government and private enterprise. They are government because they have legislative (city council), executive (mayor), and judicial (courts) power over the people; and they are private enterprise because they are incorporated much as are business enterprises. The mayor serves as the chief executive officer (CEO) and city council serves as the board of directors.

In every county, the *sheriff* is the chief law enforcement officer over the entire county, including the cities. However, in the interest of cost reduction, the sheriff permits a city a police force and a *chief of police* to handle law violations, not always including felonies, within the city limits. It doesn't happen very often, but the sheriff always has the option of taking over from the police any criminal investigation.

Every city has other rights that you should know: annexation, zoning, easement, eminent domain, and so on.

Annexation is the right of a city to expand its corporate limits by annexing adjoining land. Annexation broadens the property tax base for the city without reducing the property tax base for the county or the school district. Annexation requires that the city, as soon as possible, extend to new residents such services as police and fire protection, trash and garbage pickup, sewerage, and water.

Zoning is the right of a city to restrict the type of building or business in various areas of the city. Land is designated for heavy and light commercial use, for agriculture, for single-family homes, for multiple-family homes, for apartments, for condominiums, and so on. Zoning protects homeowners against having a business set up shop next door; it protects schools and churches from having undesirable businesses nearby. In cities with high-rise office buildings, care must be taken against new buildings blocking existing buildings from the sun and against changing the wind patterns between buildings. Before any building—commercial, office, apartment house, condominium, private home—may be constructed, the builder must seek permission from the planning and zoning commission or the city council.

Note—Just as you cover the city council, so should you cover the planning and zoning commission.

Easement is the right of a city to use private property for public use. Property owners are required to set aside a strip of land along the street for sidewalks and for utilities, above ground or underground: water, sewage, telephone, electricity, and the like.

Eminent Domain is the right of the government to take and usually pay for private property for public use, such as highways and streets and buildings.

How to Cover Tax Revenue Reports

Here are examples of some of the protections and services provided by the government:

National Government: Military defense; law enforcement and courts; immigration; purity of food and medicine; health; highways and bridges; protection of rights of authors and inventors; retirement.

State Government: Military defense; police protection; law enforcement and courts; health and medical; highways and bridges; welfare; education.

County Government: Records of birth, marriage, death, sale of property; health and medical; education; courts.

City Government: Fire protection; law enforcement and courts; medical and hospital; streets; utilities; education.

To provide all that protection and those services, government needs money. To get money, the government taxes its citizens, thereby enabling those who benefit from the protection and services to help pay for them.

Here are the major taxes that the ordinary citizen pays and what the revenue is used for.

National Government: Income tax for general operation of the government; Social Security tax for retirement and other personal benefits; excise tax on such items as telephones; gasoline tax for highway construction, maintenance, and repair; alcohol tax and tobacco tax for enforcement of alcohol and tobacco laws.

State Government: Income tax (in most states) for general operation of the government—the major source of revenue for the state—for general operation of the government; gasoline tax for highway construction, maintenance, and repair; alcohol tax and tobacco tax for enforcement of alcohol and tobacco laws.

County Government: Property tax—the major source of revenue for the county—on land, buildings, homes, vehicles for general operation of the government.

City Government: Sales tax and property tax—the major sources of revenue for the city—for general operation of the government; hotel/motel tax for attracting conventions; tobacco tax; utility tax for maintenance and repair of utilities; gasoline tax for street construction, maintenance, and repair.

School Districts: Property tax—the major sources of revenue for schools—for general operation of schools.

Those who collect the various taxes—and they are paid a fee for their work—are responsible for sending the revenue to the government tax collector.

Every month, businesses of all sorts and sizes send to the state comptroller's office the revenue from the taxes on sales, alcohol, and tobacco. The comptroller distributes to each governmental agency the amount of revenue due in accordance with the tax levied.

Revenue from gasoline taxes, which are levied by the nation, the state, and the city, is used for maintenance, repair, and construction of the federal and state highway systems and city streets.

Revenue from taxes on hotel and motel rooms, which is levied by the city, is used to attract conventions. Conventioneers are a major source of revenue for the host city because every conventioneer spends upwards of $100 a day, usually on souvenirs, restaurants, entertainment, and the like. The sales tax generated is a boost to the economy of the city.

Revenue from property taxes, collected by the county tax collector, is distributed to the financial offices of the county, the city, and the school district.

Changes in property taxes involve several governmental groups: the county tax assessor, who assesses the value of the property to be taxed, and the city council, the county board, and the school board, each of which levies a tax according to need.

Every year, every property owner pays three property tax rates (sometimes called *ad valorem* or "of the value") on an assessed value of the property and according to the needs of the city, the county, and the school district.

Assessed value of property is not always equal to what was paid for the property or what the property is worth on the market. The county tax assessor appraises the property and applies exemptions for home residence, age (over 65), disability, military veteran, and so on, thereby reducing the assessed value of the property by one-half to three-fourths for tax purposes. Thus, a house that sold for $100,000 could have an assessed value of $50,000 to $75,000 or up to $150,000, and the assessed value could be different for each of the taxing agencies.

The tax on property is in mills, one one-thousandth of a dollar ($0.001) or ten cents ($0.10) per $100 or $1 per $1,000 of the assessed value of the property. The tax on property is usually stated as pennies on $100. Thus, the owner of property valued at $100,000 and taxed at 41.46 cents ($0.4146) per $100 of assessed value, would pay $414.60. The formula is 100,000 × 0.004146.

A $100,000 house could be assessed and taxed as follows:

	Assessed Value	Tax Rate	Revenue
City	$73,230	$0.4777	$349.82
County	$73,230	$0.4146	$303.61
School	$73,230	$0.7900	$578.52
Total paid by property owner			$1,231.95

Governmental agencies that need more revenue may increase the tax or the assessed value of the property. But politicians know that, because people object to raising taxes, even in time of need, such an act could cost them their jobs. Here is a comparison of the increase in revenue from an increase in the tax rate and from an increase in the assessed value.

	Assessed Value	Tax Rate	Revenue
City	$73,230	$0.4777	$349.82
City	$73,230	$0.5277	$386.43
City	$78,230	$0.4777	$373.70

By raising the assessed value rather than the tax, politicians can campaign on the fact that they did not raise taxes. It's misleading, but, technically, they did not increase the property tax; the tax assessor increased the assessed value of the property. The result is the same, however: the property owner pays more in tax revenue.

Writing the Story

The following matrix will help you determine your lead for a tax revenue story. Answers to the all-capitals questions—WHO, DID WHAT, WHY—must be in the lead. Answers to the capital-and-lower-case questions—Where, When, How—may be placed in the first or the second paragraph.

In reporting on tax revenue, the amount collected during the reporting month is compared to the previous month of the current year and the reporting month a year earlier, showing a clear picture of the rise and fall of the economy. Provide the rise or fall in both dollar amounts and percentages.

WHO

The Who of the story is essential in stories about reports of tax revenue. This is the name of the office making the report. That is the Who you are covering. The report may contain a statement by the state comptroller or the city fiscal officer citing reasons for the increase or decrease. Such statements are used, but in the second paragraph.

Therefore, begin your story with the name of the office: the state comptroller or the city fiscal office.

DID WHAT

The Did What of the story is essential in stories about taxes. Tax revenue does one of three things—increase, decrease, remain the same—so one of these is your lead.

Tax revenue increased, by amount and percentage.

Tax revenue decreased, by amount and percentage.

Tax revenue remained the same (highly unusual).

Including the dollar amount and the percentage of change is important because it provides a graphic picture of the rise and fall of the economy by month and by year.

WHY

The Why of the story is essential because the reason for the rise and fall of tax revenue indicates the state of economy and how much people are spending, and it tells how much revenue the government has and can expect to continue providing services and protection for its citizens. Such information usually comes from the state comptroller or the city fiscal officer in a separate statement.

Where

The Where of the story is the state for statewide reports and the city for city reports. Statewide reports may include revenue comparisons for the state's largest cities. Stories that lead with city reports should include reports of the state and of nearby cities.

When

The When of the story is the day or date of the report, usually the day the report is received. But the report covers three months: the reporting month, the preceding month, and the reporting month a year earlier.

How

The How of the story is not always present. When it is present, however, it must be included.

So What

After you have written your lead, read it aloud and listen to the flow of language. Ask yourself if what you have written tells the whole story of the rise or fall of revenue, and if it gets to the point. If not, rewrite the lead.

Use the name of the month and the year instead of *this month, last month, this year, last year,* because you will receive the report after the reporting month. For example, in November 2013, you will receive the report for October 2013 with revenue for September 2013 and for October 2012. Therefore, *this month* is November, the month you are writing your story, not the reporting month, and *last month* is October, the reporting month.

The verb is *reported* because what you received from the state or the city is an official report of the office's activities.

The Story

Your lead should follow this format:

> The Texas Comptroller's office [Who with built-in Where] reported sales tax revenue [Did What] for October at $34.2 million, an increase of 14 percent over the $30 million in September and 22 percent over the $28 million in October 2012.

> The Comptroller said Tuesday [When] that the increase/decrease was a result of . . . whatever [Why].

Because the lead sentence covers so much, the reason for the increase/decrease—the Why—usually is placed in the second paragraph.

Subsequent paragraphs should provide reports of revenue from other taxes, comparing them to the previous month of the current year and the reporting month of the previous year. If the reporting office provides reasons for the increase/decrease in other taxes, include that.

How to Cover Political Campaigns

Political campaigns are not as difficult to cover as you may imagine because most of them have public relations staffs to provide reporters with as much news as they want about the candidate. Your main problem will be to ensure that you give equal news treatment to every candidate in each race. Because candidates campaign almost daily during the weeks preceding the election, you probably will write a roundup story describing the campaign speeches and activities of every candidate in each race.

There is no way that you can provide the same number of words about each candidate each day, but you can ensure that each candidate has comparable coverage on a weekly basis.

Note—Keep records so you lead with a different candidate—if possible—each day and that you rotate the order in which you present the other candidates.

Your second paragraph should list and comment briefly on each of the other candidates. Thereafter, write about each candidate in full before going to the next candidate.

Special Interest Groups

You should do weekly stories about who—individuals, associations, corporations, and so on—contributes to which candidate(s) and how much. Some states limit the amount of political contributions.

You have read books and news stories and seen television programs and movies and even campaign advertisements concerning public officials who take contributions from special interest groups and then favor or cater to those special interest groups.

By law, if anyone in government favors any group improperly, that person is guilty of fraud, or worse. The courts will take care of that.

However, candidates for public office accept contributions from anyone, including special interest groups, and special interest groups contribute to the candidates they favor.

Only in the main campaigns—president, state and national senator and representative, governor, sheriff—do candidates receive contributions from voters in general, because those offices affect every citizen directly.

In the special races—attorney general, judge, superintendent of education, commissioner of agriculture, treasurer, commissioner of insurance—voters in general have little or no interest in those races, so they do not contribute to those candidates.

Those who do contribute to special races are those who are most interested in the outcome. Here are examples of state races to which special interest groups contribute in an effort to secure the election of favorable candidates.

Attorney General: Lawyers, insurance company officials, other corporate officials (for lawsuits).

Commissioner of Agriculture: Farmers, ranchers, corporations involved in all facets of agriculture.

Insurance Commissioner: Lawyers, insurance company officials, other corporate officials, hospital officials, physicians, dentists, architects, other professional people.

Judges: Lawyers, corporate officials.

Superintendent of Education: Public school teachers, education administrators, school supply house officials.

Treasurer: Bankers, credit union officials, savings and loan officials, insurance company officials.

When you cover those candidates and campaigns, remember that the usual contributors will be "special interest" groups. When you see outsiders contributing, their reasons for so doing may produce a news story.

Keep a record of who contributed how much to which campaign so you can keep an eye on the winning candidate to determine whether special favors ensue.

15

How to Cover Business, Industry, and Labor

Business and industry are the heart of the economy, and they involve people and their lives and livelihoods. Here is how business and industry work.

Business and industry, of all kinds, are the mainstay of a capitalist society, a society in which business and industry are privately owned and in open competition in a free market. Despite infrequent bankruptcies, criminal charges against corporate officers, and other irregularities of the business world, business, overall, is good for society; it is what makes society work.

Business and industry news is big news. The news media recognize that and recruit reporters to cover the business and industry beat. Most newspapers have set aside space—even whole sections—for business and industry news stories. Some newspapers, notably *The Wall Street Journal*, and some weekly magazines, notably *Business Week*, are devoted entirely to business and industry news.

The business and industry beat produces myriad stories, most of them routine, but some of them major, and all of them of more than passing interest to the business, political, and governmental community in your circulation area. People from every walk of life want to know how and what business and industry are doing and how the economy is faring.

For example, these business and industry activities affect people in all walks of life directly through either loss of jobs or increased prices for goods and services: bankruptcy; contract negotiations with labor unions; corporate takeovers; introduction, expansion, discontinuance of products and services; mass hiring, layoffs; promotion, retirement, discharge, death of business and industry leaders; opening, closing of main and branch offices; reports of profit, loss, usually through quarterly and annual reports; stock

> **Note**—For help in understanding and using business terms, check the "Business Guidelines" section in *The Associated Press Stylebook and Briefing on Media Law*. It provides not only spellings of terms but also definitions and explanations, almost a short course in business.

activity: sales, recalls, splits, dividend increases, decreases; labor strikes and their effects; and speeches by the chief executive officer.

Even though some business and industry activity is detrimental to some people, there is almost no end to the benefits that business and industry provide. Business and industry provide jobs, produce goods and services for people, and make life easier because people do not have to grow their own food, butcher their own meat, make their own clothing and furniture, and so on.

Business and industry pay more for telephone service, electricity, water, natural gas, and sewerage, thereby making it possible for householders to pay less for the same services.

Business and industry not only provide jobs at the local level but also jobs for manufacturing, transportation, and advertising. Business and industry provide not only wages and salary for employees but also contribute to employee medical insurance and retirement programs.

Business and industry and the people who work in business and industry pay taxes at the city, county, state, and federal levels, providing for schools from kindergarten to college, law enforcement at all levels, firefighting, transportation, highways and bridges, streets and parks, and all manner of services that make life easier.

Equally important, business and industry provide the opportunity for people to share in their profits.

Starting a business or industry of almost any kind costs a lot of money, and those planning to start it usually do not have enough. To get the money, they borrow it from anyone who will lend it to them. To secure the loan, they offer shares of stock in the company and promise to pay dividends, a sort of interest on the loan. The difference is that interest is paid only until the loan is paid off, whereas dividends on stock are paid as long as the company makes a profit. Moreover, the stockholders, regardless of the number of shares of stock each owns, are part owners of the company.

To sell stock, a company must be chartered by the secretary of state. The charter describes the company and the goods and services provided, lists the officers by name and title, and cites how many shares of stock are to be sold and the price per share.

In addition, the U.S. Securities and Exchange Commission (SEC) regulates stock companies—corporations that sell shares of stock—requiring annual reports of their activities. These annual reports are public documents, available on paper and online.

All companies doing business must pay taxes to the city, county, and state, and those tax records are public documents, available in the city tax office, the office of the county tax assessor/collector, and the office of the state comptroller.

Information on all of these business and industry activities is available routinely from the public relations office and the officials of the individual business and industry.

Information on criminal activity in business and industry—embezzlement, arson, illegal waste dumping, air and water pollution, contaminated products, insider trading, and so on—usually comes from the district attorney or an officer of a federal agency doing the investigation rather than from the public relations office of the business or industry.

In covering business and industry, cultivate sources; develop contacts in business and industry, and in the labor unions. It is relatively easy to cultivate public relations people, because their task is to cultivate the news media. Both of you are working toward the same goal. Just as it is your job to gather and report news about business and industry and labor, so is it the job of the public relations staff to secure publication of news about business and industry and labor.

Get to know both the CEO and public relations officer—and as many vice presidents and division directors as you can—of every business and industry and labor union in your circulation area. On a regular basis, make the rounds, in person or by telephone, of each one.

Give each CEO, public relations director, and other company officers, along with their secretaries, your business card and invite each to contact you with whatever information they have, at any hour, day or night, on any day, workday or weekend or holiday. Emphasize that you will feel free to contact them on the same basis for whatever information you want from them. And do not hesitate to do so when the need arises.

Most public relations people know what news is and will provide it to you. You can trust public relations people to tell you the truth. They may not tell you everything they know, but what they do tell you will be true. They cannot operate otherwise. One lie, one devious report, and they lose their credibility with the news media and, therefore, their ability to disseminate news about the corporation. You would not take the word of a person who lied to you, so the public relations chief who lies is of no value to the corporation. Thus, news releases and information provided by the public relations staff will be correct, accurate, and honest. If you plan to use the news release as written, feel free to do so; it is not plagiarism. If you rewrite the news release, attribution is to the corporation or the CEO, rather than to *a news release* or to *the public relations office* or even to a public relations person by name. In general, it is better to rewrite news releases to conform to your own publication's style and to shorten them. Most news releases are too long and most bury the lead-worthy information in the third or fourth paragraph.

Sometimes, the public relations office cannot put into a news release everything it knows. If you believe that additional information may be available from others at the company, including the CEO, schedule an appointment with the individual involved. Going through the public relations office will help you make arrangements. Use the news release as a tip and see what you can come up with in an interview. It may pay off with a much better story.

In any event, read every public relations news release thoroughly, from beginning to end. Many of them are overlong and are written poorly, including burying the lead. Moreover, public relations people are trained to take a positive view of anything that goes on in a corporation. If a corporation loses money in one quarter, the news release probably will lead with a description of plans designed to produce greater profit. The loss—your lead information—will be way down in the story. News of the loss is there; you just have to look for it. Do so, and write the story with the news in the lead.

Do not forget to put the story in context. Get background information from your own files or those of the newspaper. Annual and quarterly reports, standard library reference works, and a corporation's public relations staff can provide you with the kind of explanatory material needed to flesh out the story.

Covering Labor and Labor Unions

Business and industry cannot operate without labor. Management puts up the money and gambles that the business will succeed and the investment pay off. Labor is the workforce, the people who produce the goods or services that business sells or provides. If the business succeeds or fails, so do management and labor. For reasons that you probably remember from your history courses, management historically took terrible advantage of labor, exploiting workers for profit. Eventually, the workers organized into special interest groups—called labor unions—so that, through strength of numbers, they could negotiate with management for proper working conditions and wages. If management refused to meet labor's demands, labor would strike—the workers would walk off the job—and shut down the company. A closed company earns no money.

As a result, today, workers are organized into labor unions representing all facets of labor: carpenters, teamsters (mostly truck drivers, but other workers are included), electricians, plumbers, seamen, automobile workers, seamsters, even news reporters (the American Newspaper Guild). Eventually, labor unions found that they could have even greater strength if they merged with other labor unions. Some labor unions merged as the American Federation of Labor (AFL), and some merged as the Congress of Industrial Organizations (CIO). For even greater power, those two super labor groups merged as the AFL-CIO.

In modern manufacturing plants, if one labor union goes on strike, the others usually do, too, to lend support, a sort of all-for-one approach, to negotiations. If a strike shuts down an entire plant for want of workers, management sometimes takes over and keeps the plant operating at short staff. And sometimes, management hires replacements—called *scabs*—for the striking workers, which frequently erupts into violence because, sometimes, the scabs take the striking workers' jobs permanently.

Covering labor and labor unions is similar to covering business and industry.

Get to know both the president and the public relations officer of every labor union in your circulation area. In addition, the chapter of each union elects a representative—called *chapel chairman*—to serve as liaison between that union and management to work out minor problems. From time to time, make the rounds, in person or by telephone, of each one.

Give each union president, public relations officer, and chapel chairman, and their secretaries, your business card and invite each to contact you with whatever information they have, at any hour, day or night, on any day, workday or weekend or holiday. Emphasize that you will feel free to contact them on the same basis for whatever information you want from them. And don't hesitate to do so when the need arises.

Write stories on whatever goes on in the labor community.

Contract negotiations with business management; effects of bankruptcies, corporate takeovers; effects of mass hirings/layoffs; effects of openings/closings of main and branch offices; labor union elections protected by the National Labor Relations Board (NRLB) to determine whether a group of workers will be represented by a labor union; promotions, retirements, discharges, deaths of labor leaders; strikes and their effects.

As with covering business, you will not be able to gather all the news on your own initiative alone. Most people in labor unions—except for the president and public relations officer of the local—don't talk to reporters unless they have to. To gather information about many activities, illegal as well as legal, you need contacts, people who will provide you tips, who will tell you what you want to know, but not for attribution. You must seek out publishable information from an authoritative source. And, before you can write stories of such information, you must pore over documents and interview reliable, attributable sources.

To gather information about legal activities of labor unions, you will have to cultivate the public relations chiefs and the chapel chairmen of labor unions in your circulation area.

Covering a labor union strike is much the same as covering any group activity. You won't sit in on the contract negotiations, but you may interview the negotiators after each session. And you may cover the activities of the strikers on the street around the entrance to the plant.

From time to time, a group of unorganized workers will want to try to establish a labor union at their plant. Whether management approves or not is of no consequence. The federal government, through the NLRB, will protect the right of the workers to try to organize by ordering management to provide for a free election on the issue. Usually, management will try to influence the vote against organizing into a labor union by offering greater benefits than the proposed union plans to offer or has obtained at similar plants.

Business and the Community

All this about strikes and unfair advantage and protected elections may seem as though something is wrong with business, management, and labor, that they are at odds with each other. But that is untrue. There is nothing inherently wrong with business, with doing business, with management, or with labor and labor unions. Each plays a vital role in the economic life of the community and the nation.

Business provides goods and services for people, thus serving as the economic lifeblood of the community, the state, the nation, the world. Labor unions protect the workers from unfair management practices.

What is not good is when either management or labor does something it should not, and the other reacts out of proportion. Then you have a news story, or lots of them.

Remember that most business and labor union activity is legitimate, and most is regulated by federal and state governments, providing protection for citizens as well as customers. For example, the federal Food and Drug Administration (FDA) ensures that food and medicine sold throughout the United States is pure and wholesome. Other governmental agencies are charged with regulating—and it is all for the protection of the people— banks, the environment, radio and television, insurance, beauty parlors, barber shops, restaurants, almost anything you can think of.

Also keep in mind that profit is good. People who invest their money in business enterprises, and who stand ready to absorb whatever losses come their way, have a right to profit, to make money, within reason. Profit, like interest, is pay for the use of money, like rent.

Few businesses make exorbitant profit, and fewer still make profit illegally or immorally. Profit is calculated upon the basis of investment, and it usually does not exceed 6 percent. Groceries usually return less than 1 percent profit, which is one reason for the proliferation of supermarkets and their shelves of cosmetics, hardware, books, school supplies, and whatnot. Profit from goods other than groceries is what keeps the grocery department in business.

The price marked on any item for sale includes profit, of course, but it also includes the wholesale cost—what the retailer paid the manufacturer or the middleman, for the item—overhead costs—utilities, telephone, employee salaries, retirement programs, hospitalization programs, taxes, insurance, loss through shoplifting—and the cost of keeping the item on the shelf until it is sold. That length of time varies from a day or two for perishable grocery items to several years for a piece of expensive jewelry. All of these costs above the wholesale price are called markup, and profit is only a small part of markup.

How to Cover an Annual Report

Federal law requires all corporations that sell stock to file with the SEC by April 1 each year a Form 10-K report, describing in detail the corporation's financial activities for the preceding calendar year.

Thus, the corporation's annual Form 10-K report is an official document, a public document. As such, the Form 10-K report is its own authority; that is, whatever financial information it contains is attributable to the corporation. You need not ask anyone's permission to quote from it.

The Form 10-K report is on the corporation's Web page, but it is also in a magazine produced by the corporation's public relations office as part of its publicity program. Sometimes the magazines are in full color and contain not only the Form 10-K report but also photographs of the corporation, corporate officers, and employees, and photographs of and stories about activities of the corporation and employees. The magazine is mailed to the business desk of every news medium and to every stockholder in the corporation.

To ensure that stockholders understand the Form 10-K report, the public relations office sometimes highlights, in clear, simple language on page two, the following financial activities of the corporation: net income, operating revenues, assets, the value of property and equipment, capital expenditures, and dividends per share of stock for the reporting year and the previous one or two years, and the percentage of change from the previous calendar year.

You should look at all those entries for the reporting year and the one or two previous years. If no percentage of change is listed, you should calculate it.

In addition, the magazine contains a letter from the chief executive officer (CEO) to stockholders, explaining why the corporation made or lost money during the reporting year and what the corporation plans to do in the ensuing year.

The CEO letter to stockholders is not part of the Form 10-K report, but the information it contains is available for your story, and it must be attributed to the CEO. It is not necessary to use any title but CEO, even though the CEO may serve also as president or as chairman of the board.

All of the information pertains to the preceding calendar year, and that, at the time you are reading the report, it is April of the current calendar year. Thus, three months of the current year have passed, a fact that you must bear in mind because of what is in the CEO letter.

The CEO letter is in two parts. The first two-thirds describes corporate activities during the reporting year (last year), describes changes in service or products and expansions and reductions, and presents some detail about why and how the corporation earned a profit or lost money. The remaining one-third describes corporate plans for next year (the year in which you are writing the story), the year following the reporting year. This is where you must be careful, because some of those plans may well have been realized during the three months before the annual report arrived on your desk.

In selecting quotations for your story from the CEO letter, be discerning. In public and in print, CEOs always are proud of how their officers and employees and their company performed during the reporting year, and are optimistic about the future. Most of those statements are self-serving and should not be quoted. Seek much more appropriate statements in the CEO letter. In addition, be aware of such phrases as *except for*, *subject to*, and *despite the*, because they are clues to problems.

For additional information for your story, read the stories in the magazine, particularly new items in the various areas of the corporation. And check the "Notes to Consolidated Financial Statements" section of the Form 10-K report because it explains in detail the reasons for the profit or the loss.

Because the most important thing about any corporation is how much it earned or lost during the year, that's the figure you want. That information is listed as *net income* or *revenue*, but you must write it as *profit* or as *loss* because more people understand *profit/loss* than *net income/revenue*.

Before the Form 10-K report can be sent to the SEC, it must be submitted to an independent accountant or auditor or for review. The independent accountant or auditor attests only that the financial report is presented fairly. A report of three paragraphs or one long paragraph indicates that no discrepancy was found in the Form 10-K report. Be sure, however, to read the "Notes to Consolidated Financial Statements" in the Form 10-K report.

Note—Years ago, profit was written in black ink; loss, in red ink, giving rise to the phrases *in the black*, meaning that business was good, and *in the red*, meaning that business was bad. Now, profit is listed as a plain number; loss, a plain number within parentheses or following a minus sign (−). At the top of the financial data is a notation "Amounts in millions, except for stock prices," which means that six zeroes must be added to the dollar figures in the chart. Thus, the number $107.19, in millions, is $107,190,000.

Note—Don't be too concerned with the financial report's bottom line. The bottom line of profit and loss statements always balances. It's the listings above the bottom that make news, because they show where the money came from and where it went. The "Notes to Consolidated Financial Statements" explains that, too.

Report of Independent Accountants or Auditors

This is an example of the three paragraphs written for a valid annual report. Don't be concerned if the wording varies somewhat; the wording is not fixed by law.

To the Board of Directors and Shareholders of [corporation]

We have reviewed the Statement of Financial Position of the corporation as of [date] and the statements of income, cash flows, and changes in shareowners' investment for the year. These financial statements are the responsibility of corporation management. Our responsibility is to express an opinion on these financial statements based on our audit.

We conducted our audit in accordance with auditing standards generally accepted in the United States. Those standards require that we plan and perform the audit to obtain reasonable assurance about whether the financial statements are free of material misstatement. An audit includes examining, on a test basis, evidence supporting the amounts and disclosures in the financial statements. An audit also includes assessing the accounting principles used and significant estimates made by management, as well as evaluating the overall financial statement presentation. We believe that our audit provides a reasonable basis for our opinion.

In our opinion, the financial statements referred to above present fairly, in all material respects, the consolidated financial position of [corporation] at [date], and the consolidated results of its operations and its cash flows for the year, in conformity with accounting principles generally accepted in the United States.

The report is signed by the accounting firm.

Few People Know This

More than three paragraphs or one long paragraph in a report from an independent accountant or auditor indicates a deviation or change in the method of accounting. Whatever it is, it must be checked out. Explanations are provided in the "Notes to Consolidated Financial Statements."

Most fourth and fifth paragraphs in the independent accountant or auditor's report are routine, like this:

> As discussed in Note 2 to the consolidated financial statements, the Corporation changed its method of accounting for postretirement benefits other than pensions, post-employment benefits, and income taxes.

Or this, explaining a change mandated by a federal agency:

> As discussed in Notes 1 and 10 to the consolidated financial statements, the Corporation consolidated certain subsidiaries previously accounted for by the equity method and adopted new income tax accounting principles, in accordance with recently issued statements of the Financial Accounting Standards Board.

But any other deviations must be checked out by contacting the corporation's fiscal office or public relations office before contacting the SEC.

Writing the Annual Report Story

The following matrix will help you determine your lead for an annual report story. Answers to the all-capitals questions—WHO, DID WHAT, WHY—must be in the lead. Answers to the capital-and-lower-case questions—Where, When, How—may be placed in the first or second paragraph.

What you are looking for in the annual report are how much money the corporation reported as profit or loss during the reporting year and why. The profit or loss is in the *Form 10-K* report and in the summary, and the reason is in the CEO letter.

The inverted-pyramid style of writing with its summary lead is easiest and best. And be sure to refer frequently to the "Business Guidelines and Style" section of *The Associated Press Stylebook and Briefing on Media Law*.

WHO

The Who of the story is essential in stories about corporate annual reports. In an annual report story, the Who is the name of the corporation, not the CEO or any other corporate officer, because the annual report is an official report from the corporation to the Securities and Exchange Commission.

DID WHAT

The Did What is what the corporation did. The verb is *reported* because that is what the corporation did: It reported its financial activities to the SEC.

The corporation reported a *profit* or a *loss* (not *net income*) of a specific amount of money during the reporting year compared to a specific amount of profit or loss during the previous year. The CEO letter provided the reasons for the profit or loss.

> **Caution**—Throughout the story, avoid confusion by using the name of the year—2013, 2014, 2015, and so on—rather than *last year, this year, next year.* If you are writing your story in April 2014, be aware that the CEO letter was written in 2013, so the reference to *next year* is 2014. However, to the reader of your story, in April 2014, *next year* is 2015.

WHY

The Why is the reason for the profit or loss during the reporting year, as cited by the Form 10-K report and as explained in the "Notes to Consolidated Financial Statements" and in the CEO letter. Quotations and paraphrased information from the CEO letter are attributed to the CEO; quotations and paraphrased information from the "Notes to Consolidated Financial Statements" are attributed to the corporation.

Where

The Where is the headquarters city of the corporation. For major national corporations, the Where usually is not necessary. If it is necessary, and it usually is for less widely known corporations, place the Where in the second paragraph.

When

Be careful with the When. Although the time of the annual report is April 1, the time element of your story is the day of the week that you write your story. The When should be placed no lower than the second paragraph.

How

The How of the story is not how the CEO explained the profit or loss; it is how the annual report was made. In that all annual reports are produced by the corporation and mailed to the SEC, to stockholders, and to the business desk of every news medium, there is no How in an annual report story. The Why is sufficient.

Note—The first or second paragraph should describe the product(s) or service(s) of the corporation. Most people know what AT&T provides, but few know what Raytheon provides.

Note—If the Independent Accountant's or Auditor's Report indicates no major discrepancy, there is no need to mention the report in the story.

Writing the Story

Your story should follow this format. Because of the amount of information needed, the lead paragraph typically runs to 35 words.

The second paragraph fills in the details from the CEO letter and is attributed to the CEO only.

Subsequent paragraphs should provide newsworthy quotations from the CEO letter about corporation successes, failures, and plans.

The Story

The ABC Corp., which manufactures widgets for personal computers, reported a profit of $57,952,000 because of expansion of its market during 2013, a 188 percent increase over the $20,155,000 earned during 2012.

Chief Executive Officer Marcus Price said ABC markets throughout Europe and the increase in demand for personal computers contributed to the increase in profit.

As a result, he said, the ABC Corp. is expanding its overseas markets. "We have markets in Mexico, Dominican Republic, and Panama, and are negotiating in Peru, Argentina, and Chile," he said. "We plan to move into northern Africa and India no later than 2014."

The ABC Corp. began in 1995, when Price developed an inexpensive method of manufacturing widgets and expanded nationwide by 1997.

16

How to Cover Crime, Courts, and Trials

> Covering crime is interesting, sometimes dangerous. Covering courts and trials, civil and criminal, is sometimes dull. This tells you what to look for in covering crime and the courts.

To cover crime, the police beat, and the courts, you need, not a law degree, but a working knowledge of the criminal justice system—an awareness of how the police, the district attorney, and the courts work. It only seems difficult, but you probably have been watching television shows about how the police investigate crime and how trials are conducted. Those television programs pretty much depict how the system operates. Now, you need to know your role as a reporter in the system.

The Sixth Amendment to the U.S. Constitution guarantees a speedy and public trial by impartial jury and forbids cruel and unusual punishment. Thus, everything that is said during a trial is public information, even if the judge strikes it from the court record.

There are three kinds of trial court: criminal, civil (called also *tort* and *chancery*), and juvenile.

Criminal: The government brings action against a person (the defendant) and charges the person with a crime. The verdict is either to acquit or to convict the defendant. The penalty may be either a prison sentence of more than one year or a fine or probation or any combination of the three, or execution. No defendant is ever found "innocent," because everyone is innocent until proved guilty.

Civil: The government or a corporation or a city or a person (the plaintiff) brings action against a person or a corporation or an association or the government (the defendant). The verdict is a judgment for or against the plaintiff, and the penalty is a fine. In a civil action, no one is convicted and no one is imprisoned. To sue the government requires permission from the Congress or the state legislature.

Note—Sometimes, civil matters are considered in the judge's private office (called *in camera*, sometimes *in chambers*) rather than in the courtroom. Usually, such action is closed to the public. But ask the judge if you may sit in and cover the case. If so, remember, the rules of court apply.

Juvenile: Juveniles are charged with delinquency and sentenced to juvenile detention until age eighteen. Because activity in juvenile court involves children, it is closed to all but the juvenile, the family, the attorneys, and the juvenile caseworkers. Juvenile records are sealed and erased when the juvenile reaches age eighteen. Reporters have no access to any juvenile court action or records.

Note—Juveniles accused of serious law violations may, if a judge so rules, be tried as adults, in open criminal court, which is newsworthy and should be covered.

Violations of the law, both criminal and civil, fall into two court jurisdictions—state and federal—and two categories—felony and misdemeanor. Violations of state law are tried in state court in the city or the county where the crime was committed; violations of federal law are tried in federal court. Some law violations, such as bank robbery sometimes are tried in either state or federal court or in both.

Felony is a violation of state or federal law and results in a prison sentence of more than one year in a state or federal penitentiary or a fine or probation or any combination of the three, or execution. Most felonies—especially murder, kidnapping, rape, bank robbery, and such white-collar crimes as insider trading, embezzlement, and extortion—are highly newsworthy.

Misdemeanor is a violation of a city ordinance and results in a fine or imprisonment in county or city jail for no more than one year or probation or any combination of the three. Misdemeanors generally are less than newsworthy, unless public officials are involved.

Note—Records of felony and misdemeanor trials are public and are almost always open to everyone.

State courts from the lowest to the highest level: city court—sometimes called *municipal court* or *corporate court*—serving the incorporated city for misdemeanors; justice of the peace court, serving a precinct in a county for felonies and misdemeanors; county court, serving a county for felonies and misdemeanors; circuit court or district court, serving a defined geographical area for felonies and misdemeanors; and appellate court and supreme court, serving a state for felonies and misdemeanors.

Note—Names of courts vary from state to state.

Federal courts from the lowest to the highest level are: district court, for criminal and civil cases at the federal level for all or part of each state, depending upon size of the state; twelve circuit courts of appeals, serving groups of states and territories; and the U.S. Supreme Court, serving the nation on appeals involving constitutional issues.

Note—The 12th Circuit Court of Appeals, serving Washington, D.C., hears appeals of federal agencies, which is important in mass media law. Circuit courts are so named because the judges travel from court to court within the circuit to hear appeals.

Constitutional Protections

Everyone in the United States—citizen and visitor—has the following constitutional protections of the right to life, liberty, and the pursuit of happiness against impropriety in arrest and trial. Some are in the basic Constitution; some, among the Amendments. Here are the guaranteed protections:

- The right to release from jail after three days if not charged with a crime and told about the charges (Writ of Habeas Corpus)—Article I, Section 9.
- No ex post facto laws (trial for an act committed before that act was prohibited by law)—Article I, Section 9.
- Trial by jury—Article III, Section 2, and Sixth Amendment.
- No search without a warrant describing the place of the search and the persons or things to be seized—Fourth Amendment.
- No second trial for the same offense (double jeopardy)—Fifth Amendment.
- No trial for a capital crime except by indictment by a grand jury—Fifth Amendment.

- No testimony against one's self—Fifth Amendment.
- No deprival of life or liberty or property without due process of law—Fifth Amendment.
- The right to a speedy and public trial by an impartial jury—Sixth Amendment.
- The right to be informed of the nature of criminal charges—Sixth Amendment.
- The right to confront witnesses—Sixth Amendment.
- The right to have an attorney—Sixth Amendment.
- No excessive bail, no excessive fine, no cruel or unusual punishment—Eighth Amendment.
- The right to equal protection of the laws—Fourteenth Amendment.
- The right to vote—Fifteenth, Sixteenth, Nineteenth Amendments.

Phases of Crime and Law Enforcement

Here are the explanations of the various phases of crime and law enforcement and the trial and your rights and duties as a reporter in covering them.

Crime

A crime is a violation of a state or federal law: murder, rape, robbery, burglary, extortion, kidnapping, and so on.

Most crimes are committed without a reporter's being present.

Police Investigation

Once a crime has been reported, law enforcement officers begin an investigation. They secure the crime scene, collect evidence (such tangible items as weapons and fingerprints), and testimony (statements from eyewitnesses).

It is during the investigation that reporters show up at the crime scene. Reporters are free to observe and to ask questions of the law enforcement officers and of witnesses, but should not interfere with the investigation. Although you may interview rank-and-file law enforcement officers, most of them know little because of their assignments at the crime scene. The best source of information is from the senior law enforcement officer at the crime scene.

> **Note**—The senior law enforcement officer of the county is the sheriff. Cities establish police forces, but they are subservient to the sheriff. Generally, the police investigate crime within the city; the sheriff investigates crime within the county but outside city limits.

Upon completion of the investigation, the police deliver the evidence and testimony to the district attorney.

District Attorney

The district attorney's office evaluates the evidence and testimony and decides whether it is sufficient for a conviction. If it is insufficient, the district attorney asks the police to seek additional evidence and testimony. If it is sufficient, the district attorney presents the evidence and testimony to the grand jury and requests an indictment (a charge).

You should interview the district attorney about the crime; the police investigation, the arrest, and identity of a suspect; and the district attorney's plans for prosecution. Most district attorneys are candid about their activities and plans.

Grand Jury (secret session)

The grand jury is a special group that requires special handling. It is a group of citizens selected by a court to meet weekly during that term of court (usually six months) to consider criminal charges sought by the district attorney. The grand jury has but one duty, to decide whether the evidence presented by the district attorney is sufficient for a conviction. If the evidence is sufficient, the grand jury hands *up* to the court (not down, because the grand jury is part of the court) a *true bill*, an indictment charging the suspect with the crime, and the district attorney prepares for trial. If the evidence is insufficient, the grand jury hands up a *no true bill*. Do not use the term *no-bill* as a verb.

A true bill is neither a conviction nor evidence of guilt; it says only that sufficient evidence exists for a conviction. A no true bill is neither an acquittal nor evidence of innocence; it says only that insufficient evidence of guilt exists. It is possible that the police can uncover additional evidence, in which case, the district attorney returns to the grand jury with another request for an indictment. Such action does not violate the Fifth Amendment prohibition against double jeopardy, that a person may not be tried twice for the same crime.

Caution—Grand jury deliberations are secret; members are forbidden by law to discuss their actions outside the grand jury room. Those who do are subject to fine and imprisonment. Do not interview members of the grand jury. Your best source of information about grand jury action is the district attorney.

Note—Some true bills are sealed, because an arrest has not been made, and the grand jury does not want to alert the suspect that the police are coming.

Arrest

The arrest of the suspect may come at any time, even during commission of the crime. It must come, however, before a trial.

To arrest a person after a grand jury indictment, the district attorney requests that a judge sign a warrant of arrest naming the suspect. The warrant is the authority for the police to make the arrest.

> **Note**—There is no such thing as an unidentified suspect. A suspect is an identified person who is suspected of having committed the crime. Until identification is made, refer to criminals by the crime committed: thief, robber, kidnapper, killer, and so on.
>
> Be careful how you use the term *suspect*. Suspects do not steal, rob banks, kidnap people, or kill people; it is thieves who steal, robbers who rob banks, kidnappers who kidnap people, killers who kill people.

Upon arrest, suspects are handcuffed, searched, taken to jail, photographed, fingerprinted, issued jail clothing, and placed in a cell to await *arraignment* and trial on the charges. Holding suspects in jail guarantees their appearance for trial.

Your source of information about the arrest is both the police and the district attorney.

> **Note**—You may interview the suspect. You might have to get permission from the defense attorney or the police chief, and the suspect. Be aware that the suspect is charged with, not convicted of, a crime, and that there is no law against lying to a reporter.

Arraignment

Before a trial is ordered, the suspect, accompanied by a hired or court-appointed defense attorney, is taken before the court, told the charges, and asked to plead to the charges. Because arraignment is part of the judicial system of crime and punishment, you should cover it.

In an arraignment, the suspect may plead:

Guilty, in which case the judge convicts and pronounces sentence.

Not guilty, in which case the judge sets a date for the trial.

> **Note**—Although no one can plead "innocent," the Associated Press requires "innocent" rather than "not guilty" to avoid inadvertently dropping the "not," thereby changing the plea from "not guilty" to "guilty."

Nolo contendere (or no contest, the term understood by more people), meaning that the suspect lets the judge decide guilt or not. This avoids a trial during which testimony may endanger witnesses or the family of the defendant. In such cases, the judge usually convicts and pronounces sentence.

Note—No one may be sentenced to prison or fine or probation without having been convicted.

———

Note—Judges *pronounce* or *pass* sentence, never *issue* or *hand* or *impose* or *give* sentence.

It is during the arraignment that the suspect may request release from custody on a promise to return for the trial. Release is granted under one of the following conditions:

To the custody of parents, which means that parents are responsible to ensure the prisoner's appearance at the trial.

On own recognizance (OR), which means that the prisoner is considered responsible to ensure appearance at the trial.

Upon posting of *bail* (or *bail bond*, but never *bond*), an amount of money or property fixed by the judge.

Note—Suspects who have no money or property may hire a *bail bondsman* to put up the bail money. Bail bondsmen charge a fee, payable immediately and not refundable. Thus, it is the bail bondsman, not the suspect, who posts a bond for the bail, which the court accepts.
   A bond is an IOU (I owe you), a promise to pay a certain amount of money or of property. No court would accept from an indicted suspect a promise to pay money or property for refusing to show up for the trial. But any court would accept bail from a bail bondsman. So, if the suspect does not show up for trial, the court takes the bail money from the bail bondsman, and the suspect must stand trial both on the original charge and on a charge of disobeying a court order to appear for the original trial date. And the suspect owes the bail bondsman the amount of the bail that the court confiscated.

Trial

The trial court has a judge, a district attorney, a defense attorney, witnesses, and the defendant, and may have a jury. Suspects may choose trial without jury, leaving the verdict to the judge.

The courtroom is like a theater, with space divided by a railing for visitors and for principals. Visitors sit in chairs or pews outside the railing; principals, inside the railing. Also inside the railing are the judge's bench, the witness box, the jury box, and tables for the district attorney, for the defense attorney, and for the press. The press table is farthest from the jury, so you don't want to sit there.

Since all of the action during a trial takes place on the side of the jury box and the witness box, you need to sit on that side of the courtroom, in the front visitors' row just outside the railing, so you can see and hear clearly. You may exit and enter the courtroom at will, without permission—unless the judge seals the courtroom—but do not make a disturbance.

> **Note**—Occasionally, the judge will strike a statement from the record, or tell the jury to disregard a statement, or take testimony from a witness with the jury out of the courtroom. You may use such information in your story because it was said in open court.

Trial begins as soon as the *bailiff*, the court officer, identifies the defendant and announces the charge. The first order of business is selection of a jury, a process that may take an hour or so or a few days or weeks, or even months in a high-profile case. Trial juries are selected from a *venire* of citizens, people eligible for jury duty. The first action is *voir dire*, questioning of potential jurors to determine their eligibility. Potential jurors may be struck (rejected) for two reasons: stated cause or unstated reasons. Each side has a fixed number of unstated reasons.

After the jury is selected, the testimony portion of the trial begins.

The district attorney represents the state and presents the state's case against the defendant first by calling witnesses and asking them questions and presenting evidence. The district attorney must prove, beyond a *reasonable* doubt (not beyond all doubt), that the defendant committed the crime. Most of the trial is circumstantial, based upon testimony and fingerprints, DNA, and similar evidence.

The defense attorney goes next, though the defense need not prove anything. Instead, the defense attorney tries to cast doubt on the district attorney's case.

Witnesses are *examined* by the attorney calling them to the stand and *cross-examined* by the attorney for the other side.

After all evidence and testimony have been presented, the judge sums up the case for the jury, cautions the jury what to accept and what not to accept, and gives the case to the jury. The jury leaves the courtroom for closed-door deliberations of the testimony and evidence. The jury has no time limit to consider the case.

Note—The length of time the jury needs to return a verdict may be important, but generally is of little consequence. Some juries delay returning a verdict, sometimes overnight, to take advantage of the free meals and hotel rooms provided by the court.

Caution—Do not interview jurors during the trial. Jurors are forbidden to discuss the trial, even among themselves, until the judge gives them the case. If you do talk with jurors during the trial, the judge could order a *mistrial* and hold you and the juror in contempt of court, which carries a jail term and a fine.

Once the jurors complete their deliberations, they return to the courtroom and announce one of three verdicts:

Not Guilty: Acquittal. The defendant is released.

Guilty: Conviction. The judge orders the convict jailed and directs the jury to study the possibility of the convict's future threat to society and to recommend a sentence. Only the jury can sentence a convict to death.

Note—Regardless of whether the verdict is to acquit or to convict, the Fifth Amendment forbids more than one trial on the same charge (double jeopardy). However, though it does not happen often, a person may be tried on the same charge in both state court and in federal court, because those are different jurisdictions and, therefore, different charges.

Unable to reach a verdict: *Hung jury.* The judge halts the trial and lets the district attorney decide whether to try the case again. If the district attorney declines to retry the case, the defendant is released, but the original charge remains, in case new evidence arises. If a second trial is scheduled, this is not a violation of the Fifth Amendment prohibition against double jeopardy. In this situation, the second trial is conducted as though the first trial never happened.

After the trial concludes, you may interview anyone involved in the case. In case of a conviction, you should interview both the defense attorney and the district attorney about plans for an appeal. The district attorney may appeal an acquittal, but that is rare.

Sentence

The court has the following choice of one or more of the following: a prison sentence of more than one year in a state or federal penitentiary or a fine or probation or any combination of the three or execution. A convict who violates the terms of probation may be required to serve the rest of the sentence in the penitentiary.

There are major differences between jail and prison.

Jail: For counties and cities to house suspects awaiting trial and convicts awaiting sentence. Cities use jails to house those convicted of violating a city ordinance, a misdemeanor. Jail sentences are for one year or less.

Prison, Penitentiary: For states and the nation, to house those convicted of a crime, a felony. Prison sentences are one year or more, including execution.

Appeal

Appeals from the action of a trial court are made to a court of appeal (appellate court) at the state or the federal level or both and as high as the United States Supreme Court. Arguments are always made before an odd number of justices, assuring a majority vote.

All appeals are made in open court, and you should attend to write the story of the arguments.

Appeals by the convict (through the defense attorney) are made usually on grounds of some fault with the trial—a technicality, a violation of legal procedure that may have prevented the appellant from having a fair trial.

> **Note**—In your story of the appeal, avoid writing that the appeal was made or upheld on a technicality and sent back to the district attorney. For accuracy in your story, describe the procedural violation and ask the district attorney about plans for a new trial.

Innocence is not grounds for an appeal, because the appellant, having been convicted, has been adjudged and is, under the law, guilty of the crime. Instead, the appellant must show that another person could be guilty of the crime. It is a technical argument made valid through DNA testing and other improvements in crime detection.

In arguing an appeal, only the district attorney and the defense attorney appear before the appellate court. Each side has 30 minutes to present arguments and to answer questions from the justices, and each must present a brief, an account (usually no more than 50 legal-size pages, 8½ by 14 inches) of the reason and the arguments for and against the appeal, as appropriate.

After a case has been argued before an appellate court, the justices take the arguments into consideration for study and debate. Except in the case of a request for a stay of execution, appellate decisions may not be handed down for weeks because the justices need time to study the appeal and research previous cases to reach a decision. All appellate courts have decision days, the day of the week that decisions are made public. For the U.S. Supreme Court, Monday is decision day.

In handing down a decision, the appellate court may:

Uphold the conviction, in which case the convict begins or continues serving the sentence.

Overturn the conviction and tell the trial court to erase the trial and conviction and either to schedule another trial or to release the appellant. The terms for this action are *reverse and remand* (not *remand back*). In this situation, the second trial does not violate the Fifth Amendment prohibition against double jeopardy. The second trial is a brand-new case because the first trial was eliminated.

Appellate court decisions are written and placed on file in the office of the *clerk of court*, the staff member in charge of the office of the court, not of the court itself. You should check with the clerk of court every decision day. Because much of the writing of court decisions is formal, the decision usually is in the last paragraph of the document. To help you understand the decision, read the last paragraph before you read the decision from the beginning.

Note—Do not make marks on appellate court decisions. They are official court documents, and writing on them is defacing, an act that could result in a jail term and a fine.

There will always be a majority opinion because appeals are argued before an odd number of justices. Sometimes, however, one or more justices will write a *dissenting opinion*, arguing against the majority opinion. In writing your story, be sure to include the dissenting opinion and name the justice(s) who supported it.

Note—Appellate courts have a *chief justice* and *associate justices*. Associate justices who preside over appeals are called *presiding justices*. In court documents, they are listed by last name and initials of rank: Hampden, C.J.; Emory, A.J.; and Dupas, P.J. It is up to you to know and use both the first and last names and titles of all appellate court justices: Chief Justice Andrew Hampden, Associate Justice Allen Emory, and Presiding Justice Ida Dupas.

Note—Convictions ending in a death penalty are appealed automatically. All you need do is ask the defense attorney when the appeal will be made and upon what specific grounds. If that appeal is denied, the convict may appeal as many times as new grounds for appeal are discerned.

Do not become concerned about convicts remaining on death row for as long as 18 to 20 years before being executed. It is the convict, not the system, who delays the execution date by continuing to file appeals.

Writing the Crime Story

After you have gone to the crime scene and interviewed the police and witnesses, write your story. What you know so far is this: A specific crime has been committed; the police have gathered evidence and testimony; and the police are seeking the criminal. It is up to you to tell the story objectively, accurately, tersely, and concisely, to get to the point quickly, and to tell the whole story in the first one or two sentences. It is even better if you can tell the whole story in one sentence.

Focus on the crime, the breach of the peace, the only action that is out of the ordinary. Use lively, action verbs. Do not give in to the tendency to seize upon the latest information, that the police are seeking a criminal. That is not news. The police always seek criminals. That is their job.

If no one is identified in the lead, you probably don't need attribution. The crime is a fact; it is public record.

Be wary of terms. Police speak of criminals as *unsubs*—unidentified subjects—and, erroneously, as *suspects*. A suspect is an identified person who is suspected of having committed the crime. For example, in a bank robbery, the unsub is a robber; in a kidnapping, the unsub is a kidnapper; in a murder, the unsub is a killer, not a murderer, because murder is a crime that has to be proved.

Do not write that the police "are still investigating." That *still* is an opinion word, implying incompetence on the part of the police, that hours after the crime, the police have not yet caught the criminal.

Do not write that the criminal *fled the scene*. Write that the criminal *fled*. The scene is the only thing the criminal could have fled, because that is where the criminal was at the time of the crime.

Attribute all identification to an authoritative source.

Be careful in citing charges. Do not identify a person as being indicted *for* murder, because that says that the person committed the crime and was indicted for it. Instead, write that the person was indicted *in connection with* the murder of [person's name] or indicted *on a charge* of murder in the killing of whomever.

It is not illegal to publish the names of rape victims and juveniles, but most newspapers avoid it.

WHO

The Who of the story is essential in stories about crime. This is the criminal or group of criminals. Most of the time, the identity of the criminal(s) will not be known immediately, but eventually, the police will arrest a suspect.

Crimes are easily determined facts; they are in the police report, which is a public record. Therefore, if no one is identified in the lead, there usually is no need for attribution. The crime is its own attribution.

DID WHAT

The Did What of the story is essential in stories about crime. This is a description of the crime: place, weapon, death, injury, rape, robbery, arson, whatever. This information is available from and attributable to an authoritative source.

WHY

The Why of the story is not always available in stories about crime because the reason for a criminal act is not always immediately apparent. However, when the reason is determined, it is essential and must be included and attributed to an authoritative source.

Where

The Where of the story is the place of the crime: bank, store, office, private home, street, and so on.

When

The When of the story is the day or date, and sometimes the hour, of the crime. It is never *recently*, which is vague and meaningless.

How

The How of the story is nearly always present and is essential in stories about crime. This information is available from and attributed to an authoritative source, either the senior police officer during the investigation or the district attorney later. Be careful, however, not to describe the crime in such detail that it becomes a how-to manual for committing that crime.

The Body of the Story

The remaining paragraphs of the story present, in descending order of importance, the details of testimony and examination and cross-examination.

Covering the Trial

Sit as close as possible to the railing that separates the audience from the court officials and on the side where the jury sits. That way, you can see and hear clearly because all of the action takes place near the jury.

As you cover the trial, notice everything: how the attorneys, the witnesses, and the defendant act; what they are wearing; how they look; their gestures and facial expressions; their responses, whatever. That way, you can describe the trial action in greater detail.

In describing the possible penalty for a conviction, use the maximum, because the convicted person could get less: "a maximum of 20 years in prison and a fine of $10,000."

If you use legal terms, be sure to define or explain them.

Be careful how you use such words as *murder* because they are charges to be proved. Instead, use *death, slaying, killed, strangled* (not *strangled to death*), because those terms are not charges or accusations.

Be honest with your readers; say things plainly. Criminal assault is not a synonym for rape. Rape is rape, and is always forcible (even if it is statutory). Anyone can be criminally assaulted. A punch in the nose is criminal assault.

Always begin your story with the most recent, the most important, action of the trial.

Up high in every trial story, write one or two paragraphs describing the crime and defendant's plea, which is either not guilty or not guilty by some reason. That information is necessary for a balanced and objective story. During a trial, while the district attorney is presenting its case—and the district attorney tries to paint as guilty a picture as possible—it will seem as though the defendant is guilty. But the defense has not had a chance to present its side.

In general, jurors may not ask questions during the trial, except in certain situations. The outcome of the trial depends upon the skill of the two attorneys: the prosecuting attorney and the attorney for the defense. The better attorney wins. That is how the advocacy system works. It is not a perfect system, but it is the best ever devised.

In covering lengthy trials—across several days or weeks or months—keep a copy of every story you write and a notebook of facts, names, dates, places, quotes, and so on, to help you with later stories and a wrap-up story after the trial concludes.

Caution—In the court, the judge is supreme. Whatever the judge says in court is law at that time. Even if your argument is correct, obey the judge or suffer the consequences: a contempt of court citation that carries a fine and jail term or, worse, for a reporter, removal from the courtroom. You would lose your trial story.

Kangaroo Court

A kangaroo court is one that disregards the legal system in trials or one that results in an unfair judgment.

Here is a true story from Mississippi when Douglas Starr was a newsman for The Associated Press in Jackson, covering government, politics, crime, civil rights—every news event imaginable. This is what he wrote:

> In Hattiesburg in the 1950s, a black chicken farmer was active in getting black people to register and to vote. White leaders objected and closed off the farmer's access to chicken feed. After a week or so, as his supply of chicken feed got lower, the chicken farmer took things into his own hands and stole a pickup truck-load of chicken feed.
>
> He was not a professional thief, so he was soon arrested, tried, convicted, and, presumably because of his efforts to end racial segregation, sentenced to 20 years in prison.
>
> Medgar Evers, Mississippi field secretary of the National Association for the Advancement of Colored People, telephoned me and said that the judge in the case was running a kangaroo court, a court that sidestepped legal requirements.
>
> I wrote the story, citing Evers as my source.
>
> The judge reacted and cited Evers for contempt of court and set a hearing date. In Mississippi, conviction for contempt of court carried a sentence of one year in jail and $100 fine.
>
> At the hearing, I was the only witness. The judge (no jury in a contempt hearing) asked me to describe the events. I explained about the telephone call.
>
> The judge asked how I knew that the caller was Evers.

I explained that he had identified himself and that I had recognized his voice, because I had known and interviewed him for several years in his role as a spokesman for the NAACP.

The judge asked why I accepted what Evers had said without documentation to support it.

I explained that Evers would not give me information and quotations for a news dispatch and then deny having done so.

"How can you be sure of that?" the judge asked.

Because, I replied, had Evers done that, his word would have been forever worthless to the news media, and his job would be forfeit.

Evers's attorney saw no need to question me.

The judge convicted Evers; Evers appealed to the Mississippi Supreme Court; the Mississippi Supreme Court dismissed the contempt conviction, ruling that the First Amendment gave Evers every right to say that the judge was running a kangaroo court.

17

How to Cover Science, Medicine, and Religion

Some technical stuff here, but always interesting, and you meet the most interesting people.

The term *technical news,* as applied to news of science, medicine, and religion, is sort of a misnomer, really. In fact, all news—news of science, medicine, religion, education, crime, the courts, the Congress, the state legislature, business, sports—is technical, each in its own way, especially if you do not understand it. To the uninitiated, a football game is highly technical and confusing.

To cover news of any sort requires homework. You have to study the topic, whether it be football or space shots or corporate mergers or development of an AIDS vaccine. And you do that by a combination of formal education and self-study. Before asking the first question in an interview, read about the topic in reference books, in newspapers, in magazines, and talk with people knowledgeable in that topic. And during the interview, if you do not understand the interview subject's discussion, ask for clarification. If you do not understand it, you cannot explain it to the readers. Don't hesitate to ask the subject these two most important questions:

What do you mean by that?

and

How will this affect people?

Fortunately, as in any endeavor, the longer you cover your beat, the more expert you will become in that field. When the space race began in the 1950s, few reporters knew anything about rockets and space. Before long, the reporters who covered the space shots became so expert, they were invited to speak on the topic before civic, professional, and educational groups.

How to Cover Science and Medicine

Most stories about science and medicine come from corporations and universities conducting research in those fields. Scientific research projects usually take months and years of work before results are found. Researchers are very caught up in their work; they think about it all day, and take their problems home with them at night. After the project is completed, they want people to know about their achievement. They will talk with you, explain the results of what they have achieved. Sometimes, you will get more than you need, but that is all right. You will have listened to the scientist, and that means a lot.

In addition, the corporations and the universities for whom the scientists work want publicity for the results of the research. It helps with budget requests to be able to show results and widespread interest. In addition, corporations and universities have public relations staffs whose primary function is to secure publicity, to put the research breakthrough into the news report. Those public relations people will seek you out with news releases and other information for stories.

Even so, if science and medicine are your beat, cover those offices and people as frequently as necessary to collect newsworthy information.

If you have the science beat, become familiar with the scientists and what they are studying. Get to know the scientists at the university. Remember the hard sciences—anthropology, biology, botany, chemistry, entomology, geography, geology, physics, meteorology, zoology—but don't overlook ecology, economics, fisheries, forestry, horticulture, mathematics, psychology, sociology, statistics, wildlife; they are sciences, too, and researchers are making great strides in those areas. It is not necessary to visit every researcher every day or every week, because scientific research simply does not hurry itself. But do visit with them occasionally; let them know you're around and interested in what they are doing and ready to publicize their successes. Work closely with the institution's public relations office. Staff members will tip you to newsworthy items and will provide access to the people and data you will need to complete your story. Moreover, the public relations office can provide plenty of background material.

Most stories about medicine involve advances in medical procedures and medicines, rather than epidemics or the discovery of new ailments, and they, too, evolve over months and years of research. Epidemics, such as HIV and AIDS and SARS and the annual influx of influenza, and new ailments, really are hard-news stories, rather than news of medical breakthroughs, because of the way such ailments erupt and the havoc they wreak. They are covered the same way that any natural disaster—earthquake, flood, hurricane, tornado—is covered.

If you have the medical beat, become familiar with the staff of the medical association. Attend the association's annual banquet; cover every speech made by a medical person; and maintain files of information collected from newspapers, medical magazines, medical journals, and medical corporations, particularly their annual reports. Have access to a medical dictionary, because in writing stories about medicine, you will run across medical terms understood only by those in the medical fields. It is your task to translate such terms into language the readers understand.

It is not enough to tell readers what the scientific breakthroughs will do for them; you must tell them in such a way that they understand what you are saying. If you do not understand the scientific terminology, ask your source for clarification.

Do not overlook the hospitals. They might be more than just a place to treat the ailing; they might be teaching hospitals or research hospitals whose staffs are doing newsworthy things. Almost every hospital has a public relations staff, ready to help you. Make the rounds; get to know the newsmakers.

How to Cover Religion

Covering religion is as demanding as covering science and medicine. Religion is a touchy subject. The First Amendment protects people from government-mandated religion and guarantees freedom of religion, guaranteeing that everyone has the right to practice any religious belief or none, and guaranteeing that the government will not require anyone to practice a particular religion. Thus, separation of church and state, though not mentioned in the Constitution but guarded jealously, is an explosive, emotional issue.

As a result, the demands for accuracy in writing about religion probably are more stringent than writing in any other area. People simply get more emotional about matters of religion than they do about science, medicine, education, government, business, or almost any other topic. Errors in religion stories will generate more letters to the editor than errors in almost any other type of story. It behooves you to be accurate, not only for your sake but also for the sake of your news medium. Your errors become the news medium's errors, and, for your errors, the readers will castigate you, of course, but also your news medium will receive the brunt of readers' wrath, frequently accusing religious bias.

Before you write about religions or their beliefs or their rites or their infrastructure or their clergy, seek information from an authoritative source but first check *The Associated Press Stylebook and Briefing on Media Law* under the name of the religion and under these entries: church, Mass, Protestant,

Protestantism, religious affiliations, religious movements, religious references, religious titles.

To ensure accuracy in reporting about religion, *The Associated Press Style-
book* carries thumbnail sketches of the following religions, each one re-
searched through documents and interviews with authoritative members of
the groups: Anglican Communion; Baptist churches; Buddhism; Christian
Church (Disciples of Christ); Church of Christ (not Churches of Christ);
Church of Christ, Scientist; Church of Jesus Christ of Latter-Day Saints
(Mormon Church); Congregationalist churches; Eastern (Greek, Romanian,
Russian) Orthodox churches; Eastern Rite churches; Episcopal Church
(Protestant Episcopal Church in the United States of America); Hindu-
ism; Islam; Jehovah's Witnesses; Jewish congregations; Lutheran churches;
Methodist churches; Presbyterian churches; Quakers (Religious Society of
Friends); Roman Catholic Church; and Seventh-day Adventist Church; and
the following religious movements: evangelical; evangelism; fundamental-
ist; liberal; neo-Pentecostal, charismatic; and Pentecostalism.

If you are not careful, you can fall into some rather simple errors. For example, some religious groups do not refer to their clergy as *the Rev.* and take
quite a bit of exception if you make that error in referring to their clergy.
Some religious groups refer to their clergy as *minister, brother, father, reader,
pastor, elder, rabbi*; it's your job to know which uses what. Some religious
groups have no clergy at all in the usual sense: The Church of Christ, Scientist (Christian Science) has lay readers, lay practitioners, and lay lecturers. In
most religious groups, members consider themselves members of a particular church: Baptists, for example, hold membership in a particular Baptist
Church (First Baptist Church of Houston). Roman Catholics, on the other
hand, although they may attend Mass at any Catholic Church, are assigned
to a parish church according to their geographic domicile.

Some religions have hierarchies or synods or assemblies (bishops) and
their churches are under central control (Anglican, Church of Jesus Christ
of Latter-Day Saints [Mormon Church], Episcopal, Lutheran, Methodist,
Roman Catholic). Some religions comprise autonomous churches and
have conventions (Baptist). When Baptist churches schedule conventions
to discuss church matters, the Baptist churches send, not delegates, but *messengers*, representatives who will receive the information from the convention and report to their churches. The individual Baptist churches are not
bound to accept the consensus of the convention. Some religious groups
are wholly autonomous (Jewish congregations, Pentecostal).

Religious beliefs are based upon the Bible or the Quran (or Koran). Jews
use the Old Testament; Christians, the Old Testament and the New Testament. The Jewish Torah is the first five books of the Bible, called the Pen-
tateuch. Jews worship in synagogues; Christians, in churches and chapels;
Muslims, in mosques.

All that sounds like a lot, and it may be, but accuracy is your watchword.

Note that church groups covered by the term Protestant or Protestantism include Anglican, Baptist, Congregational, Methodist, Lutheran, Presbyterian, and Quaker. The term is not applied, generally, to Church of Christ, Scientist; Church of Jesus Christ of Latter-Day Saints (Mormon Church); and Jehovah's Witnesses.

The churches themselves, in which religious groups worship, are named variously. Be careful; the names are very important. Many religions name churches after saints or holy people or religious events: St. Mary Catholic Church, St. Thomas Aquinas Catholic Church, Holy Family Catholic Church, Immaculate Conception Catholic Church, All Saints Episcopal Church, St. Andrews Episcopal Church, St. James' Episcopal Church, St. Peter's by the Lake Episcopal Church; other religious groups name churches after places and saints: First Baptist Church; Lakeside Baptist Church; Ridgecrest Baptist Church; Holy Ghost Baptist Church; Holy Temple Baptist Church; First United Methodist Church; St. Paul's United Methodist Church; Main Street United Methodist Church; St. Matthews United Methodist Church; Forest Hill United Methodist Church; Westminster Presbyterian Church; St. Luke Presbyterian Church; Trinity Presbyterian Church; Briarwood Presbyterian Church; First Presbyterian Church; Lakeside Presbyterian Church; Christ Lutheran Church; Peace Lutheran Church; First Church of Christ, Scientist; United Pentecostal Church; Martin Luther King Jr. Street Church of Christ; College Heights Assembly of God Church; and so on.

Understand such religious terminology—most of which are explained in *The Associated Press Stylebook*—as *agnostic, atheist, consubstantiation, sacrament, transubstantiation, bishop, archbishop, Bible Belt*.

Matters of interest in covering religion include:

- Gatherings of leaders and membership of religions: conventions, synods, councils, and so on.
- Ordination, appointment, resignation, death, movement of clergy.
- Change in rules of governance.
- Election of boards of deacons and other governing boards.
- Establishment of churches.
- Establishment of church-based schools and hospitals.
- Specific religious services, such as retreats and missions.
- Sermons by visiting clergy.
- Activities in the seminary.

Caution—When covering religion, remember that each religion unit—church, chapel, synagogue, mosque, whatever—is a private gathering. Regardless of how many people are present, religion activities are private. Reporters who sneak into church and report on its activities violate the privacy of the religion and of its members. For religion activities to become public, a reporter or the public must be invited to attend.

18

How to Write a Critical Review of an Art Form

This is the fun part of reporting; you cover theater of all kinds, music of all kinds, art of all kinds, architecture of all kinds, books of all kinds, even restaurants of all kinds, and tell people whether they are worth the visit.

Critics of the various forms of art are important because people are curious. People are not overly influenced by critical reviews in making a decision about whether to see a play or a movie or to attend a concert or to read a book or to listen to a musical piece. People read critical reviews because they are curious about the art form; they want to know something about it in advance; they want to compare their judgment with that of the critic; they are interested in the art even though they may not attend; and they want the literary and educational value of the criticism.

> **Note**—The critic's task is neither to praise nor to pan; it is to evaluate, to make a fair and honest judgment of the worth of the art form, its merits, and its faults.

The critic, therefore, must write, not just a review describing the art form, but also an individual judgment of the art form, based upon stated evidence, for readers to evaluate and to react to.

For the critic, although it helps to be knowledgeable about the art form, criticism does not require that you be an expert. The most important requirement for critical writing is that your opinions be your own, that they be honest, and that they be supported by fact. Your opinion may not be the majority opinion or even the opinion of any other critic or viewer. It is enough that it be your own honest, factually based opinion.

The critic cannot make or break a performer or a performance or an artist or any work of art. Artists and works of art stand, or fall, on their own merit.

Libel

In criticizing art, you need not be overly concerned about libel. As long as you criticize the art form and *not the artist*, and as long as you are fair and honest in your criticism, you are protected under the Fair Comment and Criticism section of the laws of libel.

Note—*The Associated Press Stylebook and Briefing on Media Law* has a clear explanation of fair comment and criticism, of the right of privacy, and of fair use, how much of the original work may be used in a critical review.

If you think that the artist's private life impacts on the art form, and you wish to include that in your criticism, check with your company attorney.

Ethics

You, the critic, determine your own Code of Ethics, which you may change as you wish. Your Code of Ethics is a set of directions by which you seek and attain happiness.

Compromise is not a surrender or a failure, but a seeking of a common ground in which both sides succeed, at least in part. In your writing, be truthful; be honest; tell as much of the story as you legally and morally can; avoid prejudice; do not let your biases show. Be open to criticism and willing to admit error and failure.

What Art Is

Art is difficult to define. What is art to one person is trash to another. For purposes of criticizing art, the best definition is that art is what the artist says it is. If the artist says it is art, it is art. In your critical review, you may describe the art as good or bad, but you may not say that it is not art.

Architecture: All kinds: house, office building, bridge, park, sports arena, garden, and so on.

Book, Magazine: All kinds: fiction, nonfiction, news, specific subject matter.

Dance: All kinds: live, broadcast, ballet, chorus line, tap dance, ballroom, street.

Lecture: All kinds: live, recorded.

Music: All kinds: classic, popular, jazz, country and western, live, broadcast, recorded, full orchestra, small band, single entertainer, small group, large cast, single singer, multiple singers.

Painting, Drawing, Photography, Transient (Sand Sculpture, and so on): All media: oil, watercolor, pen-and-ink, charcoal, pencil, color, black-and-white, sand, school bands in formation on the playing field.

Restaurant: All kinds: large, small, sit-down, fast food, ethnic, vehicle parked at the curb.

Sculpture: All media: marble, bronze, clay, wood, metal, stone.

Theater (Stage, Television, Motion Picture, Nightclub Act, Computer Screen): All kinds: live, broadcast, old, new, onscreen, color, black-and-white, school, Broadway, off-Broadway, little theater, road troupe, large cast, small cast, single entertainer.

The key to writing a critical review is that you write from first-hand knowledge. You must have read the book; seen the play, the movie, the television show, the dance, the nightclub act, the exhibit of painting, photography, and sculpture; walked around and through the structure; listened to (not heard) the music; attended the concert and the lecture; and eaten in the restaurant.

As you view the art form, base your evaluation upon these questions:

- What gives the art permanent value?
- What faculty of the artist makes this possible?
- Is the theme convincing? Original?
- What is different about this art?
- Is the dialogue realistic?
- Is each character true to life?
- Does the artist conceive and portray the theme correctly?
- Is the theme portrayed correctly?
- Does the action move smoothly?
- Is anything missing?
- Is anything unusual?
- Is there a reason for the work?
- How does this work compare with other works by the same artist, by different artists?

Some art forms cannot be true to life because they deal with situations that no one has experienced. With those, you must evaluate the characters and situations as seemingly true to life.

Writing the Critical Review

Your critical review will be a lot stronger if you avoid the first person—*I, me, my, mine, we, us, our, ours*—and let facts be the basis for your opinion.

Your lead should be action-packed, one or two sentences of lively description of the art form, in the active voice, and designed to capture and captivate readers. You may include your opinion of the art form, because you will provide factual support later in your review.

Above all, do not be cute or snide; you are dealing with people's careers.

In the body of the review, describe the central theme or plot of the art form in sufficient detail to be interesting and informative. For books and plays of all kinds, describe the plot in the present tense, but do not reveal the ending. Present information upon which you base your evaluation and conclusion, and include your own reaction and the reaction of the audience.

Your conclusion judges the merits of the art form, based logically upon the body of the criticism. Explain how your evaluation and conclusion were reached.

Throughout your review, be mindful of the limitations of the artist, the cast, and the producer of the art form. Students are just learning their art, whereas professionals have years of training and experience. Sometimes, there is a vast difference between the products of the two groups.

Consider the objectives of critical writing: to answer the same questions used to view and evaluate the art form. In addition, ask, "What was the reaction of the audience?"

Deal in specifics, not generalities. Be sure to describe your own reaction, your own impressions, but without the first-person singular. In general, write in the third person. If you must use jargon, explain it. Use few quotations. Do not give away the ending of the story; compare the art form with works in the same field by the same artist or by other artists.

How to Criticize Each Art Form

Architecture: Describe the purpose of the building and whether the building looks like what it is, and whether it fits into its surroundings. Describe its size, its height, its width, its length. Describe its color, its construction materials, and whether there are ornaments or carvings. Describe anything unusual or special or ordinary or unexpected.

Book, Magazine: Read the book or several issues of the magazine to determine the quality of the publication. Readers are interested in the price of the book or of a single issue of or year's subscription to the magazine. Books are both fiction and nonfiction, and you evaluate both the same way.

- Check books for copyright date, publisher and date of publication, the quality of the book, the cover, the binding, the printing, the author, and other works by the same author.
- It is a good idea to read several issues of a magazine to determine the kind of story published, the advertising, editor's note, letters to the editor, use of photographs.
- In critically reviewing a book, mention the author, the book title, the publisher, the number of pages. Describe the plot in the present tense, but do not give away the ending.
- Unlike a novel, poetry is meant to be read aloud, and listened to, so before criticizing a poem, read it aloud, with feeling, including pauses, and listen to the flow of words, the rhythm of the lines. In critically reviewing poetry, assume that readers have little knowledge about poetry. If you must be technical, simplify and explain the terms. Tell readers what mood the poem fits and how well the poet captured that mood.

Theater, Movie, Television, Stage Play, Nightclub Act, Onscreen: All of these art forms are similar in many respects, but each is different, and those differences must be considered. In writing the critical review, do not confuse the actor with the character; it is the character, not the actor, who wins the fair lady or is killed or whatever.

- Movie and television depend upon movement, both of the camera and of the actors, and the relationship between scenes. The director presents the scene from one point of view, and the audience views the scene from another and mixes the two points of view. But movie scenes synthesize into something more, a third scene, as it were, an effect called *cinematic*. That's why it's important that you tell readers your viewpoint, from what perspective you are criticizing.
- In movie and television, look for what is included, what is omitted, scene-stealers, entertainment value, human value, action, visuals, editing. Bear in mind that the director may be playing tricks on the audience through satire. In criticizing, tell readers your point of view, your perspective. Do report on how well the actor portrayed the character. As in any story, describe the plot in the present tense, but do not give away the ending.
- In theater, nothing is natural, nothing is real; all is exaggeration, all is artificial. The key to criticizing, to evaluating, a stage play is to observe your own reactions (and those of the audience) to the points of emphasis of stage productions: primarily to the opening of the play, to the closing of act one, and to the closing of the play; and secondarily, to the opening of act two.

- For a meaningful critical review, the critic should see the stage play more than once, evaluate what was seen and heard on stage, take a position as either favorable or unfavorable toward the play, and explain why. Mention the enthusiasm and energy of the actors, and mention the date and time of the play reviewed because performances vary. In writing the critical review, do not confuse the actor with the character. Do report on how well the actor portrayed the character. As in any story, describe the plot in the present tense, but do not give away the ending.
- A nightclub act is another part of theater, except that it usually features either singers or comedians. Criticize singers as music and comedians as theater.

Live Music, Recorded Music, Dance: Music and dance, regardless of how they are presented, are largely emotional and should be criticized on that basis, on how they make you feel. Be aware of audience reaction. Dance is part of music because they are presented together; they are one. As in theater, no two performances are the same, so you should attend more than one performance and compare.

- Music varies by type: classical, operatic, jazz, rock and roll, country and western, bluegrass, ballads, dance, swing, reggae, golden oldies, children's, holiday, the types continue to develop.
- Criticizing music is similar for a live concert and a recording, for a full orchestra and a band or small group. It is all music. Make comparisons to previous works by the same group or singer and to similar works by other groups or singers. In your critical review, mention by name each piece of music played in concert or in the recording. Readers want to know.
- For best results in criticizing live music, attend rehearsals and listen to what the conductor says to the musicians. During the performance, determine how well the musicians followed the conductor's instructions. After the performance, interview the conductor.
- In live music and dance, observe the conductor. If the conductor is relaxed, all is well; if nervous or giving more attention to a certain section of the orchestra, something is wrong. After the performance, ask the conductor what the problem was.

Painting, Photography, Sculpture, Transient Art: Art has four qualities: the intention of the artist; its concept, which indicates the inventiveness of the artist; its craftsmanship; and its contribution to society.

- Painting uses many media—oil, watercolor, pen-and-ink, charcoal—and is usually on canvas or wood or stained glass. A painting on a wall is a *mural*.
- Photography uses a camera—film, digital—and the photograph is black-and-white, full color, sepia, depending upon the wishes of the artist. If the photograph was enhanced, altered electronically on a computer, that must be explained.
- Sculpture uses many materials—stone, bronze, pewter, concrete, scrap iron—and ranges from pieces small enough for a tabletop to pieces 20 feet and more tall in parks and on buildings.
- Transient art is fleeting and uses many media—sand castles, ice carvings, band formations on the field, flower gardens, landscaping—and must be photographed for permanence. Landscaping involves either mowing a design into a field or sowing seeds and trimming bushes to grow a design.

Restaurant: Food is a matter of taste and is highly personal. Taste cannot be explained, but it can be described as savory, tasty, satisfying, or otherwise. And portions can be described as sufficient or meager.

- Identify by name and location the restaurant or cafeteria or fast-food eatery. Describe its color scheme, the music, the wall hangings, the lighting, the table setting (plastic or cloth, heavy or light flatware, china or plastic tableware, flower[s], candle). Describe its service, the promptness of its wait staff, its treatment of the diner.
- Describe the various parts of the meal: soup, salad, dressing(s), entrées, side dishes, breads, dessert(s), drinks. List the entrée you ate and describe the range of entrées, all including the price. Readers want to know what eating in that place will cost, usually for two, including tip.

Lecture: Covering a lecture is similar to covering a speech except that a criticism is needed. Tell the lecturer's name, title, profession, office, credentials. Describe the audience and tell why the lecturer is speaking to that group. Discuss the lecturer's tone of voice, pronunciation, gestures, speech pattern, tics, facial expressions. Describe the use, if any, of visual aids and whether the audience participated, particularly if there was a question-and-answer period after the lecture. Explain whether the lecturer covered the topic and whether explanations were understandable.

19

How to Write a Column or a Blog

You may voice your opinion, but only if you support it with facts.

A column is an opinion story, but the opinions must be based upon cited fact. A blog is an opinion piece, and the opinions should be based upon fact.

Columns are written by column writers and by reporters whose opinions are based, in part, upon experience. Columns always carry the name of the writer and, quite often, a standing headline, such as "Eyes on City Hall," "From the Statehouse," and "Capitol Comments."

The effective column contains facts and conclusions based upon those facts. However, the conclusions are not necessarily factual, because they are the opinion of the writer, but they should be logical and supported by stated fact. Moreover, the opinions usually represent only one side of the argument or issue. It is always highly likely that another writer, using the same set of facts, could arrive at a different conclusion. But your column expresses *your* opinion, reached after considering the facts.

Columns, like the other opinion pieces in the newspaper, are designed to help the readers arrive at their own conclusions. Readers need to read opinions—even those they disagree with—to help them formulate their own positions concerning issues that may affect them. News stories that present facts without conclusions or opinions are written sequentially, days, sometimes weeks, apart. Thus, standing alone, most news stories generally are insufficient to help readers to draw genuine conclusions or to develop educated opinions.

Therefore, column writers must be more than beginners; they must be professionally developed and be thoroughly grounded in the issues they write about.

Writing a column has three basic requirements: (1) know how things work, especially government and business, both separately and together, and how and why government regulates business; (2) gather the facts; and (3) be able to write a lucid, factually based opinion piece.

To gather facts, do what the reporter does: go to the source. Columns cannot be written from the office alone. Read as much as you need of the facts of the issue, but also interview people involved in the issue, especially the reporter who covered the story. Frequently, the reporter will provide unpublished information that you can use as a tip to secure published information or background.

Column writing without research, without fact-gathering, results in opinions based upon information that is usually unsupported opinion of family, friends, clergy, teachers, the Internet. What you want is factual information, information based upon research. You must go after it.

In general, the writing style of the column is crisp, terse, concise. No grandiose or sophomoric writing; no flamboyance. Don't be snide; don't be smug. Be simple. Be gentle. Be humorous. Be brief. Get to the point. Make your point. Stop. And, if you can be lively and interesting along the way, do so. Readers will appreciate it.

Most columns have three parts but no fixed length, though most don't exceed 500 words. Present the facts and the argument and draw a conclusion in as few words as possible.

1. **The Beginning:** The first one or two sentences explain carefully and completely the issue and why that issue is important. Tell readers what you are talking about and why.
2. **The Body:** The body, the middle section, presents the arguments, your side of the issue, and supports it with solid evidence and facts. In addition, the body of the column presents a key point on the other side of the issue and refutes it, based upon facts or clearly explained logic. It's important to your side to knock down the best argument of the opposite side. If the opposition's best argument won't hold water, neither will any other argument the opposition advances. Thus, the whole opposite argument fails.

   Moreover, presenting and rejecting a major opposing point gives supporters of your side of the issue ammunition to counter arguments from opponents.
3. **The Ending:** The ending, the last one or two sentences, is the key to the entire column. The ending states the position, the conclusion, drawn logically from the described facts; or it urges readers to believe something or to do something. It ties up the column neatly for the readers, providing a stopping point. If you have structured the body correctly, the conclusion should follow naturally.

Avoid using the first-person singular pronouns *I, we, us, our;* they have no place in an opinion column because they place more emphasis on the writer than on the argument. More often than not, you can proffer the same opinion without the self-serving, first-person singular pronoun. Either just omit the first-person singular pronoun or modify the sentence. For example:

Instead of writing:

I believe that the Board of Regents should . . . .

Write:

The Board of Regents should . . . .

Instead of writing:

I don't think it's a good idea for the Board of Regents to . . . .

Write:

It might not be a good idea for the Board of Regents to . . . .

Instead of writing:

I object to the Board of Regents' plan for hiring . . . .

Write:

The Board of Regents' plan for hiring . . . might not be in the best interest of students and the faculty.

Writing without the first person allows you to get the point across much more easily and without seeming to hog all the credit.

The column has these major functions.

To **Commend** or to **Condemn** actions by appointed or elected leaders, or support or decry an appointment to office.

To **Persuade** people to do something or to believe in a course of action or to behave in a certain way: to vote, to vote for a certain candidate or issue, to donate blood or money, to support a program, to write to appointed elected leaders, or to accept or reject a decision by a governmental agency.

To **Explain** complicated issues: the difference between nuclear fusion and nuclear fission, short- and long-range effects of oil spills, the effect of an increase in student tuition and fees.

To **Entertain** by describing what Groundhog Day and St. Valentine's Day are all about and how they began, and what Christmas was like in the "good ol' days." Readers like these columns because they offer relief from the turmoil that news stories engender.

Some columns are just a collection of anecdotes or news gems that, individually, are too small for a news story. Such collection columns, technically, are not columns in that they present news rather than express an opinion. Collection columns are valuable, though, because they present news items that otherwise might be omitted from the news stories or overlooked by readers.

Blogs published on the opinion page of a newspaper are similar to the column in that they follow the same rules for arriving at a conclusion. In addition, as required of columns, newspaper blogs must follow the same chain of review, must be approved by the editorial staff and copyedited for accuracy by the copydesk. The major difference is that blogs may use the first-person singular; after all, blogs are a more personal approach to presenting information and opinion.

Because newspaper blogs must follow the rules of the newspaper, they are different from citizen blogs, which have no rules to follow. The citizen blog writer, having no restrictions, may write anything, may take any position, and need not support any of it by fact. Citizen blogs can be pure opinion.

A news analysis, usually on a news page carrying news stories on the same topic, presents a logical conclusion to a series of issues or describes how a certain position was arrived at. Because its presentation is so factual, it may not be perceived as an opinion piece. But it is, because other news analysts could arrive at different conclusions. News analyses are signed by the writer and are labeled "Analysis."

At first glance, a news analysis may seem to be purely one person's opinion, but it should not be; it should be a carefully analyzed issue piece that results in a logical conclusion, a conclusion that anyone could draw from the facts.

A news analysis can draw together a number of issues—hazing on a number of college campuses, statewide or nationwide—to draw more universal conclusions. Additionally, a news analysis can explain trends and anticipate developments, such as the dumbing down of college students and a feminist backlash.

20

How to Write Feature Stories

The techniques for gathering facts for organizing and for writing features, roundups, depths, profiles.

Overview

Feature stories, the happy side of newspapers and magazines, provide a balance against the many columns of hard news about man's inhumanity to man—crime, divorce, war, intrigue—and the disasters resulting from fires, floods, hurricanes, earthquakes, airplane crashes, train wrecks, highway wrecks, and so on. In general, feature stories are "good news" stories, stories about what people do or have done for themselves or for each other, stories about people helping people, about people doing good deeds, or about people just living 100 years and remembering other times. Feature stories explain the origin of a holiday or an event or the development of a tearless onion or a new rose, or why the sea is salty, or why the sky is blue. They describe a breakthrough in medical care, in science, in technology. They profile the famous or the notorious, or the average person who has seen or done something interesting. It's easy to see why features appeal to readers; feature stories appeal to the emotions.

The term *feature story* encompasses several types of story, none of which falls under hard news or sports or other specific kinds of story. Within the category *feature story* are several types, depending upon the approach you care to take.

Feature stories generally are happy stories, and are generally about people and animals. They appeal to the emotions.

Roundup stories and **depth stories,** though feature stories, are not necessarily happy stories. They may involve either the good or the evil that people do, or they may explain the damage from natural or man-made disasters.

Profile stories are about individuals, about personalities in the news, explaining how and why they achieved whatever status they have.

Gathering Information

Before you can write any feature story, you must gather information. Information comes from three sources: the subject person, people who know or work with the subject person, and published documents. Use as many of them as you need.

The information you get depends upon the questions you ask, the answers you get, the place of the interview, your interview notes, and documents you research. Here are the steps.

Pick a topic, and pick a subject person to interview.

Write in a notebook the questions you plan to ask, listed in the order you plan to ask them. If you need assistance with questions, ask colleagues, the CEO, anyone. Here are some suggested question areas.

Goal: What were/are you trying to achieve? What was/is the purpose of your program?

Obstacle: What problems did/do you face? What problems did/do you anticipate?

Solution: How well did/will you handle the problem? How did/do you plan to overcome the problem?

Start: When did/does the program begin? Whose idea was it?

Set up the interview. Contact the subject person and set a date, a time, and a place. The task of interviewing can be disheartening to a beginning interviewer. But, an interview is merely a conversation between two people; you ask questions; the interview subject answers. So, don't worry, your subject person most probably is experienced in the interview, and will help you.

Take with you your notebook with the questions on the beginning pages. Use the rest of the notebook for taking longhand notes. Take two or three pens; one may run out of ink. Take a digital camera for random shots of the interview place and of the subject person. If you plan to use a voice recorder, test it before you go to ensure that it works.

Dress appropriately for the interview. Arrive at the interview site 15 minutes ahead of time. That will give you time to review your questions, and you may get to begin a few minutes early, all to your advantage. Above all, mind your manners; be polite, smile.

In the office, take a seat alongside the subject person's desk; that's less confrontational than directly in front.

Remember, you are in charge of the interview. In the interview site, don't ask permission, simply set up the voice recorder and begin to ask questions. If the interview subject objects to the recorder, explain that it is necessary for accuracy. After a while, both of you will forget that the recorder is on.

In fact, don't turn the voice recorder off and on during the interview. Let it run, and don't turn it off until after you have departed the interview site.

Ask each question specifically, without such preambles as "Let me ask you this." Above all, don't interrupt the speaker's answers. If the speaker does not answer your question, simply ask it again.

This is vital: Listen to the answers and continue taking longhand notes. Your subject person may introduce a new angle, one that you had not thought of. Continue along that new line as long as necessary. You haven't lost contact; you can always return to your listed questions.

> **Note**—Never mention *off the record* or *just between us*. You are not there for off-the-record information. If the interview subject proffers an off-the-record statement, explain that you cannot use it and request that it be on the record. Once you accept an off-the-record statement, you are honor-bound never to reveal the information.

After the interview, gather your belongings, but do not turn off the voice recorder until you have departed the interview site. Your last question should be "Is there anything else that you'd like to say?" You want that answer on the recorder.

After you have written your story, it's a good idea to send a copy to the interview subject to be read for factual accuracy. If the interview subject changes your writing style, don't worry; you have the original. What you want is accuracy.

After the story is published, send your interview subject a copy or a *tear sheet* from the newspaper or magazine and a thank-you note.

Writing the Feature Story

As diverse as feature stories are in topics, all of these story types—feature, roundup, depth, profile—are handled the same way as any other story.

Gather the facts, interview people as appropriate, take notes, find a peg to hang the story on, and write the story, this way:

- Organize the information; omit what does not pertain.
- Lead with information that will attract the reader into the story.
- Describe quickly the main point of the story or the news event upon which the story is based.
- Explain why the information is important or significant or relevant to the reader.
- Write clearly and simply, in terms that people can understand.

There is no required length for any feature, but, remember, onscreen or on paper, one page double-spaced is 250 words.

Some questions that should be answered:

- What does this mean?
- What will be the effect, the result?
- Who will be affected? How?
- What will happen next?
- What does this mean to the average person?

Describe the background and summarize the information.

The ending may summarize the story, refer to the lead, stop, or project into the future.

Of course, you must write a reader-catching lead and an interesting story, tersely and concisely, using proper grammar, punctuation, syntax.

Keep in mind two admonitions: one firm, one perhaps. The firm admonition is that you should not deliberately strive to write, or think that you must write, a prize-winning feature story. Most feature stories are just good yarns, stories that appeal to the average reader. In the beginning of your writing career, you're not likely to write any kind of prize-winning story. But you needn't worry about that just now. Just now, the goal is to write an acceptable feature story, a publishable story.

The perhaps admonition is that you should avoid writing a feature story about something or someone personal in your own life. If you do write something from your own life, that story probably will fall short of your expectations. That's because (1) in general, few people, if any, care about what affects you personally, and (2) the topic is too subjective; you're too close to the story and to the people involved.

Now and then, some exceptional it-happened-to-me stories are published, but those stories are relatively unique and really outstanding: attacked by a grizzly bear, adrift at sea, that sort of thing. Even stories growing out of Hurricane Katrina or of 9/11, or of whatever, emotion-packed as they are, pale by the fact that whatever happened to one person in those instances probably happened to hundreds more. If you're going to write something like that, write about what happened to one person or to one family. You can handle a story about someone else more objectively, and the story will be quite believable. Let someone else write the story about you or about your family; you can provide the details.

In writing these feature stories, remember, there are no dull stories, only dull writers. There are no fixed rules for handling feature stories; each set of facts, each story, usually will dictate the type of lead and the approach that fits best. Look for that. Above all, don't be stuffy; don't be afraid to experiment with the lead, to try different approaches, to surprise the readers, to have fun. In writing any of these stories, the inverted pyramid of news writing is not necessarily the best approach.

Sometimes, the story can be written best in chronological order, like an English essay, or following an anecdote or a vignette, a short sketch that focuses on the main topic of the feature story. *Reader's Digest* uses anecdote and vignette leads frequently, and successfully. And don't forget, rewrite and revise as many times as needed to make the story the way you want it. You're going to do a lot of rewriting and revising of your stories before you're satisfied, and a lot more before your editor is satisfied, but that's what it takes to be a writer.

A feature story is not something you write on the run. It's a precision piece, a story crafted over time, word by word, sentence by sentence, graf by graf, each handled lovingly and carefully, as though each might crumble if used incorrectly. As in any story, the lead is vital; it's the showpiece of the story, the part that grabs the readers and entices them into reading the rest of the story, and, with any luck, all the way to the end. In general, write in conversational style; use third-person pronouns—*you, your*—as frequently as the story will permit; it helps draw readers into the story.

Any feature story has a good many approaches to the lead. Use a story, an anecdote, a vignette, a description, a quotation, even a shock word or phrase ("a teddy bear lying in a pool of child's blood"), anything that will grab readers' attention and lure them into the story. Another approach is to lead by telling the story from one person's perspective. Sometimes called *The Wall Street Journal* format after the newspaper that uses it extensively, this is a way of personalizing or putting a face on a complicated or an abstract story.

As in any story, select your words, particularly the pebbles of the language, with great care. Make certain that each word fits the sentence precisely, that each word says exactly what you mean to say. Remember, words are either boulders or pebbles. Boulders are the main words: nouns, pronouns, verbs, adverbs, adjectives; pebbles are the small words: articles, conjunctions, prepositions. Although small and seemingly unimportant, pebbles can wreak havoc with your story if used incorrectly.

After the lead, provide readers a *nut graf*—sometimes called *justifier*—telling exactly what the story is about and why it is important.

Another suggestion for a good feature story is to provide many quotations, allowing your subjects to speak for themselves, bringing your story to life. Be sure that the quotations are accurate, quotable, and appropriate.

As in any story, feature stories usually focus upon one topic. That helps readers identify with what the story is telling them. If you see that your story is moving at a tangent, think about using that tangential topic as a separate story. It may be worth it.

Remember to work statistics into the story, rather than to focus mainly on them. If a hurricane dumped 8.4 inches of rain onto a city in 12 hours, knocked out electricity in 75 percent of the city, killed 9 people and injured 48, and left $438 million in damages, that's important and interesting, of course. But it would be far more interesting to readers—especially those away from hurricanes—to describe the hurricane from the vantage point of a victim: the rain lashing the trees, the noise of the wind ripping apart buildings and blowing away homes, the ever-present danger of injury or death by falling objects. That's what interests readers. You can work in the statistics as support.

Write in terms of people. It's one thing to write about 8.4 inches of rain. But who knows what that is. In New Orleans, which gets 6 feet of rain every year, hurricane or not, 8.4 inches is just over one month's average. Tell readers what those 8.4 inches of rain did to the town: flooded streets, overflowed creeks, and surged knee-deep into homes, soaking furniture and beds and rugs; turned low sites into automobile-swallowing lakes; that's what's of interest. Tell readers that the wind blew steadily at 85 knots—whatever that is—and gusted to 120, but add the moan and the howl as the roof blew off the pastor's rectory, centuries-old trees were uprooted and tossed against churches and schools, automobiles scattered haphazardly like children's toys after play. Tell readers the size of the hurricane, but explain it. A 300-mile-wide hurricane that centers on New Orleans causes damage from Lafayette, La., to Mobile, Ala., and from New Orleans to Jackson, Miss., and everything in between. That covers a lot of readers.

In feature stories of all kinds, much of the time, attribution can be dispensed with. If your interview subject tells you that she believes in going to the source and tells you that she went to the source and secured the information, you need not attribute all that. Simply write that your subject received the information from the source.

Above all, be accurate. Spell names correctly. If you are unsure about the spelling of a person's name, ask the person. If you are unsure about the spelling of the name of a store, check online or in the Yellow Pages of the telephone book or with the store manager.

Roundup

Every spring, cowboys go on the range and collect the cattle, round them up from fields and gullies and copses and drive them to holding pens for branding and whatever before shipping them to market. In a similar manner, news writers round up information from various sources and put it all together into a story.

Basically, the roundup is a result of an informal survey of various people or departments concerning related developments on a particular topic or event. It is a collection of opinions about a common element. Roundups are of three general types.

Developing: Strikes, disaster, gasoline shortage, epidemic, sports, the economy, the job market.

Reaction: Development of cold fusion, abortion laws, wars.

Trends: Fashion, tax increase, specific crimes, universal medical protection, rise/fall of interest rates.

Roundups can be written on any topic, but in general, these command the most attention:

Business: General business, inflation, recession, new home construction, results of tax increases, strikes, job layoffs, rise/fall of tax revenues, particularly sales tax and gasoline tax.

Crime: Generally, major crimes, but minor crime if it is pervasive; serial killings; the death penalty.

Disasters: Weather, hurricanes, tornadoes, floods, fires, explosions, earthquakes, epidemics, epizootics (among animals), traffic accidents and fatalities.

Government: Potential effects of proposed legislation, actual effects of enacted legislation.

Holidays: How birthdays are celebrated in various places or by various groups of people, and in other times; how other holidays are celebrated.

Politics: Campaigns, candidates, platform promises, elections, winners.

Science: Energy, environment, medical advances.

Society: Fashion, entertainment, television, theater, the arts.

Sports: Before the weekend games are played: relative strengths and weaknesses of the teams, and prediction of outcomes; after the games: description of the games in brief.

War: Battles, invasions, peacekeeping, deaths, injuries.

The basis of roundups is a survey, a collection of appropriate information from multiple sources, sometimes in multiple cities. You must ask each source the same questions, because what makes the roundup interesting and newsworthy is either the similarities or the differences in the responses.

To ensure that you do not overlook any questions, write them in your notebook and mark each one as answered. This is necessary, because people will add information that you had not thought of, information necessary to the roundup. In such case, you add that to your list of questions, and you need to ask every person you interviewed about that issue.

There is no fixed number of people interviewed for a roundup, but the list should be broad enough to represent all sides of the issue and to cover possible differences of opinion. Therefore, make a list of people you plan to interview. Ask colleagues for suggestions for both people to interview and questions to ask. Don't be reticent; you can't think of every angle yourself.

For example, to do a roundup on the possible effect of lower interest rates, you need to interview the president of every bank in the city, the director of every savings and loan association and every credit union, the president of the Chamber of Commerce, a university professor of economics and finance, and the state banking board. If that is too much for you, you might enlist assistance from colleagues or find a representative sample of individuals who can provide the needed information.

If you are unable to contact some subjects, make that plain in the story. If some subjects decline to be interviewed, make that plain in the story.

Your lead focuses on the common element of the survey topic; the body of the story provides the detail of the responses; and the end of the story just stops. There is no conclusion; that information was in the lead. If you must have an ending, select an appropriate and meaningful quotation.

For example, for a roundup on the possible results on city revenue of a two-cent increase in the tax on cigarettes, you would contact two sources in every city: the mayor and the head of the city accounting department. Your lead would focus on the overall result: how many mayors and accountants favored/opposed/had no opinion on the tax increase, and what the additional money was to be used for. Of course, mention the name of each city in the roundup, but also the populations of those cities.

Include whether the interviews were in person, by telephone, or online. Select appropriate quotations to bring your roundup to life.

Depth

A depth, like a roundup, has its basis in hard news, in some event that has affected or might affect or will affect people. The depth goes into detail about the results of a news event, puts the news event into focus, tells what the news event is all about and what it means. The depth explains, but does not take sides. Basically, the depth tells the WHO, the DID WHAT, the WHY, the How, and the THEN WHAT, presenting a lot of detailed information on the WHY and the How of the news event.

Depths require a lot of research, interviews with more than just the main persons involved. So, seek out specialists in the field, colleagues, rivals, competitors, relatives, friends, various publications and documents, as many of all that you need. Don't worry that you are not an expert in the topic of the story. All you need to know is how to ask questions until you understand the situation. If you are alert to what your interview subject is telling you, you can write a meaningful depth story.

In that you are writing from the vantage point of an observer, you may write much of the depth story on your own initiative, without much attribution. Be sure, however, that you base projections, conclusions, and consequences upon fact, and be sure that the facts are stated in the story. In all probability, you must include alternate views, alternate conclusions, alternate projections. But that's all right.

Profile

A profile is about people, but it is not a biography—that deals with the entire life of a person—nor is it a result of a question-answer interview. A profile describes and explains why readers are interested in the subject person today, in what the subject person has done lately. It focuses on the here and the now. The best profiles are those that are tied to the news of the day.

Before you can write a profile, you need biological information; you need to interview the subject, ask questions, get answers, but you need more than that. You need information about the subject person, which is available from knowledgeable sources, from people who know and like and know and dislike the subject person, who work with the subject person, who are neighbors of the subject person. You need information from previous articles written about the subject person. All of that means that you will move around quite a bit to get your story.

During the interview, don't be afraid to ask tough questions, ask about failures as well as about successes; ask about why the subject person got into such a situation. More often than not, you will receive answers, good answers. If you don't? Well, perhaps you can get answers to those questions from other sources.

Thus, you need to research three areas for your profile: (1) published material: newspapers, magazines, books, Facebook, online; (2) official records: court documents, property records, professional and business affiliations; and (3) financial records. All of that is available; you just have to search.

As you do your research, seek and listen for anecdotes and information for vignettes that will make your profile sparkle with life. Look at your subject person and surroundings. Describe your subject person for readers—appearance, height, weight (not for women), hair and eye color, dress, gestures, expressions, smiles, frowns, mannerisms—and describe the surroundings—the office, the home, the home office, automobile(s), family, friends. Make your subject person come to life on the page. After all, your subject person is a human being.

Be careful, though; don't just write that your subject person is this or is that. Instead, describe how your subject person *acts*, so readers can arrive at the conclusion you want them to.

Some profiles describe a day in the life of the subject person. This requires following that person for nearly 24 hours a day, from the alarm clock's ring to bedtime. Some use breakfast as a beginning before launching into the meat of the profile. Your approach depends upon you and your subject person.

Summary

- **Features** tend to be happy stories, good news that balances the harsh realities of daily events.
- **Roundups** contain a collection of opinions from experts on a trend, development, or event.
- **Depths** go into great detail about a news event, focusing primarily on the WHY and the How.
- **Profiles** are personality stories about one person and should contain sufficient detail so that readers empathize with the subject person.
- **Feature leads** can be vignettes, anecdotes, shockers, sometimes even full quotations, but they must be interesting to grab the attention of readers.
- The **nut graf**, the justifier, explains the reason for the feature.
- Use appropriate, meaningful quotations to liven up the story.
- Don't write; tell your story in terms of people. Talk to your keyboard. The more you write in conversations style, the more interesting and readable your story will be.

Writing Tips

- Write conversationally. Use the active voice: subject, predicate, object.
- Use proper attributive verbs, action verbs; use "to be" verbs sparingly.

- Use the dictionary to look up definitions and usages of words.
- Prefer the familiar word to the far-fetched, the concrete word to the abstract, the short word to the long.
- Avoid such redundancies as *revert back, while at the same time, is presently, and also, past experience.*
- Avoid such meaningless words as *somewhere, sometime, earlier this month.*
- *There* never is the subject of a sentence. Avoid it.
- Reserve *feel* for sense of touch.
- Above all, rewrite. As many times as needed to make the story glow.

21

Freelancing and How to Do It

Now that you know how to write feature stories, why not sell some of them to magazines and make a little extra money?

Freelancing, a term from the days of knights whose lance was his own, not in the service of the king or a lord, applies to people who write stories for publications without being on the payroll. Most magazines have one or two writers on the payroll, depending, in the main, therefore, on freelance writers because it is cheaper to pay a writer for one story than to have the writer on the payroll. A freelance writer is an independent contractor, responsible, not only for freelance expenses, but also for medical insurance, income-tax withholding, Social Security payments, retirement program, vacation, workers' compensation insurance, and so on, all of which the magazine pays for its employees.

It is safer for you to have a day job and do freelance writing during your own time; at least you will have a steady income. If you work for a newspaper or a magazine, be sure to get permission from the company before you do any freelance writing for other publications. No publication wants its employees working for the competition.

Freelance writing focuses on feature writing because magazines generally do not publish hard news. And with thousands of magazines published in the United States, freelance writers have a ready market, if they are good enough and follow the rules.

Many books about freelance writing are available in bookstores and libraries of all kinds. One of the most complete books on freelancing is *Writer's Market*, published annually by Writer's Digest.

Almost every library (including university libraries) lists *Writer's Market* as a reference book and restricted to use only in the library. In that all libraries have copier capability for a small charge, copies of appropriate chapters or pages can be made inexpensively, and you always have the current information.

Writer's Market covers the details of the freelance business, listing for each magazine the name, title, address, and so on, of the person to whom to send the story; the required/suggested length of the story; whether photos are needed; and the payment (by the word or by the story) and when payment is made: upon acceptance (in two or three months), upon publication (in four to six months), or on *spec* (speculation)—an agreement to consider, not a guarantee of, publication—and whether expenses are paid.

Before submitting anything to a magazine, study the magazine. Study every story for each of the previous 12 months, for several reasons, but primarily because no magazine will publish a story on the same topic within a year. By studying the magazine, you should gain firsthand knowledge about what stories and what advertising the magazine publishes, something about the typesetting style of the magazine: what to abbreviate, to capitalize, to hyphenate, and so on. To be certain of the style, ask the magazine for a copy of its style sheet.

Look at the photographs and other artwork to learn what kind of art (photo [color or black-and-white], line drawing, whatever) the magazine uses. Magazines usually pay a bonus if the photo is used on the cover.

How to Submit a Freelance Story

The first requirement is a query letter to the managing editor suggesting a story topic and asking if the magazine is interested. The letter should describe the proposed story in fair detail, including the credentials of people to be interviewed.

Take great care with the query letter because it is representative of your writing style, and the managing editor will use it to judge your writing ability. If you submit a query letter for a long story, attach a sample chapter so the managing editor can form an idea of your writing ability and the tenor of the story.

If you have a short story, shorter than 500 words, you may save time by dispensing with the query letter and submitting the story along with a cover letter only.

Stories submitted electronically are single-spaced and hard copy is double-spaced.

Whether electronically or on paper, prepare a cover page to the story, containing the following information:

- On the top left corner of the page: "To be paid for at usual rates to" and list your name, postal address, office and/or home telephone number, fax number, and email address.
- On the top right corner of the page, in all-capital letters: "FIRST NORTH AMERICAN SERIAL RIGHTS ONLY." That assures the magazine of the following: The magazine will have the right of first publication only, and, after publication, the story reverts to you for sale elsewhere; and the magazine may circulate the magazine throughout North America: United States, Canada, and Mexico. *Serial* refers to magazines, as distinct from newspapers and books.
- Centered on the page: a suggested title to the story on one line with your byline below.
- Centered on the page and below your byline: a 30- to 40-word abstract of the story; a statement that the people quoted in the story have read the story and initialed it as accurate; the number of words of the story; whether photographs or artwork are included; and the identity of the photographer or artist.

Note—Newspaper reporters have long objected to allowing sources to read their stories prior to publication, holding that it is an insult to their professional ability. Magazines want to be certain that freelance copy is accurate. Besides, the Internet can publish corrections the same day, and newspapers can publish corrections the next day. A magazine needs four to six months to publish a correction.

Note—That 4- to 6-month lag from layout to publication of the magazine means that seasonal stories must be planned six months in advance, requiring you to submit Christmas stories in June and summer stories in December.

22

How to Handle the Press

Reporters are a touchy bunch. They are not your friend, so handle them with care. Never lie to or mislead a reporter.

The press—newspaper, radio, television, and the Internet—is an essential part of life today, keeping people informed about activities they need to know about: government, politics, business, industry, education, medicine, and so on.

Today's press is so pervasive and so tenacious and the equipment so sophisticated that it is virtually impossible to hide anything from a reporter, even for a little while. So do not try. Besides, it is to a public relations professional's advantage to take the initiative and release bad news before being asked. It gets your side into the first story, and it enhances your credibility.

No matter how bad things seem for you, remember: News is perishable; it lasts only as long as it's published, on paper, on the Internet, on radio, or on television. Tomorrow is another news day, bringing other news. Then, today's news is old, and will be forgotten. So, in general, all you have to live through is the first day.

So what do you do about all that? Here are the rules.

Play the game the way the reporter plays it. When a disaster occurs, and reporters show up in your office, they aren't looking for a story; they already have one; they just want your side. So give it to them. It's to your advantage because it means that your company's side gets into the first story.

Never consider a reporter your friend.

On the job, reporters have no friends, not even other reporters; they have contacts, sources of information. They neither like you nor dislike you; they just want a story. And you are the one who can give them the story, the one who has the information they want. Treat the reporter as politely and as candidly as possible.

Just as it is the reporter's task to get a story, so is it your task to tell the story of your company, to describe what happened, to explain what is occurring.

How to Have Good Press Relations

Never lie to or mislead a reporter. If you do not know the answer, or if you prefer not to answer, or if you are forbidden to answer the reporter's question, say either that you will secure the information and contact the reporter later or that the information is confidential.

Give service. Be available whenever reporters need you, 24 hours a day, 7 days a week. Provide appropriate information, stories, and photographs in a timely manner.

Never argue with a reporter. You cannot win. Never become defensive or lose your temper. Adopt a pleasant demeanor. Smile as appropriate. Remain calm. Use up-and-down gestures and nod your head to emphasize positive points.

Do not beg; do not complain. If your story is not newsworthy, it will not be published. Nothing irritates a reporter or editor more than begging to have a story published, unless it is complaining that a story was not published.

Do not ask for kills. Asking a reporter to kill a story is an insult.

Do not flood the news media. It is not true that increasing the number of releases you send in increases your chance of publication. On the contrary, reporters quickly recognize that your copy is not newsworthy and tend to discard your submissions without even opening the envelope.

If you do not want something published, do not tell it to a reporter, not even "off the record." Do not mention "off-the-record" if you can help it. Generally, reporters will abide by a promise of keeping information off the record, but, too often, they forget and inadvertently publish off-the-record information. But, accident or not, an off-the-record statement has a good chance of being published.

Be careful with yes-or-no questions. Add as much qualifying information as you wish.

Other Suggestions

Do not call a news conference if you can possibly do otherwise. Once you open a news conference, the reporters are free to ask any questions they wish about any topic. If you do open a news conference, treat the situation as an interview, but with multiple interviewers.

Instead of a news conference, issue a public relations statement or a news release.

Long before any disaster hits, your company should have a written crisis plan, what to do when disaster hits. The company public relations office usually develops the crisis plan.

One of the keys in any crisis situation is to designate one person to represent the company and respond to all questions from the press. Then keep that person wholly informed, informed of what not to say as well as what to say. Remember, the company representative is just that, the company representative. The company representative is on your side.

Most people fear the television camera and the radio more than the newspaper. That is a mistake for several reasons:

- Television and radio news disappears as soon as it is aired.
- Newspaper and Internet news is archival; it lasts as long as that issue of the newspaper lasts and as long as the Internet site is available.
- However, both print and broadcast media file their stories, their video, and their audio on their Websites, making all news archival. Fortunately few people seek television and radio news from the Web.
- Television news reporters show you speaking your own words, giving you considerable control over what is said. Radio news reporters let the audience hear your voice speaking your own words.
- Newspaper reporters interpret your words, making your task much more difficult, requiring that your explanations be subject to one interpretation only.
- Television and radio news reporters almost always tell you in advance the questions they plan to ask. They must, because they want you prepared to provide responses short enough to fit the time requirements of the news segment. That gives you and your public relations staff an opportunity to develop exactly the kind of responses you needed.
- Newspaper reporters never tell you in advance the questions they plan to ask. They have no time or space restrictions in writing their stories. Because you do not know exactly what is wanted, planning is more difficult.

There is, however, one area for concern in television news: Very little can hide from the television camera. Anxiety, nervousness, stage fright, anger— all normal emotions—are magnified by the camera. But, so are smiles and chuckles and twinkling eyes. Use your personality to your and your company's advantage.

Neither television nor radio nor newspaper reporters will show you the stories they have prepared before it is aired or it goes to press. Do not bother asking to see the stories; they won't show them to you.

The Interview

Despite everything, you can learn some control of the press, print and broadcast. Here is how you can, and should, advise your CEO.

The interview is one of the basic tools of the newsgathering process. All reporters use the interview to collect information. Depending upon the reason for the interview, it can be either a pleasant conversation between the reporter and you, or an intimidating interrogation by the reporter.

In either case, keep in mind that, in any interview, you are not talking to one person, to the reporter only; you are talking to the public, to every person who reads that newspaper or the Web page or tunes in to that radio or television station.

Play the game the way the reporter plays it. The reporter records the interview, both by pencil notes and by recording. You should do the same. You need a record of the questions and your answers. Plug your own recorder into a wall socket and let it run throughout the interview session. And have the public relations director and your secretary present and taking notes.

If the interview concerns a disaster—fire, explosion, airplane crash, deaths, injuries, crime—admit it. You cannot hide it; you may as well admit it. Admitting disaster permits you to get your company's side of the affair into the first story, to stress what the company is doing, not just to make amends, but also to ensure that that disaster never happens again.

It is important to get your side of a disaster into the first story published or aired. Waiting until after the story is published or aired puts you and your company on the defensive.

Do your homework. Before the interview, be sure you know as much as possible about what you *will be* and what you *might be* asked. And have a few points or a statement you or your company wish to make.

You can control the interview somewhat, because you have the information. If you do not like the question or the way the question is asked, you do not have to answer the question directly. Use the question to lead into your own statement about the company or the situation.

Do not be goaded into answering before thinking. Take as much time as you need to formulate your responses. Do not worry about periods of silence. Television and radio reporters will skip over periods of silence, and periods of silence do not matter to newspaper reporters.

Frequently, questions are stated negatively, putting you and your company on the defensive. Before you respond, restate questions positively.

If the reporter asks several questions before giving you time to respond to any, pick one that lets you make the most positive statement, and ignore the others.

If the reporter interrupts your response, say that you will address that issue later, and continue with your original response.

You can even take the initiative, saying you think the audience would be interested in knowing such and such, and presenting your own information.

If the reporter precedes a question with background information that you deem negative, interrupt and say that the reporter is not there to make a speech, but to ask you questions.

How to Handle a Hostile Interview

Interviews are hostile if reporters seek information or ask questions in a manner deemed harmful to the company. If you face such a situation, these suggestions will help you cope.

- Have your secretary present to take notes and to record the entire interview.
- Recognize that everything you say will be published or aired.
- Do not say anything off the record.
- You need not answer any question directly.
- Challenge questionable statements and assumptions and dubious sources.
- Personalize your answers and put them into language that people understand and relate to rather than into company jargon.
- Speak to the camera, rather than to the reporter.
- Do not overreact to abrasive or unfair questions, but, if necessary let your indignation show, in moderation, of course.
- Do not speculate.
- Do not answer hypothetical questions.
- If the reporter makes a negative speech in asking a question, interrupt immediately and say, "You're supposed to ask me questions, not make a speech."
- If the reporter makes a negative statement and then asks a question, restate the negative statement into a positive statement before you answer the question.
- If the reporter asks a question that implies guilt regardless of the answer, qualify your answer, or refuse to answer such a question.
- If the reporter asks a yes-or-no question, provide as much information as you deem necessary.

- If the reporter asks a loaded question, do not repeat adverse information, but do set the record straight.
- If the reporter asks several questions at once, answer one you like and ignore the rest.
- If the reporter interrupts your answer with another question, either ignore the interruption or say that you will answer that question later. Continue with your initial answer. Insist upon your right to complete your answers.
- If the reporter predicates a question upon information from an unidentified authority, refuse to answer the question unless the authority is identified.

Off the Record

Never use the words *off the record* or *just between you and me* in any circumstances while talking with reporters. You should assume that everything you say is on the record.

The reporters' assignment is to get information on the record for a story. They cannot use off-the-record information. They are honor-bound to not reveal that information nor to seek that information from another source.

If, during the interview, you decide that something you said earlier should be off the record, you may ask that that information be off the record. But the rules are that anything said openly cannot later be placed off the record.

Once on the record, always on the record.

Understand also that reporters who show up at your office for an interview already have a story and now want your company's side. In such a situation, a "no comment" answer merely goads reporters into digging deeper, a situation that may be detrimental to your company.

If you cannot respond to a reporter's question, instead of "no comment," say that you are forbidden to speak about that topic and explain the reason. It may be a legal reason. Whatever the reason, be honest with reporters.

Remember the suggestions for how to have good press relations.

How to Handle Quotations When the CEO Is Unavailable

In news reporting courses, students are taught that quotations are sacred, that they may not be changed. If the speaker said the words, those words are reported as spoken and placed within quotation marks. No changes allowed! See *The AP Stylebook* under "quotations in the news."

But, in the field of public relations, that admonition does not hold. Public relations professionals frequently are called upon to make up quotations for the CEO, to ghostwrite speeches and letters, to make up statements from the CEO—in short, to speak for the CEO.

The task of serving as the voice of the CEO is difficult for the newcomer to public relations. It seems unethical for the public relations professional to fabricate and enhance quotations for the CEO.

It's not unethical. Public relations professionals are not writing news. What they write is not news until it is published by a news medium.

It is the public relations professional's job to polish the words of the CEO and to ghostwrite—not fabricate, because *fabricate* implies lying—statements to be attributed to the CEO.

In top echelons of the public and private sectors, the following are not at all uncommon.

- A news reporter telephones the public relations professional for a statement from the CEO. The public relations professional ghostwrites a statement and tells the reporter, "Quote the CEO as having said that." The reporter does, knowing that, even though the CEO, personally, did not say it, it is the CEO's position.
- The CEO is scheduled to deliver a speech, but the press of routine duties makes it impossible for the CEO to research the issue and write the speech. The public relations professional conducts the research and ghostwrites the speech for the CEO to deliver. Copies are delivered to reporters in advance so they can prepare their stories.
- The CEO needs advice. The executive committee, individually or collectively, provides both written and oral suggestions. The CEO accepts the suggestions.
- The CEO needs to make a routine response to a letter. The CEO's secretary drafts the letter, and the CEO signs it. Sometimes, the secretary signs it for the CEO.

In each situation, each employee, each adviser, has a thorough knowledge of the CEO's policies and thought processes and can imitate the CEO's thought and speech patterns. The statement, the speech, the suggestion, the advice, and the letter are prepared as though the CEO prepared them.

And, once the CEO has signed the letter or spoken the words, they belong to the CEO, not to the originator.

The ethics of the advice—making up quotations for the CEO—proffered by the public relations speech ghostwriter equals the ethics of the advice—suggesting policy positions and writing letters—proffered by others in the office.

There is a downside for error. All of those advisers, ghostwriters, and secretaries know that they will lose their jobs if they issue statements or documents contrary to the CEO's policies and positions. And no CEO, particularly holding a political position, will, under any circumstances, deliver a speech, ghostwritten or not, contrary to stated policy or position.

In public relations, the public relations professional represents the CEO and ensures that what the CEO says is what the CEO means. This relieves the CEO of the burden of researching and writing speeches and dealing with reporters on routine matters.

Whether the public relations professional must clear ghostwritten statements with the CEO is an internal matter, depending upon how closely the CEO and the public relations professional work and the sensitivity of the CEO's position.

For example, public relations professionals working for the national or state attorney general probably clear everything with the attorney general because of the sensitivity surrounding such statements and the consequences of error or contradiction.

Ultimately—and this is understood by the reporter and the public relations professional—when the CEO delivers the ghostwritten speech or does not retract the ghosted statement, that speech and that statement are accepted as having emanated from the CEO.

The ethics of all this may be argued, but to no avail. This means of handling quotations for the CEO has existed since before there were public relations professionals, and no doubt will continue. People in positions of power must depend upon ghostwriters because their jobs are so demanding that they don't have time to research and write every speech.

The fact of the matter is that, if you plan a career in public relations, be prepared to represent your CEO, to be a ghostwriter for your CEO, and to put together quotations to be attributed to your CEO. It is a major part of the job in public relations.

To be proficient at those tasks, be prepared to know everything you can about your CEO, including thought processes, speech patterns, and word use.

Other Suggestions

Follow the suggestions detailed earlier in this chapter:

- Advise your CEO to not call a news conference if possible.
- Instead of a news conference, issue a statement through your public relations office.
- Long before any disaster hits, your company should have a written crisis plan, what to do when disaster hits.
- One of the keys in any crisis situation is to designate one person to represent the company and respond to all questions from the press. Then keep that person wholly informed of what not to say as well as what to say.

Favorable Editorials

You may be able to secure favorable editorial comment and news stories—or less unfavorable editorial comment and news stories—if you cater to the editorial writers and the editor, the executive editor, and the managing editor of the newspaper.

This is not a guarantee, but it helps.

What you want for your organization and your CEO is a fair shake from the reporters and the editorial writers. You want your CEO's side presented in the original story and in the original editorial.

Therefore, whenever your organization develops a new program or product or service or whatever, or when your CEO travels to another city, ask the newspaper to schedule a meeting between its editorial writers and reporters who cover your organization and your CEO (and you, of course). It is a good idea to invite the editor, the executive editor, and the managing editor, and appropriate special editors (business, education, agriculture, government) to sit in on the conference.

At the meeting, have documents and materials to distribute. Have your CEO make a general statement and explanation of the reason for the meeting, and open the meeting to questions from the newspaper people. Your CEO must be totally candid, but need not provide private information.

Of course, your CEO should be well briefed on the information and possible questions that should arise.

What will happen is this: Having received this information from your CEO, the reporters and editorial writers will gain insight into your CEO and how he operates. They will gain information they can use in their editorials and news stories.

Thereafter, when an issue arises, the writer will have your CEO's side of the story already and will be able to work it into the initial editorial or news story. That way, both sides get into the first editorial or news story. Moreover, having the background from your CEO will mean that the writer will know what questions to ask during subsequent surfacing of issues and what is likely to be accurate and what bombast.

It is all to the benefit of your CEO and your organization. The result may not always be favorable, but it will not be unfavorable. It helps guarantee that your organization and your CEO will get a fair shake.

A Quick Reference for Handling the Press

- Never consider a reporter your friend.
- Reporters have no friends; they have news contacts.
- Never lie to, or argue with, a reporter.
- Tell the reporter as much as you legally can.

- If you cannot provide some information, explain why.
- Never tell a reporter anything you do not want published.
- Release bad news as well as good news.
- Take the offensive.
- Do not be goaded into responding before thinking.
- Restate negative questions positively before responding.

23

How to Write in Public Relations

> Everyone in your business is interested in what your company is doing;
> so, write about everything your company does.

Every public relations professional writes news releases, sometimes called
press releases, but news releases are not the only things they write, and, although they write a lot of them, that may not be the bulk of what they write.

If you want your news releases published, make them conform as closely
as possible to news dispatches written by reporters for the news medium
you send them to. Make news releases factual, terse, concise, and, usually,
no more than 100 words. Make certain you tell the whole story in the lead,
because that may be the only part of your news release that is published.

When you submit a news release to the news media, it passes out of your
control because it belongs to the news media. When you publish information in an internal publication (your company magazine), you retain complete control of that information.

Note—You are part of the organization. If you interview an employee, and the
employee asks that you change or delete a quotation or information, you are
bound to abide by that request unless you can persuade the employee otherwise, but only if using the information is not detrimental to the organization.

Caution—Although you must act like a reporter, you are not a reporter. The
reporter is an outside agent and under no obligation to your organization.

Most of the news releases you process will be good news, positive news, upbeat information. But, eventually, you will face the prospect of processing bad news for news releases. Do not hesitate; it will be to your and your organization's advantage to release bad news promptly and completely. Bad news is sure to get out. You cannot prevent that. But you can turn it to your organization's advantage or, at least, prevent its becoming a disadvantage.

If you wait until the news media learn of the bad news and go after the story, you and your organization will be accused of suppressing news, and, worse, you and your organization will be on the defensive. Even worse, the initial bad news story oftentimes is published without your organization's balancing comments.

If you release the bad news yourself, you ensure that your organization's balancing comments are published in the same story, and you and your organization are not on the defensive.

Moreover, you will become known as a true public relations professional, one who releases bad news as well as good news. If all you release is good news, the news media soon will reject everything you submit.

Letters to the Editor

If you are being stymied in your quest for publication of your information, or if the newspaper story did not fully explain your organization's side of the issue, do not overlook the Letters to the Editor page of the newspaper.

Anyone—including governmental officials, company officers, and public relations people—may write a letter to the editor of the newspaper and have a reasonable chance of getting it published. In fact, the chances of publication are greater for people of importance in the community.

Caution— In your letter, do not be vitriolic; be factual. You are seeking a forum, not a fight. Write your letter the way you would write a news story. State your position and your support for that position. Be logical and complete. Offer to provide additional information, as appropriate.

Some Things You Will Write and Where You Will Publish Them

The following publication outlets are available to you: daily and weekly newspapers and radio and television stations, and their Web pages on the Internet; your own internal publications (magazines and newsletters); and trade and professional publications that carry, to businesses and industry in your field of interest, information about your field of interest. The trade and professional publications provide a superior channel of communication about your organization's activities. They carry various types of writings.

News Releases (Press Releases): Published in daily and weekly newspapers, on radio and television, on the Internet, and in internal publications. Write each in the form required by the medium and rewrite and submit the print versions to the trade and professional publications.

Columns and Editorials: Published in daily and weekly newspapers and on radio and television, and their Web pages on the Internet (generally in response to an opinion piece, the opposite side of which you support), and in internal publications. Some of these may be offered to the trade and professional publications. These opinion pieces usually are about activities that affect your organization, but they are not necessarily confined to that. You may write opinion pieces about almost any topic.

Feature Stories and Profiles: Published in daily and weekly newspapers, in internal publications, and, quite often, in trade and professional publications. Feature stories and profiles are written about activities of personnel in your organization. Topics range from activities on the job to activities at home and on vacation and hobbies.

Some Topics You Will Write About

Topics and their treatment can vary considerably.

Promotions, Transfers, Retirements, Resignations, New Hires, Deaths: In public relations, the activities of personnel, especially top echelon personnel, is news to others in the community and in the state and, perhaps, the nation. Offer news releases of such activities to the news media in your geographical area, and to trade and professional publications.

People in allied and competing fields of interest are intensely interested in the activities of their contemporaries. The news release may not command much space in the newspaper or much time in the newscast, but it will almost certainly be carried.

Expansions, Reductions, New Products or Services, Research Results, Open Houses, Tours, Contests: The same need to know is true of all of these activities of your organization. Publicize them in the various media and in trade and professional publications. Invite the news media to visit.

Speeches: Whenever your CEO or other top official of your organization makes a speech, people in allied and completing fields of interest, and in state and national government, are interested, have a need to know.

When the CEO makes a public address, it is either a policy statement or a discussion of the organization's activities, both of which topics are of vital interest to allied and competing groups in your field of interest and in both your geographical area and nationally, and particularly in trade and professional publications.

How to Act on the Job

As a public relations professional—regardless of your actual title—you are both a professional and a member of the organization. Your first loyalty is to the truth; your second, to the organization.

Protect your own credibility. Never lie to or mislead the news media; never write a piece that you know to be incorrect or untrue or misleading.

You should consider yourself a reporter whose beat is your organization and obey the rules of news writing and reporting. You gather news of your organization in the same manner as a reporter gathers news on the beat. You visit fellow employees—at all levels—and talk with them about activities in their offices and divisions.

Designate correspondents in each division of your organization and task them with providing you information about the activities of their groups.

The Fact Sheet

The Fact Sheet is an easy way to provide information about a speech or a news event from which a reporter can write a news story. Written in the future tense about an upcoming speech or news event, the Fact Sheet provides information for advance publicity; written in the past tense about a delivered speech or news event, the Fact Sheet provides information for publication.

Except for the tense, the information presented about the speech and the news event is the same. In both cases, the Fact Sheet enables the news medium to write its own story.

The Fact Sheet is a simple form: one page on office letterhead, with your name and contact information at the top. Be sure to list your email address and your cell and home telephone numbers. Down the left side of the page are listed the W and H questions, Other (for appropriate information), and Quotations (for appropriate and applicable quotations from the speech). If one page is not enough, do not write on the back of the page; use a separate sheet.

Treat the Fact Sheet as you would a news story: Answer the most important questions (WHO, SAID WHAT, WHY) as though you are writing the lead sentence of a news story; use appropriate verbs of attribution; state fact, attribute opinion; write tight (you do not have much room).

Email the Fact Sheet to the appropriate news media, both newspaper and broadcast. It is not appropriate to send a Fact Sheet to the trade press or to post it on your Web page. The trade and professional publications and your Web page deserve a full story.

The Fact Sheet

Douglas Starr   Office   123-456-7890
Vice President for Public Relations   Fax   567-890-1234
The ABC Co.   Cell   908-765-4321
P.O. Box 123   starr123@gmail.com
Dallas, TX 12345-6789

WHO?	Name and title of your speaker and the name of the corporation, governmental agency, university. Avoid acronyms unless they are widely known: NASA, FBI.
SAID WHAT?	Summarize in one or two sentences what your speaker said or recommended or suggested or called for, and so on. The verbs *spoke, discussed* are unacceptable; they tell readers nothing.
TO WHOM?	The name and size of the group before whom your speaker spoke.
WHY?	The reason for what your speaker said, recommended, and so on.
WHERE?	The place of the speech, as appropriate: city, county, state, street address, hotel.
WHEN?	The date, time, and occasion for the speech: annual banquet, political address.
HOW?	The mechanics of accomplishing what your speaker wants done.
OTHER	Anything pertinent: descriptions, explanations, background information, invitation to reporters to attend.
QUOTATIONS	List appropriate and applicable quotations from the speech.

24

How to Write News for the Company Magazine

Here's where you get to shine as publisher, editor, and writer, all in your own magazine.

Writing is the most difficult work imaginable. The writer must not only know everything possible about the topic but also must be able to explain and describe, without opinion, information about which the readers may have little or no information.

Because of those demands, writers, real writers, do not "love to write," they love "to have written." Real writers write because they must, because they cannot imagine doing anything else. Moreover, real writers do not just write, they rewrite, revise, recast. Anything less is just typewriting.

For writers today, rewriting is essential. It tightens the writing and reduces the length of the copy by cutting out unnecessary words and by rearranging sentences for greater impact.

The Company Magazine

Most corporations have either a monthly company magazine or a weekly or twice-monthly newsletter. The monthly magazine is published; the newsletter is produced in-house; both are produced by public relations department personnel.

Two photographic agreements are needed: one to use photographs of employees and one to hire an independent photographer. The best photographic agreements are drawn by your company attorney, but here are some suggestions about photographic agreements that you could use.

A person's name and image are considered, in law, to be property rights, and photographs of them may not be used for commercial or trade purposes without their permission. To do otherwise is an invasion of privacy and could lead to legal problems.

If you plan to use a photograph of an employee in the company magazine or for company advertising purposes, you need a *photographic consent release* signed by the employee before or at the time the photograph is made.

The photographic consent release gives the company (and/or you) the right to use the photograph not only for the use for which it was made but also for other uses later. Without a photographic consent release, you or your company may not use the photograph for any purpose other than that for which it was made and only as long as the employee works for the company.

Both you and the employee should sign and date two copies of the photographic consent release, one copy for each of you. A witness is not necessary. The pronoun *I* in the consent release refers to the employee, the subject of the photograph.

The Photographic Consent Release

The employee certifies to being an adult and, in consideration of whatever amount of money or other considerations provided, if any, authorizes the company the unqualified right and permission to reproduce, copyright, publish, circulate, or otherwise use the photograph(s).

The authorization and release covers the use of photograph(s) in any published form and in any medium of advertising, publicity, or trade in any part of the world for 10 years—the usual length of time—from the date of the consent release or as long as the employee remains with the company.

The employee and heirs, executors, administrators, or assigns transfer to the company and to its successors and assigns all rights, title, and interest in all photographic reproductions taken by representatives of the company.

The agreement fully represents all terms and considerations, and that no other inducements, statements, or promises were made to the employee.

Independent Photographer

When you need a photograph, or several photographs, it is easier and cheaper to hire an independent photographer. This frees the company from having to provide retirement programs and medical insurance; to deduct and pay Social Security taxes; to withhold income tax; and to provide workers' compensation insurance, sick leave, vacation, and other benefits.

But you need an agreement, a contract, between your company and the photographer because it gives you many advantages.

The best photographic agreement, of course, is one drawn by the company attorney. But any such agreement should contain certain provisions and set forth specific terms and conditions. Here is a sample photographic agreement. *You* and *your* in the consent agreement refer to the photographer; *company* refers to your company. Both you and the photographer should sign and date two copies of the photographic agreement, one copy for each of you. A witness is not necessary.

The Independent Photographic Contract

1. You will not be an employee of this company, but will act as an independent contractor.
   This frees the company from providing retirement and hospitalization programs, deducting and paying Social Security and income taxes, and providing workers' compensation and other benefits. It enables the company to make only one lump-sum payment for services.
2. Your duties will include photographic assignments for the company in (name[s] of place[s]), performed under the direct supervision of (name[s] and title[s]).
   This gives you control of the photographer's activities and authorizes you to direct the photographs to be made. It does not prevent the photographer from making suggestions that you may accept.
3. For each day of your services as photographer for the company, you will be paid the sum of (amount) and all reasonable expenses for food, lodging, and travel incurred in the performance of your assigned task(s), and the entire cost of printing, if desired, incurred in the performance of your assigned task(s). To secure payment, you are required to submit an itemized bill and an itemized expense report.
   You will need such documents to present to the company financial office and for your own office records. Moreover, by stipulating the exact amount of each day's pay, you know exactly how much the assignment will cost the company.
4. All photographs taken by you in the performance of your assigned task(s), including the disc or film, shall be or remain the property of the company. In addition, the company shall have the right to use all photographs taken by you in the performance of your assigned task(s) in any manner whatsoever, without limitation or restriction.
   This is the most important part of this agreement because it gives the company the disc or film and the right to reprint and use the photographs repeatedly in any way that you or your company wish.

5. This agreement becomes effective on (date) and shall remain effective until you have completed your photographic assignment(s) for the company. Either party may terminate this agreement at any time upon notice to the other party. Termination of this agreement shall in no way affect the terms and conditions set forth in Paragraph 4.

   This permits either you or the photographer to break the agreement, but gives you and the company the right to keep and use the photographs taken.

Both you and the photographer should sign and date two copies of the agreement, one copy for each of you. A witness is not necessary.

The Second-Day Approach

Writing for the company magazine is not the same as writing for a newspaper. A newspaper reporter covers an event today and writes it today for the newspaper's Internet page and for tomorrow's newspaper.

Public relations writers cover an event today and write it today, but not for tomorrow's publication. In fact, your story may not be published until next week or next month or two months from now. By the time readers read your, story it's old news.

Moreover, everyone in the company will have heard the information through the grapevine—which is 85 percent accurate and very fast—long before the company magazine is published. In general, the company magazine serves as verification of the grapevine.

Your task, then, is to make your past copy current in the future.

To do that, use the approach afternoon newspaper reporters have perfected: the Second-Day Approach: Seek the next action.

For example, if your company receives a contract for $20 million for a new product, that's news. But there's no way to prevent the grapevine from spreading the word quickly. Long before your magazine is published, nearly everyone in the company will have heard about the contract, and some departments might even have begun tooling up to produce the product. The contract itself no longer is news.

The news, therefore, is not the fact of the contract; the news is what happens next.

So, in writing your magazine story, seek the next action; lead with what the company is doing to meet the contract, how far along the preparation is, who is in charge, what progress has been made so far, what the next step is, what the contract will mean to the company, whether additional employees will be or have been hired, the list is endless. All it takes is your imagination.

And don't worry about getting the details of the contract into the lead. You're not writing legal matters; you're writing a story. Begin with what happens now that the contract is signed; save the contract details for later in the story.

Don't forget to get a quotation from the CEO about the value of the contract to the company.

Writing Tips

Here are some suggestions to help ensure that your writing is the best you can produce.

- Use short words; they are more powerful than long words.
- Use short sentences; they are more powerful than long sentences.
- Use short paragraphs because of the narrow columns your copy will occupy. Readers want plenty of white space in their reading matter. Short words, short sentences, short paragraphs provide the necessary white space.
- Rely heavily upon the six traditional questions, and usually in this order:

These first three questions constitute the most important information in the story:

WHO: The person or group you are covering, writing about.

DID WHAT: What the person or group did.

or

SAID WHAT TO WHOM: (in case of a speech or an interview) This is a summary of the speech or the interview, not a statement that the speaker spoke or delivered a speech.

WHY: The reason that the person or the group did what it did.

Of secondary importance are these three:

Where: The city where the story took place.

When: The day of the week that the story took place.

How: How the person or the group did or plans to achieve what it plans. Not every story has a How.

The second three questions, though they constitute important information, can be saved for the second paragraph. In fact, the Where may be built into the name of the city council or of the county government agency.

And one more: **So What:** This is important in that it helps the writer decide whether the story is really news.

Above All, Get to the Point. Right Away.

For example, if your board of directors votes for a 4 percent increase for all employees effective next fiscal year, don't write that the board met and voted in favor of a 4 percent raise. Boards—groups of all kinds—do nothing but meet and vote. Readers want to know what the board voted for. So write that the board authorized a 4 percent raise for all employees. You may write so because when the board voted "aye," what it approved became effective.

Use action verbs rather than "to be" verbs; they are more powerful. The predicate—the verb—is the focal point of the sentence, the strength of the sentence.

Write in the active voice, in which the subject does the action, because that's conversational style.

Polish Your Writing

After you've written your copy, read it aloud and listen to the flow of language. Listen to the words: Do they merge into a meaningful whole? Do they flow smoothly? Does the language get into the way of the information?

Rewrite. Make the writing sing to you; readers will appreciate it. They may not realize it consciously, but they will appreciate it unconsciously, because, as they read silently to themselves, their mind's ear will tell them whether the language is pleasing.

Use a Copyeditor

You could copyedit your own copy, but it is far better to use a copyeditor because the copyeditor is like readers, but without your intimate knowledge of the topic.

If you want to edit your own copy, set it aside for a day or so before you do so. You will tend to forget the details, making copyediting possible. Not easy, possible.

Whoever edits your copy should look for errors of style, spelling, punctuation, grammar, and so on, of course, but also for misuse of words and incomplete and incorrect information.

Proofreading, Copyediting, Editing

Proofreading, copyediting, and editing have different meanings and usages.

- **Proofread:** to read and mark corrections on printer's proofs, etc., to ensure that the typeset version is identical to the writer's final draft. But, if the final draft contains deliberate errors, so must the published version.
- **Proofreading:** done by two people, one to read aloud the writer's final draft; the other to follow and correct the typeset version.
- **Edit:** to revise and make ready for publication a writer's work by selection, arrangement, and annotation.
- **Copyedit:** to edit and correct the grammar, punctuation, etc., of articles or manuscripts, as in a newspaper or magazine office or publishing house.

Editing and copyediting are done by one person well versed in grammar, word use, spelling, punctuation, syntax, all the requirements of fine writing. That is the final step in publishing; the final step in helping guarantee that the writer's work is accurate.

It is extremely difficult to copyedit your own work. The best way to copyedit your own work is to set it aside for a day or two, letting the details of the work slip away from your active memory. Even so, you will miss a lot.

Use the Right Word

Use the proper writing aids: your style sheet and the dictionary—particularly the dictionary.

Speaking English as your native tongue does not guarantee knowledge of the language. You may be misusing words without realizing it. Look up words, even words you think you know. You may be surprised.

If you use a thesaurus, use it in conjunction with the dictionary. Don't use a synonym from a thesaurus without checking the dictionary meaning. For example, the thesaurus lists *prevent* as a synonym for *stop*. But it would be silly to say, "Prevent your car at a red light" when you mean, "Stop your car at a red light."

Avoid unnecessary approximation of numbers. Few numbers are ever round: $20,000,000, $250,000, $2,500,000. More than likely, numbers are $20,583,451, $249,737, $2,522,475. When you round them off, you do so because the detailed amount is not as important as the general size of the number.

Some numbers, such as distances, rarely are exact. If your company is building a plant outside of town, "five miles" is sufficient. "Approximately five miles" is unnecessary detail. And spell out numbers at the beginning of a sentence.

When you do round off numbers, don't insult readers by telling them so. They understand.

Moreover—and more important—in listing numbers, you may forget to approximate every rounded number, which may confuse readers into thinking that the non-approximated number, however round it appears, is accurate.

The same admonition holds for use of *he or she, him or her, his or her.* If you forget and use just *he,* you confuse readers into thinking that only men are meant. Instead, pluralize your nouns so you may use plural pronouns.

Stay Out of the Story

It is unprofessional to use the first-person pronoun—*I, me, my, mine, we, us, our, ours*—in copy, except as part of quotations. Non-quoted usage of first person bestows upon the writer unwarranted expertise and detracts from the editor's prerogative of writing opinion.

Write as an observer, not as a participant.

25

How to Ghostwrite a Speech for Your CEO

> If you look for a good speech now, you undo me:
> for what I have to say is of mine own making.
>
> —William Shakespeare, 2 Henry IV, *Act V, Epilogue*

Speech ghostwriting, like any other art, is mastered through practice. There are, however, techniques of writing that may be applied to most speechwriting situations, enabling you to produce a well-crafted speech.

Don't be too concerned about speech ghostwriting; you're not writing major orations. Most speeches last 20 minutes, particularly those after luncheons, because people have to return to work, or after banquets, because, after eating, people are rather lethargic. A 20-minute speech is 2,500 words, 10 pages double-spaced.

The key to ghostwriting a speech is that the speech be the speaker's ideas, the speaker's words, and the speaker's speech pattern—that it sound as much as possible the way the speaker talks, because speechwriting is talk writing. Master your speaker's conversational style, and you will succeed.

Every speech ghostwriter—indeed, every writer, because speechwriting is just another form of writing—ought to be well grounded in the principles and techniques of spelling, punctuation, grammar, and syntax, and the rhythm of the language. To help you, you should have, and use:

- A book of grammar rules.
- A dictionary, at least the collegiate edition.
- It is not a good idea to use synonyms. They could confuse listeners. And repetition reinforces understandability.

- A book on the basics of speechwriting.
- A book on the art and craft of writing.

You need to begin writing the speech, so here are the steps that make it a bit easier.

- Ask your speaker's secretary for the name and telephone number of the program director of the group inviting your speaker and whether and what topic was suggested.
- Contact the group program director concerning the topic, the speaking situation, the makeup of the audience, your speaker's credibility with the audience, and the name of the person who will introduce the speaker.
- Complete the Audience Analysis form (found later in the chapter).
- Schedule an interview with your speaker about the speech topic and whether your speaker prefers a different topic. Most groups inviting a speaker leave to the speaker the choice of the topic. Using a voice recorder and pen-and-paper notes, interview your speaker about details of the speech topic. This is vital because you want to know not only what your speaker says but also how your speaker says it so you can include in the speech your speaker's own words and speech pattern.
- Notify the group program director of the speech topic chosen by your speaker. Provide a title for the group's internal bulletin and prespeech publicity.
- Conduct research on the speech topic, using files and interviews with knowledgeable people on staff.
- Complete the Speech Progress form (found later in the chapter).
- Prepare the first draft of the speech, incorporating as much of your speaker's own words and language habits as possible and avoiding words and phrases that your speaker has difficulty pronouncing. For a 20-minute speech, prepare 2,500 words, 10 pages, typewritten, double-spaced.

Here are some things to do and to not do in ghostwriting a speech.

The major difference between writing a speech and writing most other material is that a speech is written for the ear, not for the eye. The speech is written to be delivered orally—to be listened to. The listener, unlike the reader, has no point of reference and cannot call for a repeat of any portion of the speech. Thus, the speech must be understood the first time or not at all. Not only that, but each sentence must be clearly understood, or listeners trying to interpret one unclear sentence will miss the next sentence or two.

To help you achieve clarity, your writing must be concrete, precise, appropriate, simple, and, of course, grammatically correct.

Concreteness: Use specific terms. Instead of writing *building*, describe the building; instead of writing *large*, provide exact measurements; instead of writing *pretty*, describe the object or person.

The predicate delivers the power of any sentence, so, to convey meaning, try to avoid the weak "to be" verbs and use action verbs and expressive verbs rather than adverbs. Instead of *walk drunkenly*, use *stagger* or *lurch* or *stumble*. Help the audience gain a mental image of what you are trying to convey. Do not tell; show.

Precision: Do not ever become complacent about the meaning of words. Use the dictionary; look up words, even those you think you know or those you have been using for a long time. When you check the meaning of a word, check its roots.

For example, *podium*, from the Latin *pod* for *foot*, is the platform on which the speaker stands. To lean on the podium is to lie on the floor. Speakers stand on a podium and behind a lectern. They place their lecture notes on the lectern, not on the podium. And *convince* and *persuade* are not the same. *Persuade* is followed by an infinitive, *to*; *convince*, by *of* or *that*.

Appropriateness: Use words and phrases that are appropriate to the occasion, to the audience, and to the topic of the speech. Never talk up or down to an audience.

Simplicity: Winston Churchill put it nicely: "Old words are best; short words are better." Do not use a long word where a short word will do. Use simple sentences because that is how people speak. Simplicity is one of the key rules for clear writing.

Ear-writing, writing for listeners, has the following requirements, all of which are easily mastered:

- Use the active voice, subject, predicate, object, because that is conversational style, the way people speak. Active voice is easier to understand than passive voice.
- Use plenty of commas. Commas indicate a pause, however slight, in the flow of language, giving listeners a chance to absorb what was said.
- Use periods instead of semicolons. A semicolon joins two thoughts, creating a compound sentence. Substitute a period, and you have two simple sentences. Two simple sentences are easier to understand than one compound sentence, and listeners do not know the difference, except that the period indicates a longer pause than does the semicolon.
- Seek ways to convert compound sentences into appositives for a smooth flow of language. Instead of "Bill Beckett served four years in the Coast Guard, and he graduated from college in 1995," write: "Bill

Beckett, who served four years in the Coast Guard, graduated from college in 1995."

- Quotation marks are unnecessary. Speakers should not read them, should not say "quote" and "end quote." If the exact words are necessary, handle it one of these ways: "Let me tell you what the Senator said. He said, and these are his exact words . . . ," Or, "The Senator put it this way . . ."
- Seek a conversational style in your speechwriting. Listen to how your speaker talks about the topic of the speech.
- Use dashes instead of parentheses. They indicate a long pause. Set them off with a space on each side to open up the sentence.
- Use short, simple sentences.
- Use the second-person pronoun: *you, your, yours.*
- Use contractions, but be careful of *n't* words because many of them don't emphasize the *n't.* When you want to emphasize the *not,* use two words: *do not, did not, is not, are not, was not, were not, have not, has not, had not.* Say aloud, and listen to *don't, didn't, wasn't, weren't, haven't, hasn't, hadn't.*
- Where appropriate, use slang and jargon to help establish rapport with the audience, but always explain unfamiliar jargon.
- Use fragmentary sentences. Like this one. Such sentences make the listener fill in the blanks mentally. They force listeners to participate in the speech.
- Keep your modifiers close to the words they modify. For example: "He joined the Coast Guard in 1992, where he learned his trade." Written that way, *where he learned his trade* modifies *1992* instead of *Coast Guard.* Recast the sentence: "In 1972, he joined the Coast Guard, where he learned his trade."
- Avoid splitting compound verb forms unless it sounds natural and is understandable. For example: "He bottled up the bill in committee" is more natural and understandable than "He bottled the bill up in committee."
- In compound verb construction, repeat auxiliary verbs; it facilitates understandability. For example: "He said that, by the time he had had his first visitor, he *had* gone to the locker room, *had* changed into his jogging suit, *had* run a mile before lunch, and *had* been at his desk an hour." Read that aloud with and without the three italicized *had* words and listen to the clarity of the sentence.
- Repeat prepositions in series.
- Repeat the *to* in a list of infinitives.
- Repeat articles (*a, an, the*) in lists.
- Repeat participles, as in "Having studied and having worked in the field, he was considered an expert."

- Use connectives, transitional words or phrases that help maintain a smooth flow of language and thought.

Examples

We can classify connectives by type.

Temporal connectives: *previously, formerly, earlier, at the same time* (never *while at the same time*)*, already, during this time, meanwhile, at last, finally, later, since then, thereafter.*

Demonstrative connectives: *thereby, in this case, under these circumstances, here again, in connection with this.*

General connectives: *first, second, third, and so on; in the first place, second place, third place; in general; to continue; to return to; to resume; once more; as I said; then; in fact; as a matter of fact; at any rate; by the way, incidentally; namely.* But, not *firstly,* unless you follow it with *secondly, thirdly,* and so on.

Reference connectives: *with respect to, as related to, concerning, as for.*

Be careful of pronoun antecedents; the noun and the pronoun must match in number. For example: "The team is going to New Orleans, where they will play in the Sugar Bowl." In the first part of the sentence, *team* is singular (verb *is*); in the second, plural (*they*). The pronoun should be *it.* Or recast the sentence.

Ask the audience questions, but provide the answers immediately; do not give the audience time to think of an answer. And suggest that your speaker nod while providing the answer. That affirmative action draws the audience into the speech by forcing agreement. People who participate in a decision tend to adopt the decision as their own.

Omit detailed statistics. Round off figures to the nearest whole number. Insofar as the audience is concerned, it is of little importance whether your company's annual budget was exactly $198,472,349 or $200,000,000. The audience will tend to remember the rounded-off number longer than the precise number.

Refer to and use quotations from the Bible, great people of history, and historical documents. In the United States, 80 million people are members of organized churches, and millions more are not only familiar with the Bible but are also followers of its word, though in a less-structured sense. Historical people and documents are known to countless millions of people throughout the nation. Moreover, when you include such references, your speaker will receive credit for being familiar with the cited works.

Use fewer different words. Do not make changes in your sentence structure and use of words to avoid using the same word or construction more than once in a sentence or paragraph. Such repetition facilitates understandability of the speech. Repeat key statements and key ideas. Repetition is a great aid to memory. Moreover, a general audience, one comprising a cross-section of the city, has an average understandability at the eighth-grade level.

Dr. Martin Luther King, Jr., did not hesitate to repeat powerful phrases, phrases that he wanted to emphasize. Read, better yet, listen to his "I Have a Dream" speech, delivered before the Lincoln Memorial in Washington, D.C., in 1963. In that speech, he used *I have a dream* seven times, and *let freedom ring* ten times. The effect was overwhelming.

Use **allness** words—*all, never, none, always.*

Use **qualifying** words—*but, however, nevertheless, although.*

Use **pseudoquantifying** words—*many, some, much, very.* These words are vague, but you can fit them in and still be concrete by using such a construction as this: "Most high school students in this city, in fact, 87 percent of them, will attend college, and 74 percent of them will graduate."

Use **consciousness-of-projection** words—*it seems to me, apparently, clearly.* This puts the personal touch into the speech and helps develop rapport with the audience.

Be careful with the words you use. In themselves, words have no meaning; in usage, they stand for something. Words do not transmit meaning; they stir up meaning already present in the listener. In addition, words do not mean the same thing to all groups of people.

Counsel your speaker about gestures. To emphasize affirmation, nod the head and/or use an up-and-down motion of the hand and arm; smile at appropriate times during the speech.

Thus is the speech tailor-made, not only to the topic but also to the audience, and how that topic might affect that audience.

After you have finished writing the speech, read your draft aloud, listening for alliteration, sibilants, tongue twisters, and awkward phrasing, all of which must be eliminated through rewriting.

Read and rewrite as many times as necessary and as time will allow.

Prepare and send a smooth copy to your speaker for corrections, suggestions, changes, additions, deletions, and so on.

Make the corrections, additions, deletions, changes, and so on, marked by your speaker.

After you and your speaker are satisfied with the speech, prepare a final reading copy for your speaker. To make it easy for your speaker to read the speech, use a sans-serif font, 14 to 18 points, double-spaced. Check with your speaker for preferences.

Give your speaker the reading copy of the speech and the completed Audience Analysis form for last-minute information on the speaking situation and those planning to attend.

Prepare as many single-spaced copies of the speech as needed for the news media who attend the speaking situation, and one copy for yourself so you can follow the speech during delivery.

Prepare a Speech of Introduction, two minutes, 250 words, one page, typewritten, double-spaced. The Speech of Introduction should be brief enough not to take up the time allotted for your speaker. Contact the group member who will introduce your speaker and suggest that your Speech of Introduction be used. Request a FAX number or an email or a postal address and send it. If the introducer prefers writing the Speech of Introduction, request a copy and show it to your speaker.

Attend the speaking situation, distribute copies of the speech to the news media, and be ready to respond to questions. During the speech, note changes in the delivered speech, additional information, deletions, and so on.

Complete the Speech Evaluation form in detail (at the end of the chapter).

As soon as your speaker concludes the speech, secure your speaker's reading copy of the speech for your files. It will have your speaker's notes between the lines and in the margins, all highly useful for future speeches.

As soon as possible, write two versions of a news story about the speech and the speaking situation: write a print version and send it to newspapers and Websites and to the trade and professional magazines, and write a broadcast version (no more than 100 words) and send it to radio and television stations.

Upon your return to the office, file your speaker's reading copy of the speech, your typewritten copy, the Audience Analysis form, the Speech Evaluation form, the Speech Progress form, copies of the print and broadcast versions of the news story, and whatever other information is pertinent. Later, add to the file: clippings of newspaper and trade press stories about the speech.

For the next speech you will write, the information in your file will be invaluable.

No One between Speaker and Speech Ghostwriter

When Douglas Starr was in the Coast Guard Reserve, he said, he was called to CG Headquarters in Washington, D.C., because an admiral was having trouble with his speeches. It seemed that his speech ghostwriter never could get the admiral's language, sentence structure, and word use correct.

It took a half hour of discussion with the speech ghostwriter (a civilian) to discover the difficulty. The ghostwriter described his routine: He would interview the admiral, record and write his ideas, his language, and his word pattern, and produce the speech. Then, because of the military chain-of-command rule, he would submit the speech to his immediate superior, who made changes and submitted the speech to the next higher officer. That's where the trouble lay.

Each officer in line, seeking to emphasize and enhance his position, would make changes in the speech, have it typed for use, and send it to the next superior. When the admiral received the speech, it was not his language, his words, his word pattern, his sentence structure; it was awkward to read from.

After Starr's report to the admiral, the admiral stopped the chain-of-command requirement and made the speech ghostwriter report to him only.

In any situation, the speaker and the speech ghostwriter must be one-on-one—no one in between. The speech ghostwriter may interview others for information, but the speech ghostwriter must have full control over the writing of the speech. Only the speaker may make changes in the ghostwritten speech.

Here are the forms you need to help with preparing for and writing and evaluating the speech.

Audience Analysis

Organization

Name of group _____

_____

Type of group (professional, political, religious, service, etc.)_____

_____

Date of meeting _____ Time of meeting _____

Place of meeting (complete address, hotel room, city, state)

_____

_____

Group Officers

President _____

Vice President(s)

_____

_____

_____

Secretary _____

Treasurer _____

Other(s) (names, titles) _____

_____

Introducer (name, title) _____

Special guests expected (names, titles) _____

Others at the head table (names, titles) _____

_____

Suggested topic for speech _____

Time allotted for speech _____

Occasion

Purpose of meeting (regular, dedication, installation of officers, etc.) _____

_____

Premeeting reception?	Yes	No
Will alcoholic beverages be served?	Yes	No
Does meeting include a meal?	Yes	No
Are spouses invited?	Yes	No

Attire: Men _____

          Women _____

_____

Are news media invited?   Yes   No

Who are they? (names, news media)

_____

_____

_____

_____

Audience

Type of meeting room (auditorium, small dining room, large banquet hall, etc.)

_____

Public address system available	Yes	No
Light at the lectern	Yes	No

Number of people expected ___ Range, average of ages of audience _____

General educational level of audience _____

Major occupation(s) of audience _____

Anticipated knowledge of speech topic by audience _____

Primary interests / desires of audience _____

Fixed attitudes / beliefs of audience _____

Attitude of audience toward speaker _____

Attitude of audience toward speech topic _____

Anything else? _____

Program

Copy of program attached?   Yes   Not Available

What else is on the program? _____

_____

_____

Others on the program _____

_____

What is before / after the speech? _____

_____

What else is planned for the speaker? Debate / Question-Answer Session / Panel Discussion?

_____

Make certain that the speaker speaks before any other item on the program.

Speech Progress Report

Speech Particulars

Date of speech _____

Place of speech _____

Group _____

Type of audience _____

Size of audience _____

Subject of speech _____

Topic suggested by group _____

Actual speech topic _____

Status of preparation _____

Research assigned to _____

Date research to be completed _____

Speechwriting assigned to _____

Date first draft due _____

Date final draft due _____

Date reading copy submitted to speaker _____

Date press copies prepared _____

Remarks _____

_____

_____

Speech Evaluation Form

Speaker _____

Title of speech _____

Date/time of speech _____

Name of group _____

City, State _____

Evaluation of Speaker (1 is least; 5 is best)

Forcefulness of delivery	1	2	3	4	5
Impact of message	1	2	3	4	5
Facial expressions, animation	1	2	3	4	5
Gestures	1	2	3	4	5
Voice, tonal range	1	2	3	4	5
Enunciation	1	2	3	4	5
Visual contact with audience	1	2	3	4	5

What specifically distracted you or diminished maximum impact of the speech?

_____

_____

_____

What specifically impressed you about the speech or delivery?

_____

_____

_____

What words, sentence construction did the speaker have difficulty pronouncing?

_____

_____

26

How and Why to Write the Speech of Introduction

> Every speaker needs an introduction, but a Speech of Introduction goes much farther than just identifying the speaker.

It is the rule. Every speaker, even the president of the United States, must be introduced before beginning a speech. Of course, the president's Speech of Introduction is brief, only nine words: "Ladies and gentlemen, the president of the United States."

That is because everybody knows who is the president, and because people attend a presidential speaking situation to hear the president, not the introducer.

But every other speaker, without exception, must be introduced in more detail, even though the audience knows who is to speak and the topic of and the reason for the speech.

Unfortunately, too often, the Speech of Introduction is left either (1) to someone who does not know the speaker or the speech topic and, therefore, cannot provide a realistic Speech of Introduction; or (2) to someone who knows the speaker too well and laces the Speech of Introduction with tales better left to private reminiscing. Either way, as far as the speech topic is concerned, such a Speech of Introduction is at best a disaster and at worst embarrassing.

The Speech of Introduction is not a biographical sketch of the speaker; it is an integral part of the speaking situation, serving two major purposes: (1) It sets the stage for the speech, telling the audience what to expect from the speech; and (2) it explains why the speaker is qualified to speak on that topic.

Therefore, if you are wise, you will write the Speech of Introduction as well as the main speech itself, crafting both into a meaningful whole. You should contact the person designated to introduce your speaker and send a copy of the Speech of Introduction with a request that it be used. More often than not, the introducer will be receptive to your doing the work.

The Speech of Introduction

The Speech of Introduction should not intrude on the main speech, neither giving away details of the main speech nor encroaching upon the time allotted for the main speaker. To accomplish this, here are some suggestions on writing the Speech of Introduction.

Write the Speech of Introduction after you have completed the main speech. That way, you will have a better idea of what to include in the Speech of Introduction to lead the audience to the speech.

It should be no more than 250 words (one typewritten page, double-spaced), no more than two minutes of delivery.

It should mention the name and title of the main speaker frequently. It is no secret who is to speak. Nearly everyone in the room knows who is to speak and has spoken with the main speaker, either during the reception or as the meeting began.

It should include the topic of the speech, the reason the speaker was selected to address the group, why the topic is relevant to the group, and the main speaker's qualifications to speak on the topic.

It should tie in to the theme of the speech, serve as a lead-in, a teaser that will arouse the interest of the audience in the main speaker.

It should *not* include the main speaker's life history; date and place of birth, education, marriage and family, and employment generally are unimportant, as far as the speech is concerned. However, background—employment, experience, education, and so on—that is applicable to the speech should be included. Briefly.

If applicable, it should remind the audience of the main speaker's latest achievements.

One other point: For a political speech, choose the introducer with care. The introducer should be someone who is well-thought-of by the group because people tend to favor friends of friends. For a political speech, the introducer should be of the same political party.

27

How to Get Publicity
for Your CEO's Speeches

It's up to you to provide publicity for the CEO's speeches to all the news media, to professional magazines, and throughout the company facilities.

Speech ghostwriters have three major routine tasks with regard to writing speeches: (1) to write the speech, (2) to write the speech of introduction, and (3) to secure the widest publicity for the speech.

Writing the speech involves hours, sometimes days of collecting information, conducting research, interviewing, reading, taking notes, and writing, rewriting, polishing the speech. Your speaker delivers the speech in 20 minutes to a group logy with the late hour and the aftermath of a cocktail reception and a heavy banquet. The next morning, one newspaper carries four inches of copy about the speech and the speaking event, and half of the story contains unnecessary information, such as the name of the speech and the theme of the convention.

That is not enough publicity. The speaker and the speech demand far more than that. Every speech carries information wanted and needed by peers, by colleagues, by competitors, by leaders in government and business, by employees, and by the general public. Therefore, the speech ghostwriter must provide both pre- and postdelivery publicity on the speech: predelivery publicity to help ensure coverage by print and broadcast reporters, and postdelivery publicity to spread the information broadly, among the general public and among every person and organization affected by or interested in what the speaker said. To do that, understand that every speech has three audiences.

The **primary** audience—the smallest of the three—comprises the people listening to the speech as it is delivered.

The **secondary** audience—the largest of the three—refers to the people who read or hear about the speech through the news media: newspapers and news magazines, radio and television stations, and the Internet.

The **tertiary** audience—the most influential of the three—includes the people who read about the speech in trade and professional magazines and journals. This audience—leaders in the business, industry, political, and professional communities—needs to know what speakers are saying publicly because of their leadership position in business, industry, government, and the professions.

The news media—online, on paper, radio, television—are hungry for well-written, timely, information-laden stories about the various communities: business, military, religion, medical, education, scientific, legal, and so on. The news media do not have the staff to cover all of the news events they need to cover, so they depend upon public relations professionals to provide them with news stories. That's you.

Trade and professional magazines and journals are even hungrier for news about activities in their field. Like the newspaper, they must depend upon public relations professionals to serve as their reporters. Again, that's you. Thus, publication of a speech story in trade and professional magazines and journals is almost guaranteed. The story may be rewritten or shortened, but it will circulate among people of influence nationally.

And, of course, the company magazine is a prime outlet for news about the company speaker and what the company speaker said.

Here are suggestions on how to reach those audiences, how to get wider exposure for speeches. These suggestions are not guarantees, and they are not difficult, but they do provide favorable odds.

After the speaker has approved the final version of the speech, prepare a single-spaced copy for every news medium—online, on paper, radio, television—in the company's geographic area and for your company Web page.

If it is desirable to distribute to print and broadcast reporters in your city a predelivery copy of the speech, do this: On the top of page one of the speech, type an embargo to prevent premature release of the information: FOR RELEASE AT 8 P.M. SATURDAY OCTOBER 15, 2013. That tells the news media not to release a story about the speech before that hour on that date because the speech has not been delivered.

Sometimes, the news media will publish an advance story that the speaker will speak on a certain topic before a certain group in a certain place on a certain date. That's good publicity, and it helps guarantee attendance at the speaking situation.

At the speaking event, and before the speech is delivered, distribute copies to the reporters attending. If you are lucky, a wire service reporter will be among the reporters assigned to cover the speech and the speaking event, guaranteeing even wider publicity for the speaker and the speech. Of course, reporters will write their own stories, but you should be available before, during, and after the speech for whatever help the reporters need.

Obviously, only a few reporters will attend the speaking event, and the speech deserves more broad distribution than in city only. Therefore, you must arrange for publicity. Either you or your public relations/public affairs office must serve as the reporter for all the publications and broadcast stations that do not send reporters. The task is to write the story, covering the speech and the speaking event as a reporter would. Be sure to include the name of the host organization and audience size, the frequency and length of applause, whether there was a question-and-answer session and what questions were answered, and so on.

To help guarantee publication, the speech story must be written in two versions: one version in the news style of the newspaper for newspapers and their Web pages and one version in the news style of the broadcast station for radio and television and their Web pages. The print version should not be more than 250 words; the broadcast version, 100 words (omitting as unnecessary information the name of the speech and the theme of the convention or conference). The broadcast version differs, too, in the approach because it is written to appeal to the ear, rather than to the eye.

It is worth the effort to provide a broadcast version because broadcasters appreciate having their needs taken into consideration.

Email a copy of the story and a copy of the speech to every news medium in the geographic area. And put a copy of the speech and the print and the broadcast stories on the company Web page.

Write a longer story about the speech and the speaking event, providing greater detail than the newspaper version, and email both a copy of the speech and a copy of the story to every trade and professional magazine and journal in the company's field of interest and to the publication of the organization before which the speaker spoke.

If the speech is of more than parochial interest, that is, if it is of interest to a broader audience, email a copy of the speech, not of the news story, and the speaking situation to *Vital Speeches of the Day*, P.O. Box 1247, Mount Pleasant, SC 29465 or online to vitalspeeches@bellsouth.net. That publication carries verbatim copies of speeches that have widespread effect, and includes details of the speaking situation.

To know how successful your publicity efforts were—how widespread your publicity was—and to tell your speaker, you should scan the newspapers for the story. You won't be able to know how exactly the broadcast media handled your speaker's speech story, but you can know how it fared among the daily newspapers and trade and professional magazines and journals. For a broader reach among newspapers, your company should subscribe to a clipping service, agencies that subscribe to and scan appropriate newspapers daily to find stories for subscribers.

Make copies of each clipping, with the name and date of each publication. Put the original in your file and send the copies, with an appropriate memo of explanation, to the speaker. And post copies on the various bulletin boards in the company facilities.

28

How to Write and Deliver a Briefing

Delivering a briefing requires a lot of work, but it's easier than you think.

A briefing is just that, a short speech designed to present to colleagues a series of facts and ideas on a single issue. Sometimes, however, a briefing may encompass two related topics. At most, it is 10 minutes long: 1,250 words, five typewritten pages, double-spaced.

The briefing is presented by the person most knowledgeable about the topic because those attending the briefing need complete and accurate information, and they may ask questions after the presentation.

Before Preparing the Briefing

If you are asked to prepare a briefing for you to deliver, do this:

- Become thoroughly familiar with your topic; review your information.
- Determine the purpose of the briefing, the goal.
- Analyze the audience. Know the education and background of all the members, including the job rank and duties (in general, of course, not in detail), and their knowledge of company matters.
- Check the briefing room for layout, arrangements, facilities, equipment. Ensure that you have plenty of room for the speaker as the focal point of the audience.
- Make arrangements for equipment: computer, connectors, screen, easel, slide projector, overhead projector, whatever you need.
- Make certain that the public address system works. In a small room, before a small audience, you will not need one.

Preparing the Briefing

Organize your material in logical sequence. Even if you use the computer and multimedia, prepare a typewritten copy, double-spaced, on one side of the page only for distribution to those who have a need to know.

Prepare a separate document that provides a detailed analysis of the topic of the briefing. Set it aside for later distribution to those who want more information.

In the briefing, state your main points right away. No guessing. Tell your audience what you are going to brief them about. Then explain and describe. You are explaining, not trying to persuade, though that may be the result.

At the conclusion, summarize your main points.

Use simple words, simple sentences, active voice (subject, predicate, object), oral language. After all, this is an oral presentation, a talk to colleagues.

Use language that fits your audience. Do not talk up or down to them. Do not use words or terms they will not understand, unless you explain them.

Design simple visual aids (charts, graphs, multimedia, and so on) to explain and reinforce your main points. Use bold, vibrant, contrasting colors, few words, simple drawings, rounded-off numbers, few details. This is a briefing, not a detailed analysis; your detailed analysis is in your office.

Rehearse and time and rewrite the presentation to trim it to 10 minutes. You may have to repeat this step several times.

Delivering the Briefing

If you are new at speaking before a group, you probably will have stage fright. It's natural. Nearly everyone, even veteran professionals who stand before an audience, has some degree of stage fright. Just remember, you have everything going for you: You are the expert; your audience knows you are the expert; your audience is interested in your message; your audience wants you to succeed.

Take a deep breath. Speak slowly and naturally. Lower the pitch of your voice. Enunciate your words so that every word is understood. Use plenty of pauses and plenty of facial expressions and gestures.

This is a talk; the audience is your colleagues. Relax.

Be sure to tell your audience what you want them to do or to believe, what message you want them to carry away with them.

When you present your main points, nod your head or make up-and-down hand and arm motions. This encourages agreement among the audience. If you can get your chief executive officer (CEO) to nod, too, that will help.

Maintain eye contact with your listeners; let your eyes sweep the audience regularly. Do not concentrate upon just one or two listeners; it makes them nervous.

Above all, do not read your briefing. Children like to be read to; adults feel insulted. Speak from notes or from a full text, but use the full text only as a guide. After all, you are the expert on this topic. You should know the information.

After the Briefing

Remind your audience that full information on the topic is available in your office—make certain that it is—and invite them to get it from you later.

Call for questions from the audience. Respond as briefly as possible: one minute or so, at most, to each question.

Distribute to each member of the audience appropriate handouts, information that emphasizes and explains your main points in the briefing. This ensures that they will retain the information you presented.

Notes

When using visual aids, do not leave them in view any longer than necessary. Otherwise, your audience will tend to focus on them and not listen to what you are saying. As you finish with your visual aid, cover it, or turn it off.

People listen for facts rather than for ideas. Visual aids help them assimilate facts from which they will formulate ideas.

29

How to Plan for a Convention

Convention planning is detailed and demanding, but you will have a lot of help.

Preface

Planning for a convention of any size is not so much difficult as it is exacting. It demands that the planner formulate and follow a schedule, maintain and keep up with a tickler file of what needs to be done, and maintain a meticulous record of what has been done and by whom.

Although visits to the convention site are not essential, they are most helpful in planning for meals, meeting rooms, local transportation, entertainment, coffee breaks, and other events expected and unexpected at any convention.

Moreover, personal visits to companies and company representatives who provide services (meals, motels, transportation, and so on) are more efficient than telephone calls only and do provide a bridge to later telephone calls.

A visit to every site needed in the convention will give the planner information not available in any other way and will help offset any problems that may arise.

Planning

Planning for a convention should begin at least one year in advance—as soon as you know that your group will host the next gathering. The main reason is that planning for the convention really is only part of your normal work assignments.

One person should be assigned overall responsibility and authority for planning the convention. To that person should be given whatever information is available from previous conventions—the whole file—to study. This is not to say that the next convention should be a carbon copy of the last one. On the contrary, changes may be demanded simply because of the passage of time. But the file will be of great help to the basic planning.

Everyone involved in the convention should be told as soon as possible who is in charge of planning. This includes the person in charge of the facility where the convention is to be held. Keeping everyone informed reduces problems and makes the planning easier.

The host group's senior official should give the planner a letter stating the facts about the convention (dates, number of delegates and other attendees, purpose, and so on) and naming the convention planner and requesting whatever assistance is necessary. This facilitates the work of the planner and provides easier access to those the planner needs to work with.

One of the first steps the planner must take is to prepare a month-by-month schedule of assignments, of things to do, and to ensure that the schedule is followed.

Here is a sample schedule for a convention.

Step One

Obtain authority to host the convention.

Obtain permission from the convention site to serve as headquarters for the convention.

In conjunction with the planner and the lodging reservation manager, fix the overall dates of the convention. Remember, convention dates are fixed by the national group, but delegates and other attendees arrive before the convention begins and leave after the convention ends. Provision must be made for those additional lodging dates.

Visit the convention site and determine what is needed and what is available.

Step Two

Send letters to potential delegates, identifying the planner and apprising them of the place and dates of the convention.

Write letters to or visit appropriate people at the convention site and make plans for rooms, Internet access, meals, coffee breaks, parking for coaches and private automobiles, use of athletic facilities during noon hours and before and after working hours, and assistance in securing publicity.

If the convention has such facilities, seek entertainment and other activities pertinent to the site.

Make arrangements for local transportation from and to airports and from and to motels and the convention site.

Make arrangements for the special luncheons and dinners and the annual banquet.

Reserve appropriate rooms for office work and for meetings.

Make arrangements for entertainment as appropriate.

Invite the guest speaker(s), and ask to be provided a copy of the speech(es) for publicity purposes. Ask for a biographical sketch and a color photograph, online, for publicity purposes.

Set a deadline for return of the information.

Step Three

Invite VIPs.

Apprise those who need to know of the dates and place of the convention.

Step Four

Ask each convention delegate for items to be placed on the convention agenda.

Set a deadline for return of the information.

Step Five

Send each delegate a preregistration form to be completed and returned (see section on Delegates). Set a deadline for return of the information.

Ask each delegate to cite special needs, particularly medical and dietary needs.

Set a deadline for return of the information.

Step Six

Ensure that liaison (see section on Liaison later in the chapter) makes arrangements for securing personnel to assist with the convention, for establishing check-cashing facilities and authority, for making arrangements for parking vehicles and coaches, for security, for Internet and computer hookups for delegates and other attendees and the press, for copy machines, and for office supplies.

Ensure that liaison makes arrangements for tables, chairs, and computer hookups for the secretarial staff.

Step Seven

Issue final call for all agenda items, for list of delegates and their spouses and guests and their needs.

Set a deadline for return of the information.

Prepare nametags for delegates and other attendees.

Step Eight

Prepare a packet of information for each delegate and attendee, including agenda, name tag, information on the area and maps as appropriate, notepaper and ballpoint pen, preferably one bearing the name of the convention.

Set a deadline for return of the information.

Step Nine

This is the month of the convention.

Take information packets to the convention site for distribution to delegates and other attendees upon arrival.

Prepare luncheon, dinner, and banquet seating charts for VIPs.

Conduct the convention.

Clean up after the convention ends.

Step Ten

Write letters of appreciation as appropriate: to VIPs, speakers, lodging managers, and those who provided entertainment, transportation, and publicity.

Conduct postmortem on the convention and take detailed notes on how to improve the next convention. Send a copy to the host of next year's convention.

Step Eleven

Prepare a final report on the convention, including the budget, and send a copy to the host of next year's convention. As appropriate, disseminate copies among all delegates and potential delegates and others. Remind delegates that they may purchase copies of speeches and other presentations and provide the address and the price.

Step Twelve

Clean up all the loose ends.

Convention Components

Delegates

The best method of estimating in advance the number of delegates to be expected at the convention is to check the attendance records of the past several conventions. Your convention should draw about the same number of people. In fact, it should draw most of the same people.

In the early stages of planning for the convention, you may use last year's attendance list to estimate the number and identity of those likely to attend. As time progresses, however, you will need precise numbers and names of delegates and other attendees.

The most effective method of collecting such information is to send each delegate from last year a preregistration form and ask that copies be made for others in the office or city who plan to attend. Set a deadline for return of the information.

The preregistration form serves many purposes.

- It identifies the delegate by name, title, company; office address; office, home, cell telephone; email address.
- It describes the delegate's date, time, mode, and place of arrival and of departure. This is essential for the transportation crew to provide pickup and delivery service.
- It describes the delegate's preference for seminars and workshops.
- It describes the delegate's health and dietary needs and preferences for lodging (kitchenette, single room, double room, number of beds and size, and so on).
- It lists all meals and special events the delegate and spouse and guests plan to attend.
- It states health and dietary needs of the spouse and guests.
- It states the registration fee and other costs of the convention and requests payment either by check or by credit card.

Attach to the preregistration form an agenda-item form asking the delegate to submit items for the convention agenda and appoint a person to supervise that agenda item.

Speakers

In all probability, you will need more than one speaker for the convention. You will almost certainly need a main speaker, a keynote speaker, to address the main banquet, and on a topic not necessarily as technical as the convention itself.

In addition, you probably will need at least one speaker to address the group on a highly technical basis, in keeping with the professionalism of the convention.

You cannot begin too soon to invite speakers. An early beginning helps ensure that your invitation will be accepted, or, if not accepted, that you will have time to invite replacements.

This is particularly true if you invite speakers who normally are in great demand as speakers, such as political and governmental leaders. Sometimes, such speakers are scheduled as long as three years in advance. Moreover, because of situations beyond their control, speakers who accept your invitation may be forced to cancel. So, be prepared to seek replacements on short notice.

Finding professional speakers is somewhat easier than finding speakers in the public domain. Many professional speakers, though excellent speakers, are not in the same demand as are political and governmental speakers. And professional speakers demand, and get, fees of several thousand dollars plus expenses. Be sure to ask.

One of the best ways to find professional speakers is to ask another professional in the same field for recommendations. Such professionals are found in business, industry, government, and universities. Many university faculty members are eager to speak on their topic of interest because it enhances their reputations.

Once you have a list of speakers, review their qualifications and rank-order them. As soon as possible, send a letter of invitation to the first name on the list, explaining the convention and the topic that the speaker would be expected to discuss.

Urge a quick reply. This is essential because you must publish the agenda and you will need to include the name and topic of the speakers. Speakers understand this.

In addition, you will need a photograph for publicity purposes.

If your first choice declines, you still have time to invite the second, and third, choice.

Caution—Sometimes a political speaker, or even a nonpolitical speaker who has been in the public eye, may have a background that is unacceptable to the focus of the convention. Check the background of every potential speaker.

Budget

One of the easiest methods of developing any budget is to use the previous budget and build upon that. However, for a convention, this is not always possible because of several variables: Prices have risen in the past year; the convention is in a different city with a different cost of living and of doing business; the number of delegates and guests will vary; local transportation needs will vary, and so on.

Therefore, the best method of determining a convention budget is to determine first what will be needed: local transportation, tent and lighting for an outdoor evening meal, coffee and pastries for coffee breaks, mementoes for delegates, gifts for guests and speakers, entertainment, meals for entertainers, fuel for vehicles, printing of reports and agendas and other items, envelopes, press kits, postage. It is a long list.

Once you have the list in hand, ask the supplier of each item for an estimate of maximum and probable price. Make sure the supplier does not give you the current price, but projects the price to the dates of the convention. Develop your budget with both maximum and probable costs in adjoining columns. This gives you a range within which to work.

Ask your fiscal office how much money the organization has set aside for the convention and make a comparison. If your projected expenses are less, all is well. If they are greater, you will need to trim, beginning with nonessentials. If you cannot trim, ask for more money.

The sample budget does not include salaries and wages for personnel or the cost of utilities. If salaries and wages and utilities are to be included, they must be added, but only for the days of the convention.

Keep in mind, however, that some personnel will be needed several days before and after the convention, and that those lodging and meal costs must be included.

As you deal with suppliers of equipment and services, get a signed contract that includes the prices agreed upon. This is necessary because prices change from month to month over a year's time.

If you cannot get a signed contract with fixed prices, ask the supplier for an estimate of what the price is likely to be at the time of the convention.

Do not forget to determine and include a registration fee for delegates to the convention. This fee is used to pay for coffee breaks, meals of speakers and guests, lodging for speakers and guests, gifts for speakers and guests, press kits for delegates and other attendees, and incidentals that might arise.

Because registration fees will arrive months before the convention, set up a combination checking and savings account in a credit union and deposit the incoming fees and other money. You will use some of the funds before the convention, of course, but much of it will generate interest income that you will need.

Have each check or credit card account made out in the name of the convention.

Liaison

It is almost indispensable to have at the convention site a liaison officer between the planner and the convention site officials, particularly a liaison who is acceptable to the convention site officials.

Such a liaison can handle many of the on-site preparations that are difficult, if not impossible, for a planner in a city hours away.

The liaison need not be on a full-time basis, but should be available when needed, and around the clock.

As the date of the convention nears, the liaison will be of incalculable service by serving as a local contact for convention site officials to ensure that all arrangements are on schedule and that no difficulties remain.

Moreover, if changes are to be made, or if problems arise, the liaison can handle them on the spot and with dispatch.

Even so, problems may arise that the liaison cannot anticipate or handle. Arrangements made months in advance for reduced rate or free admission to places of interest may collapse without notice and the permission withdrawn. For example: A promise to lend automobiles for VIP transportation may be nullified at the last minute if the person who made the promise leaves the agency.

Because the liaison lives in the convention city, making different arrangements in such situations becomes easier.

The liaison is especially valuable in providing or hiring personnel to work the convention. Every convention needs office help: typists, messengers, drivers for speakers and VIPs, an accountant to keep records of income and expenses, and, perhaps, even child caretakers.

The liaison can make arrangements for a copying machine, desktop or laptop computers and a printer, a room for both broadcast and print reporters, parking spaces, and special events involving local activities.

And, by being at the site, the liaison has a better grasp of the problems that may arise and will be able to recommend solutions quickly.

Lodging

Using your best estimate of the number of delegates, guests, speakers, and other attendees, ask the convention hotel reservation manager to reserve at least that number of rooms for the convention. Be sure to include the preconvention arrival and postconvention departure dates. If the hotel cannot guarantee as many rooms as your convention requires, ask the hotel reservation manager to reserve rooms in a nearby hotel or motel and to advise you of the name of the hotel/motel and the name and contact information of the reservation manager.

Visit the convention hotel and the overflow hotel/motel because you will need to describe in your preregistration packet the rooms and their appointments, the meal facilities and times, arrangements for medical needs, distance from the convention hotel, and anything else a delegate may need to know about lodging accommodations. The delegates should obtain their own rooms, but your duty is to make arrangements for paying for rooms for the speakers and special guests.

Try to secure a convention rate for all rooms, including the suites for speakers and VIPs. Ask that complimentary rooms be included, the number determined by the overall occupancy of the convention group. After all, you are reserving several scores of rooms, guaranteeing a tidy profit for the hotels and motels.

Meals

Every convention requires provision for three meals and, usually, two coffee breaks, every day of the convention. Some meals are paid for in the registration fee; some are the responsibility of the delegates and other attendees.

Normally, delegates are left to their own devices for breakfast, and most of them eat in the hotel or motel before the convention proper begins for the day. That leaves to you the duty of making provisions for lunch and dinner each day of the convention and the convention-ending banquet. Generally, lunches and dinners include speakers, and the banquet includes the main speaker and entertainment, such as a choral group, or musicians, or the like. Those people must be fed, too. All information about meals must be included in the convention schedule.

To set up meals, meet with the restaurateur or catering manager for the bill of fare, the hours of service, and the list of choice of entrées, vegetables, salads, and desserts. Try to include some local dishes in the meals and promote them in your mailings to delegates. Ask for the best estimate of the price of the meals to be expected at the time of the convention, and ensure that the price of the meals includes the tax and the tip.

For meals that are not part of the convention, but for which it is convenient for delegates to eat in the hotel or motel dining room, make arrangements with the catering manager for the additional customers so additional food can be prepared.

For the banquet, you should confer with the chef about the meal and special dishes the chef may recommend.

In selecting the foods to be served, it is wise to leave much of that to the restaurateur whose business it is to be expert in that regard.

If alcoholic beverages are to be available during a predinner social, you will need to decide between a cash bar and an open (free) bar and the beginning and ending times. For a cash bar, each person pays for the drinks, and the convention pays the bartender an hourly wage. For an open bar, the hotel charges a specific amount per hour for each delegate (the same number to be served at the dinner), and the convention pays that amount. Obviously, a cash bar is less expensive for the convention.

In fixing the times of the social hour and the dinner, take into consideration the time the delegates quit their last afternoon activity, because they need to return to their rooms to clean up and change clothing, and return to the dining room.

Remember, the social hour is usually 6 to 7 p.m., and the dinner, 7 to 8 p.m. The master of ceremonies begins addressing the gathering as dessert is being served or eaten, and the speaker begins 10 minutes later.

Be sure that the speaker begins immediately after the meal and before any entertainment or lottery or such. Speakers who follow entertainment find that the audience pays little attention because of the aftereffects of the entertainment.

If you have convention information to pass along to the delegates, do that after the speaker and before the entertainment. This way, if the speaker needs to leave, or if the reporters want an after-speech news convention, they can still make their evening news deadlines.

In some situations, considering your delegates, you may schedule a chaplain or parson to deliver the prayer before the meal. This is not mandatory, nor is it forbidden, but, if it is expected and it is not provided, you may be chastised.

Transportation

You must make arrangements for two forms of transportation for the convention: private vehicles for the VIPs and coaches for the rest of the attendees. You must provide transportation between the airport and the lodgings for the VIPs and between the lodgings and the convention sites for the attendees.

Because you know from your preregistration forms the time, date, place, and mode of arrival of each person attending, you can schedule a pickup service. To do this, assign one person as transportation officer with the sole duty of arranging the transportation schedules and ensuring that the schedule is followed.

You need one driver for each private vehicle. For best effect, have the VIP's name and rank on a placard on the dashboard, visible through the windshield, and have that vehicle and driver assigned to that VIP throughout the convention.

In arranging for coaches for the rest of the attendees, you normally have a choice: a school-bus type with Spartan appointments, and, for only a little more money, a coach with more luxurious appointments, including more comfortable seating and a restroom at the rear.

Most coaches carry 45 to 49 passengers.

You may hire the coach by the trip or by the day. The price includes both the coach and the driver. You need not feed the driver at any meal.

If you use coaches by the day, you must make arrangements at the convention site for parking the coaches. If you use coaches by the trip, you need not make parking arrangements because the coaches will arrive shortly before the time to load and park in the loading zone during loading and unloading.

In any case, you must make parking arrangements for VIP private vehicles and attendees who wish to use their own vehicles. However, attendees should be urged to use the convention coaches.

Before the convention ends, poll the attendees to ensure that their departure schedules remain the same as they listed in their preregistration packet.

Coffee Breaks

Every convention should have coffee breaks in the morning and in the afternoon. After listening to discussions, attendees need time away from the convention to stretch and relax and to discuss with colleagues what they learned during the discussion.

Coffee, fruit juice, and pastries should be available before the first morning session, but midmorning and midafternoon coffee breaks should provide coffee, soft drinks, fruit juices, and various forms of Danish pastry and doughnuts.

To arrange for coffee breaks, contract with the catering manager or the person in charge to provide whatever is needed for the number of people attending. The convention site will set up the coffee break according to your schedule and will remove the equipment and clean up afterward.

Office Help

No convention runs by itself; they all need office help. You probably will need the following types of office workers for a smoothly running convention:

Convention Planner: That's you. You should be present throughout the convention because you know more about the functions and the logistics than anyone else. You are the spokesperson for the entire event. If a question arises that you cannot answer, refer it to the senior convention official.

Liaison: A local representative in case problems arise with the various convention sites and in case new situations warrant help.

Assistant Liaison: To assist in resolving problems.

Transportation Officer: To provide a private vehicle and driver for each VIP.

Messenger: One or more, as needed, to ensure that messages to and from attendees are delivered.

Typist: One or more to type and reproduce reports of seminars and workshops, to prepare nametags and notices and convention packets, and to do whatever office work is needed.

Receptionist: One or more to receive and record preregistration forms and payments and to issue receipts and convention packets.

Fiscal Officer: To handle fiscal matters and to resolve bookkeeping difficulties.

Photographer: To record noteworthy attendees, visitors, speakers, events, and so on.

Equipment: Several laptop computers and printers, copy machines, identification tags, letter-sized paper, note pads, post-it notes, voice recorder, registration table

Meeting Rooms

You will need several rooms for the convention: a large room for the general meeting or the plenary session, a press room for reporters, a room for attendees to socialize in between and after sessions, and as many smaller rooms as you have seminars and workshops scheduled.

Contract for those rooms when you contract for the convention site.

If, during the convention, meeting rooms must be changed, assign that duty to the liaison.

Entertainment

No convention is all work and no play. Attendees need relaxation so they can approach the next day's events with a rested mind. Therefore, schedule entertainment during the evenings for attendees. For spouses, schedule such daily entertainment as off-site visits and tours of sites of interest.

If facilities are available, make arrangements for the attendees to use convention site facilities for jogging, tennis, swimming, racquetball, and working out during the lunch hour and evening.

Ensure that the attendees do not interfere with the normal use of the athletic facilities. That should not be difficult if you make arrangements well in advance.

Entertainment could include visits to and tours of museums, parks, and historical sites, and performances of choral groups, dancers, jugglers, magicians, and so on, before the evening meal.

For ideas about entertainment, ask the catering manager of the convention site or the chamber of commerce. Get brochures and maps. You may have to make transportation arrangements for off-site visits and tours.

Spouses particularly appreciate special entertainment and guided tours during the day when delegates are in meetings. Get brochures. Hire a tour company to provide buses and guides.

Because you have a large number of attendees, you may be able to secure reduced rates for admission to some attractions. Ask well in advance.

Certificates of Appreciation

After the convention ends, send a letter and a certificate of appreciation to every person who contributed to the success of the convention, whether it be through sales or donations or assistance: the convention site supervisor, the catering manager, the chef, the coach company, session leaders, panelists, speakers, and, of course, your staff: liaison, assistant liaison, transportation officer, drivers, messengers, typists, receptionists, and fiscal officer.

Recipients probably will file your letter in their personnel file and will hang your certificate on their office wall, thereby providing considerable free publicity for your organization.

The next time your organization needs help from those people, they probably will be more than happy to oblige.

Finally

With key personnel in your organization, conduct a postmortem of the convention and its successes and failures.

Prepare and file a final report on the convention, including what went well and what did not. Provide a list of attendees, the schedule of seminars and workshops and entertainment, the speakers and their topics, the meals, the coffee breaks, transportation, the dates and place of the next convention, the letters and certificates you sent, the budget, equipment used, everything, and your own evaluation of the success of the convention.

To provide such information, you must keep detailed notes throughout every day, beginning with the first planning session.

Send a copy of your final report to those involved in the postmortem and to your supervisor and the convention planner for next year.

Convention Checklist

In public relations, one of your tasks will be to set up conventions. Check off each item as you complete it. Put next to each item the date completed and the initials of the person verifying completion.

Before the convention begins, check with people assigned to determine their knowledge of the procedure and details.

You will need to know the convention policy on accepting checks and the policy on refunds.

The size and length of the convention will determine which of the following items apply.

General Information

Information desired on registration cards: special needs, diets, medical care of delegates, spouses, guests.

- Information desired on members, guests, speaker(s), badges.
- Convention registration fee.
- Single ticket prices.
- Convention program.
- Dates for the convention.
- Tickets, schedule of events.
- Total number of convention registrants expected.
- Number of rooms needed (singles, doubles, suites).
- Reservations confirmed.
- Transportation needs for convention speakers, local dignitaries, guests.
- Invite local dignitaries (mayor, legislators, chief of police, sheriff, et al.). Does mayor wish to welcome convention delegates?

Hotel(s)

You should keep track of all of the necessary lodging arrangements.

- Date majority of group arriving.
- Date majority of group departing.
- Date uncommitted hotel rooms are to be released.
- Name of convention hotel and number of rooms assigned.
- Name, telephone number, and email of caterer assigned.
- Hospitality suites needed.
- Rates for hospitality suites.
- Bars, snacks, service hours, dates.
- Names, addresses, telephone numbers, and emails of contacts for hospitality suites.
- Name(s) of hotel(s)/motel(s) for overflow of delegates, and number of rooms assigned in each.
- Room rates in each hotel/motel.
- Arrangements for child care in each hotel/motel.
- Arrangements for child activities.
- Procedure for emergencies.
- Floor plan of convention.

- Seating plans for banquet, luncheons, dinners.
- Meeting rooms, schedules.
- Coffee breaks
  ○ Before morning session.
  ○ Midmorning.
  ○ Midafternoon.
- Reception, hors d'oeuvres, canapés, music, decorations.
- Meals
  ○ Breakfast.
  ○ Lunch.
  ○ Dinner.
  ○ Banquet.
- Serving times for meals.
- Menu for each meal, alternate meals for special diets.
- Prices of meals, including gratuities.
- Extra services (flowers, decorations on tables).
- Exhibits (number, dates, hours, sites).
- Needs of exhibitors (electricity, booths, guards, and so on).
- Piano (tuned), organ.
- Copying service.
- Dressing rooms.
- Parking, garage facilities.
- Automobile rentals.
- Flags, banners (hotel usually furnishes flags of United States, Canada, Mexico, state).
- Cover charges.
- Cover charges guaranteed.
- Cloak room and staff.
- Assistance at check-out time.
  ○ Transportation from/to airport.

Reception Desk

Since the reception desk is where any event starts, track all relevant meet-and-greet information.

- Stenographers.
- Telephones.
- Computers, printers.
- Signs for registration desk, hospitality rooms, members only, tours, tours for spouses, welcome, and so on.
- Registration cards.
- Tables for registration (number, size).
- Accommodations for delegates arriving after registration desk closes.

- Wastebaskets.
- Water pitchers, glasses.
- Letter paper, notepaper, pencils, ballpoint pens, felt-tip pens, sundries (ask secretary).
- Bulletin boards (number, sizes, stands).
- Cash boxes (number, size).
- File boxes (number, size).
- Name tags for members, speakers, guests, spouses.
- Reception group for out-of-town dignitaries.
- Special notes to be placed in guest hotel boxes.
- Photographer.

Equipment Needed

Be prepared to account as well for the availability of, access to, and, if necessary, maintenance of all necessary equipment.

- Closed-circuit television.
- Radio/television broadcasting.
- Lighting and operators as appropriate.
- Staging.
- Chalkboards, flannel boards, magnetic boards, stands.
- Lectern light (test it), gavel, block, teleprompter.
- Small flashlight if lectern light fails.
- Public address system. Test it.
- Recording equipment, operator.
- Projection equipment, blackout switch, operator.
- Flowers, plants, other decorations.
- Buses to transport delegates from/to airport, to/from convention hotel.
- Arrangements for sightseeing trips, tours.

For Publicity

As a general rule of thumb, make sure the following are addressed:

- Visit news media in advance to ascertain needs.
- Press room with tables, chairs, paper, ballpoint pens, pencils, sundries, at least one computer, Internet access for several computers, press liaison.
- Prepare news releases and distribute them in advance of each event.
- Prepare copies of speeches and biographical sketches of speakers and dignitaries and distribute the copies in advance of each event.

Miscellaneous

It is critical to have on hand the name, address, telephone, and email of the contact person for convention information.

30

Public Relations in a Crisis

> Reporters who show up in your office, already have a story; they just want your side, and it's your job to see that they get it.

When reporters show up on your job site or at your office, asking tough questions about what caused the disaster at your company and how many people were killed and injured, and who was at fault, they already have a story. What they want now is your company's side.

If you refuse to comment, to release information, your company loses, because the story of the disaster will be printed and aired—you cannot prevent it—and the story will be one-sided—usually the bad side—with no balancing information from your company.

If you refuse to comment, you excite the news media; they think there's a cover-up. Nothing excites reporters more than digging up information they think is being concealed. Moreover, the concealed information, which reporters eventually will dig up anyway, rather than the efforts of your company to resolve the difficulty and restore order, becomes the focus of their stories.

If you delay releasing information, and try to play catch-up, you lose, because you will be on the defensive, a bad position.

However, if you cooperate with the news media and give the reporters full information, telling them everything you legally can, both the good and the bad, you win, because your company will be seen as caring, compassionate, and helpful.

Good business practice demands full disclosure in crisis situations. Today's news media—Internet, newspapers, radio, television—and your company employees are so pervasive and so tenacious that it's virtually impossible to hide anything from them for more than a little while. And there is really no way to cover up an explosion and fire that rips through your plant, kills and injures workers, and causes widespread property damage. And, in the case of a fire, there is all that smoke and firefighters and fire trucks and paramedics and ambulances and police officers; you can't hide all that.

Too many people know about every crisis situation almost as soon as it happens. Employees tell their families; their families tell their relatives and their neighbors and their friends. The police and firefighters and paramedics and ambulances race to the scene of disasters with lights flashing and sirens screaming. Sometimes, federal auditors and regulators converge upon erring companies. Eventually, all of these agencies file public reports.

In the newsrooms of the newspaper and the television and radio stations, police scanner radios are broadcasting information about the disaster and dispatching police officers and firefighters and paramedics. Before reporters are sent out to get details, a story of the disaster is already on the air. Within minutes, the whole area knows something is up at your company, and it's not good.

Families of employees begin telephoning the company for assurance that their loved ones are safe. The curious drive out to the plant site to watch the activities. It's almost a holiday atmosphere.

There is simply no way to keep any of this from being published or aired. To try to cover it up only results in what is called *bad press*.

There is a silver lining, however.

No matter how severe your disaster, the news media and the public will remember it only a short while. Right now, your disaster is hot news, but news is a most perishable commodity. Tomorrow, certainly next week, a new disaster will replace yours.

In reality, the news media are not out to get you; they are out to get a story. It's your task to help them and, by helping them, you help your company. Your task is getting the best publicity you can as quickly as possible.

Your first task is to recognize what a crisis is. It is anything that upsets the routine of business: explosion, fire, bomb threat, environmental disaster, health problem, financial failing, strike, injury, death, corporate takeover, law suit, large-scale layoff, plant closing.

Long before any crisis, your company should have a written crisis plan, what to do when disaster hits, how to cope with any contingency. The company public relations office usually develops the crisis plan.

One of the keys in any crisis situation is to designate one person to represent the company and respond to all questions from the news media. Keep that person wholly informed, informed of what not to say as well as what to say. Remember, the company representative is just that, the company representative. The company representative is on your side.

To accomplish all that, your company needs a crisis communication team charged with developing a written crisis communication management plan, called also a *crisis plan* and *crisis public relations*.

The objectives of the crisis team and plan are to minimize losses, to remedy the crisis situation quickly, to disseminate information about the crisis, to take criticism early if the company is at fault, to avoid legal entanglements, and to ensure that the public understands that the company is doing everything possible to set things right.

The crisis communication team can comprise either staff public relations people or outside public relations counsel. Either is fine, but your company must have one. It's good insurance.

The Crisis Communication Team

- Identifies the community's opinion leaders, including the key people in the news media, including the editorial writers.
- Explains to management the functions and needs of the news media.
- Identifies potential crises and controversial situations within the company.
- Studies how other businesses handled emergencies, marking successes and failures, and evaluating effects upon corporate credibility.
- Develops a written crisis communication plan, and ensures that it is understood at all levels of the company.

The Crisis Communication Plan

- Designates one person with sufficient credibility and knowledge and command of information to represent the company and to present the company viewpoint.
- Keeps that person wholly informed, informed of what not to say as well as what to say.
- Maintains background information on the company and its operation.
- Maintains a list of names, titles, and telephone numbers of key company personnel.
- Establishes a program of crisis goodwill.

Objectives of a Crisis Plan

- To minimize losses.
- To remedy the crisis situation quickly.
- To disseminate information about the crisis.

- To take criticism early if the company is at fault.
- To avoid legal entanglements.
- To ensure that the public understands that the company is doing everything possible to set things right.

Crisis Goodwill

Before any time of crisis, the crisis team builds crisis goodwill by educating reporters and editorial writers and community opinion leaders about the operations and activities of the company, by providing paper, Internet, and video information about the company, by conducting tours of the company and open houses to which the community is invited, by sponsoring sports teams, by setting aside company land for a public park.

Goodwill so established will mark your company as one of the good guys, as a company interested not only in the public welfare but also in the welfare of its employees. As a result, when a crisis occurs, the attitude of the public—and the news media—toward your company will be positive.

When a Crisis Occurs

Remember, a crisis is anything that upsets the routine of business. Some crises are planned—employee layoff, plant closing, strike. Some crises are unexpected—explosion, fire, bomb threat. Some crises are expected but not planned—hurricane, tornado, earthquake. Some crises come to life after lying dormant long enough to have been forgotten—law suit, environmental disaster, health problem.

Regardless of the type of crisis situation, each is handled in much the same way insofar as the news media are concerned. Reporters wanting information and photographs will show up at company headquarters or at the disaster site or in both places. Your job is to provide as much as you legally can.

Just as it is the reporter's task to get a story, so is it your task to tell the story of your company, to describe what happened, to explain what is occurring.

Regardless of what the crisis involves, admit it. You cannot hide it. The story will be published and aired with or without your company input.

Admitting disaster permits you to get your company's side of the affair into the first published version of the story, to stress what your company is doing, not just to make amends but also to ensure that that disaster never happens again.

It is important to get your side into the first story published or aired. Many people read or listen to only the initial story. So, if the company presents the company side after the initial story is published or aired, many people will not get that information. And those who do read the next-day story only will believe the company is on the defensive.

Give reporters and photographers as much access to the disaster scene as is safely possible. Assign an employee to accompany and assist them.

One of the basic tools of the newsgathering process is the interview, either you and one reporter or you and a group of reporters. But the format is pretty much the same. You should deliver a prepared statement providing as much information as you legally can about the crisis and open the floor to questions from the reporters.

Keep in mind throughout the interview that when you speak to the reporters, you're not talking to them only; you are talking to the public, to every person who reads that newspaper or tunes in to that radio or television station or reads the Internet account. Every reporter present will go out and tell thousands of people what you said.

Never consider a reporter your friend. On the job, reporters have no friends, not even other reporters; they have contacts. They neither like you nor dislike you; they just want a story. And you're the one who can give them the story; you're the one who has the information they want. Treat reporters as politely and as candidly as possible. Be honest; never mislead a reporter.

You should control the interview, answering questions from reporters as you wish. If there is a large group, it may help if you repeat each question before answering. And, because reporters frequently pose questions negatively, restate such questions positively before answering.

If you don't like the question or the way the question is asked, you do not have to answer the question directly. Use the question to lead into your own statement about the company or the crisis situation.

Do not be goaded into answering before thinking. Take as much time as you need to formulate your responses. Do not worry about periods of silence. Television and radio reporters will skip over periods of silence, and periods of silence don't matter to newspaper reporters.

If a reporter asks several questions before giving you time to respond to any, pick one or two that let you make the most positive statement, and ignore the others.

If a reporter interrupts your response, say that you will address that issue later, and continue with your original response.

You can even take the initiative, saying you think the audience, the readers, would be interested in knowing such-and-such, and presenting your own information.

If a reporter precedes a question with background information that you deem negative, interrupt and say that the reporter is there, not to make a speech, but to ask questions.

Never lie to, deceive, or argue with, a reporter. If you do not know the answer, or if you do not want to answer, or if you are forbidden to answer a reporter's question, say either that you will secure the information and contact the reporter later, or that the information is confidential. Avoid "no comment" responses; they alert the reporter to dig deeper for the information. If you are legally forbidden to respond to a question, tell the reporter that.

Throughout the interview, adopt a pleasant demeanor. Smile as appropriate, and never become defensive or lose your temper. Remain calm. Use up-and-down gestures and nod your head to emphasize positive points.

If you do not want something published, do not tell it to a reporter, not even off the record. Never tell a reporter anything off the record; do not even mention "off the record" if you can help it. Generally, reporters will abide by a promise of keeping information off the record, but, too often, they forget and inadvertently publish off-the-record information. Thus, accident or not, an off-the-record statement has a good chance of being published.

Be careful with yes-or-no answers. Add as much qualifying information as you wish.

Other Suggestions

Unfortunately, in a crisis situation, you must conduct news conferences to ensure that all reporters receive the same information at the same time, without showing favoritism.

Be aware, though, once you open a news conference, reporters are free to ask any questions about any topic. Of course, you don't have to answer every question, but those you don't answer become red flags to the reporters.

Even though you conduct news conferences, you should have situation statements prepared by your public relations office to distribute to the reporters.

It is always a good idea to record any news conference. Have a secretary present to record the conference both by notes and by voice recording. Your voice recorder should be plugged into a wall socket and let run throughout the news conference.

31

Now What?

> The future of the United States looks good, but only if you do what
> every citizen is supposed to do: Keep up with what government is doing
> and planning.

What does the future hold for the news media and for the United States?

For one thing, daily newspapers are becoming a thing of the past, because
most people don't subscribe, and those who do, don't read past the first
seven or eight sentences of any news story. That's frightening, because it's
only the free press that keeps the United States strong and great, that keeps
us the people free.

To survive, the United States needs the free press, and the free press, par-
ticularly the newspaper, needs us. From almost the beginning of the United
States, we have been guaranteed six freedoms; they are listed in the First
Amendment to our Constitution.

> Congress shall make no law respecting an establishment of religion, or pro-
> hibiting the free exercise thereof; or abridging the freedom of speech, or of
> the press; or the right of the people peaceably to assemble, and to petition the
> Government for a redress of grievances.

Those 45 words—the most important 45 words ever written—give
everyone in the United States six freedoms: freedom *from* religion (no
government can establish or require membership in a religion), freedom
of religion (the people have the right to believe or not believe whatever
they want), freedom of speech and of the press (no government can deny
the people the right to say and to publish anything they want), freedom

to assemble (people can get together almost wherever they want), and freedom to petition the government.

No other nation has those freedoms, those protections that guarantee each of us what the Declaration of Independence says are our "unalienable Rights, that among these are Life, Liberty and Pursuit of Happiness."

And the most important freedom, the freedom that helps preserve those protections and all the others in the Constitution and the Amendments and the laws of the nation and the states, are these seven words: freedom of speech or of the press.

Those seven words are a guarantee that the news media, written and spoken, can inform the people about what their governments are doing and planning. That way, if we the people don't like what our governments are doing and planning, we the people can take remedial action; we can make changes.

But, because of the electronic revolution, people are giving up newspapers and turning to other news media: radio, television, Twitter, Facebook, blogs, the Internet, news magazines. Let's see how they compare to newspapers and how they help us.

Radio provides little news. Most news stories are fewer than 70 words, three or four sentences. That's the beginning of a newspaper story, two inches of type in a narrow column.

Television news is not much better; in fact, in a way, television is worse. Television news stories are the same length as on radio, but they seem longer, because television adds video. Unfortunately, television newscasters add plenty of unwanted opinion through their facial expressions and body language, and some even takes sides blatantly.

Even worse, radio and television don't provide much news about governments. Government activity is complicated, and, on the whole, most listeners and viewers don't find it entertaining or interesting enough to listen to.

Twitter and Facebook and citizen blogs, and other online sources of information by citizen journalists, are the least reliable. They are protected, not by freedom of the press, but by freedom of speech. At best, their postings are mostly gossip and based upon opinion—not upon stated fact, but upon nothing but the writer's beliefs. What those sources of information do provide are tips, information that legitimate reporters can investigate and, perhaps, turn into news stories. Even so, a lot of people are so enamored of electronic gadgets that they read Twitter and Facebook and citizen blogs and think that they get news from them.

If all you do is tune in to radio and television news programs and read Twitter and Facebook and citizen blogs, you don't know much about what governments are doing and planning.

News magazines provide good, detailed, responsible, factual, balanced news about international, national, and state governments. Their news stories put major events into perspective at an understandable level. But the downside is that news magazines are weeklies, so much of the news is six or seven days old.

Internet news provides plenty of news about governments immediately and in great detail and all written by professional reporters. But there's a bit of a downside: the cell phone and iPod screens are small and difficult to read, and laptop screens are vertical, an awkward position for reading. Hyperlinks and advertisements surrounding the news stories onscreen are distracting; they blink and change continually. And onscreen, although a list of stories is shown on the side, only one story is called up to read.

That leaves newspapers as the best source of news about government, even though they are a day late. On the Internet, news stories are available minutes after the news event occurs. In the daily newspaper, the stories are in tomorrow's morning edition, hours after the news event. And in weekly newspapers, the stories are in next week's edition.

Even so, newspaper news is reliable, because of how news stories are developed for publication. News events are covered and written by educated, trained, experienced, dedicated reporters. Their news stories are reviewed by educated, trained, experienced, dedicated editors, thereby ensuring accuracy and objectivity and that equal play is given to both sides.

But, today, because of the electronic revolution, people consider daily newspapers to be the least important source of news, so they stop reading and subscribing to them. Fewer subscribers means less advertising revenue, because the rate for advertising in newspapers is based in part upon the number of subscribers. As a result of this loss, a number of daily newspapers have shut down or reduced to three days a week, and many have gone online only. Those that remain on paper have smaller and fewer pages, providing less news of any kind.

Even more frightening, daily newspapers lay off staff and have fewer reporters assigned to cover government at any level. Weekly newspapers continue with smaller staffs, but their subscribers tend to remain loyal.

Fewer daily newspapers, fewer reporters, and less news about governments puts the United States in jeopardy, because our access to news about governments is what makes our democratic government work and keeps us free. So far, however, some newspapers are doing their job of providing the kind of news we need.

But this is what is frightening: If all newspapers—daily and weekly, on paper or online—were to shut down, we the people would be unable to read news about what our governments are doing and planning, leaving us unable to take any kind of remedial action. And worst, our government representatives in Washington and in the states and territories would take charge, and government by the people would change to government by the government, a totally undesirable situation. We would lose three freedoms and protections that make the United States strong and great.

1. The first freedom to go is freedom of the press. The government will control the news, will dictate to the news media what information will and will not be published.
2. The second freedom to go is freedom of speech. The government will permit no criticism of the government, even in private conversation.
3. The third freedom to go is freedom of religion. The government will permit no sermons critical of the government.
4. And the penalties for disobedience are severe: prison, torture, death.

If all of that sounds harsh, it is, but that's what happens every time a government takes over a nation.

To prevent any of that from happening in the United States, we the people, we the government, must keep up with news about what our government representatives at all levels are doing.

The only way we can keep up with the news is for daily and weekly newspapers to continue to do their job, to provide accurate, objective, balanced coverage of all news, especially news about governments, and not take sides in news stories. And, we must subscribe to and read newspapers.

Citizen journalists, those who write blogs and those who shoot photographs of news events, cannot compete in the reporting process, because, unlike professional reporters, they don't have the credibility, the resources, the background, the knowledge, the education, the training, the contacts, the desire, or the time to cover news events.

Reporters do have the credibility, the resources, the background, the knowledge, the education, the training, the contacts, the desire, and the time to cover news events. As they cover the daily news, reporters become known to and recognized by newsmakers, and are expected at and are readily admitted to news events. They cover the news; it's what they do.

What it all comes down to is this: The future of the United States really is in jeopardy, and it's up to the news media and to us the people to preserve our nation. It may be difficult, but this must be done and quickly, because our future as a nation is at stake:

Newspapers—daily and weekly, on paper or online—must continue to do their job of reporting accurate, objective, balanced news about government at all levels.

We the people must continue to subscribe to newspapers—daily and weekly, on paper or online or both.

We the people must read news about what our governments are doing and planning.

We the people must voice our opinions at the polls when it's time to vote.

So, part of the responsibility is ours. *We* must read news about government on a regular basis and help take remedial action and make changes as needed. Our nation needs us.

32

Find a Job

After it's all said and done, it's time to apply for a job. Whatever field you pick—reporting or public relations—here's what you do to apply.

Now that you've walked across the stage and received your college diploma, your next step is to use all the information and suggestions that you've accepted in classes and in internships and go on a job hunt. The procedure is not difficult, but it is demanding, and you must follow the guidelines.

To get a job in news writing, photography, advertising, or public relations, you must have a college education, an interview, and the ability to do the job you are seeking, and you must show the interviewer not only that you can do the work but also that you would fit well within the company. For a newspaper job, apply to the managing editor; for a public relations job, apply to the company public relations department executive.

The first step is to prepare a cover letter, a résumé, a list of references, and a portfolio, and to prepare yourself for the interview. The following pages show examples of the format of the cover letter, the résumé, and listing of references.

The résumé alone will not get you a job, but it will help get you an interview.

You will get a job based upon two things: your skill in writing and photography and design and layout, and the impression you make during the interview.

Make your cover letter and résumé attractive. Read them several times, including backwards at least once, to make certain that they contain no errors of any kind. To find overlooked errors, ask an outsider to read and comment on your cover letter and résumé.

Caution—Everything you submit is typed; only your signature is handwritten.

———

Caution—Never give up an original document.

The Portfolio

Your portfolio is a collection of the work you have done and the work you have published. It should include stories, photographs, advertising layout and design, magazine covers, letters of accomplishment from supervisors—anything that you have completed.

For this stage in your development, your portfolio may be simply a three-ring binder containing copies of your work. **Never give up the original of any document.**

The Interview

The interview is where you explain whatever needs explaining and where you show your personality. Remember, a ready smile and the four magic words—*sir, ma'am, please, thank you*—go a long way in your favor.

Adopt a positive attitude; make strong eye contact; believe in yourself; present a firm, confident, friendly handshake; do not fidget with your hands or pens or touch your nose; do not jiggle your foot or leg.

Do not ask about vacation or sick leave; they are fixed and guaranteed. You may ask about workday hours.

You might be asked what salary you would like. To prepare for that question, in advance of the interview, check out the city and the rent for the neighborhood and kind of apartment that you, living alone, would prefer, would feel safe in. Your monthly salary should be no less than four times the rent.

The Cover Letter

Because a résumé describes your past, if you wish to cite your career objective, put that information into your cover letter. Be careful, though; never state your career objective as an entry-level job, because it indicates that you may not be prepared to do the work required by the office.

Make certain that every document you submit has no errors of any kind: spelling, typographical, grammatical, factual. Make the formatting of each document visually attractive.

In the cover letter, you may make whatever changes you wish except in the first and last paragraphs. Do not thank the addressee for reading your cover letter, and do not begin the first paragraph with the pronoun *I*. The last paragraph should not say that you are eagerly awaiting a reply, but should read as follows: "I will telephone your office and make an appointment for an interview."

Many interviewers believe that if you are not interested enough in the job to schedule your own interview, they are not interested in you.

You may end the cover letter with your full name, but you should sign it with your normal signature.

Example of Cover Letter
Douglas Perret Starr
4123 Chestnut Street
Collegetown, Texas 12345
d-starr@tamu.edu

[date]
Grace Hopper
Vice President for Public Relations
The ABC Co.
P.O. Box 123
Dallas, Texas 12345–6789
Dear Ms. Hopper:

Since high school, when I learned about the public relations successes of the ABC Company, I have been preparing myself to join that effort. Explain that sentence, the preparations you made, the additional and applicable courses you added to your college work, that sort of thing.

Explain how your job or internship helped prepare you.

Explain jargon and unusual terms, terms not in general use.

Make the reader understand your eagerness for the job.

Last paragraph, write this, and this only: I will telephone your office and make an appointment for an interview. Do not write that you are eagerly awaiting a telephone call from the addressee.

Sincerely,
[This is where you sign your name.]
Douglas Perret Starr
Attachments
   Résumé
   Names, addresses, telephone numbers, email addresses of references
   Examples of work

The Résumé

The following personal items should **never** be put into a résumé, nor should your interviewer ask you questions about them:

- A photograph of yourself.
- Your age.
- Your date of birth.
- Your place of birth.
- Your marital or engaged status.
- Your gender.
- Your sexual orientation.
- Your physical or mental disability.
- Your religion.
- Your political preference.
- Your membership in or work with religious or political organizations.

The key listings in your résumé are the following: Education, Work Experience, Skills. Secondary listings are Honors (Dean's List, Scholarships, Citations, and so on) and other language(s) and how well you read, write, and speak it/them.

In listing education, begin with your university and cite your degree (Bachelor of Arts/Bachelor of Science) and the month and year of graduation. You should list appropriate courses: Media Writing I and II, Copyediting, Public Relations Theory and Practice, Public Relations Methods, Electronic Media Production, Web Writing.

In listing experience, begin with current or most recent job and list jobs and internships backward in time.

Describe duties, not responsibilities, and write everything in the past tense.

Do not explain the obvious or such common jobs, such as waitress, cashier, lifeguard.

Do not put at the bottom of your résumé that references are available upon request. Of course, they are, if you want the job, that is. So, include a separate page listing three to five references, cited by name, title, company, postal address, city, state, ZIP code, complete telephone number, and email address. Do not write *email* before the email address.

Ensure that dates are accurate and complete.

Thus, your résumé packet should contain the following: cover letter, résumé, list of references, and five or six examples of your work, all stapled in the upper left-hand corner.

Because most students hold jobs during their four years in college, you probably will, too. If you have a job, you probably will pay for at least 25 percent of your education. Therefore, between the listing Work Experience and the first listing, type this: "Through work, scholarships, and loans, I paid for X percent of my college education."

Example of Résumé

Your Full Name (centered)

School Address   Home Address
1002 Williams Street   917 Baylor Street
Collegetown, Texas 12345   Houston, Texas 12345
555-123-5432   555-456-7632
                          m-dupas@tamu.edu

Education

Dec 2006   Texas A&M University, Bachelor of Science (Public Relations), cum laude.

Appropriate courses: Media Writing I and II, Copyediting, Public Relations Theory and Practice, Public Relations Methods, Electronic Media Production, Web Writing.

Do not list your grade-point average unless it is above 3.5/4.0.

May 2002   Houston Magnet High School, with honors.

Experience

Through work, scholarships, and loans, I paid for 75 percent of my college education.

Write all of your duties, not responsibilities, in the past tense.

Summer 2008   Office of U.S. Sen. Mary Roe, Texas, Washington DC. Public Affairs writer, intern, supervisor
May 2007–Dec 2007   H.E.B. supermarket, cashier, supervisor John Doe
Sep 2005–May 2006   Smith Florist, bouquet designer, sales, supervisor Mary Doe.

Job Skills

Qualified operator PC—Microsoft Office, InDesign, Illustrator.
Qualified operator Macintosh—Microsoft Office, InDesign, Illustrator.
Photographer—digital and film cameras.
Fluent in Spanish, read, write, speak.
Speak Italian, read enough to get along.

Honors

Graduated Cum Laude
Dean's List, Fall, Spring 2006; Fall, Spring 2005; Fall, Spring 2004.
Brahman Cattle Scholarship, $5,000, 2006.

Lions Club Scholarship, $250, Fall 2005
Paul Smith Scholarship, $1,000, 2004.
Houston Magnet High School Medal of Honor Scholarship, 2002.

Foreign Travel

| Summer 2006 | Vacationed in Paris, France, two weeks. |
| Fall 2005 | Study Abroad Program, Santa Chiara, Italy, 12 weeks. |

Memberships

Public Relations Student Society of America, Vice President, 2005
Society of Professional Journalists
Texas Horse and Cow Society, Vice President, 2006; Secretary, 2005
Alpha Phi Omega service fraternity

References

List three to five.

After the Interview

A week after the interview, type and postal mail a thank-you note, thanking the interviewer, not for the interview (that's part of the job), but for clear and complete explanations of the job requirements and the tour of the facilities. It puts your name back on top of the pile of applicants.

How to List References

Douglas Perret Starr, City Editor
The Collegetown Journal
P.O. Box 123
Collegetown, Texas 12345-6789
office 555-123-4567 (Write *office*, not *telephone*)
fax 555-123-9876
dpstarr@journal.com (Do not write *email*; the @ indicates an email address.)

All listings are from the most recent backward. In Memberships, list the year(s) of offices held, not the years of membership,

Do not concern yourself that your résumé runs to more than one page. If you list everything that is appropriate, it will.

In addition to listing everything of note since birth and a list of references, you will attach copies of five or six different stories showing your best writing, your best photography, your best page layout and design. And,

Note—Do not list family members or clergy personnel.

———

Note—Do list high school or college teachers, supervisors of jobs or internships, or neighbors who have known you for some time.

———

Note—Follow the order shown on the résumé example: Education, Experience, Skills, Honors, Foreign Travel, Memberships, References.

if you have them, attach a copy of any letter of commendation for a job or an internship well done.

Attire for the Interview

Women

- Matched skirted suit: wool or silk (lined) or wool-silk blend; black, bright blue, navy, taupe, gray.
- Heavy silk or cotton blouse: accented colors (red, cobalt blue, turquoise, emerald green, fuchsia, off-white, shell pink).
- Scarf that picks up the colors of major pieces.
- Shoes: classic leather pumps, black, navy, taupe, cream. Avoid straps.
- Jewelry, 14k gold or sterling silver: no more than one ring per hand (college ring is acceptable), elegant pearls, wristwatch (tank or oyster shape); no dangling earrings; preferably no studs in nose or tongue or eyebrow.
- Hair above the shoulder or put up. Nails manicured, but no color polish.
- Handbag: leather, smallest functional size, black, brown, burgundy.
- Briefcase: leather, smallest size functional, black, brown, burgundy.
- Make-up: subtle, well-blended, eye make-up important; lip color whitens teeth.

Men

- Two-piece suit: navy, gray, charcoal, wool or wool blend.
- Shirt: long-sleeved, cotton or cotton blend, white or light blue or small pinstripe.
- Tie: silk or blend, color to contrast with suit and shirt, burgundy, navy, small print or stripe.

- Shoes: polished, slip-on or lace-up wing tips, black.
- Briefcase: leather, brown, black, burgundy.
- Jewelry: no more than one ring per hand (college ring is acceptable); gold, silver, or stainless steel watch; no bracelets or chains or studs in nose or tongue or eyebrow.
- Belt: leather, black, burgundy.
- Hair and beard: trimmed, combed, short sideburns; preferably clean-shaven, but if otherwise, beard and mustache trimmed.
- Nails: manicured, but no polish.

Job Mentor

This advice is so important, particularly as you begin your career or any new job, that some corporations not only require it but also even provide assistance for you to attain it. What you need is a job mentor to help you assimilate into your new assignment, your new workplace.

A job mentor helps you navigate through the maze of information about your employer, about your job requirements, about your role in the corporation, about fellow employees, about office politics, and even about office intrigues.

Properly used, your job mentor serves as your safety net by providing the benefit of experience to guide you along the right path.

What your job mentor does for you is to provide institutional information, information about not only the company and its role in the business or political world or both, but also your role therein. It gives you an expanded learning curve, and it's all to your advantage.

But, be careful. The job mentor you choose should be in your career field and should be someone whom you trust and with whom you feel comfortable. It might not be essential, but it would help—and you would be more comfortable—if you and your job mentor are of the same race or the same ethnicity and the same gender.

In addition, you may need a backup job mentor, especially in the beginning, to consult while your primary job mentor is unavailable. As with the primary job mentor, you must choose your backup job mentor with the same care and consideration.

Eventually, if you remain in that job and with that corporation long enough, you may—perhaps you should—become a job mentor to a new employee.

Appendix 1

Verbs of Attribution
and How to Use Them

Verbs of attribution don't always mean what you think they mean. Here is how to make certain that your verbs are accurate.

Writing news requires accuracy and objectivity on the part of the reporter: accuracy not only in fact but also in word use, and objectivity in that the reporter's opinion must not be in the story, even through inadvertent use of incorrect words. Definition of words is important, but so is the *usage* of words. Do not change words, especially verbs of attribution, merely, as some say, to keep readers from being bored with repetitions of *said, said, said.*

For writing news, *said* is the most useful verb of attribution; it is the only verb that fits in any situation. *Said* has no hidden meanings, and it hides in the sentence, allowing the sentence to focus on *what* was said rather than on *the way* it was said.

Synonyms for *said* carry other definitions and nuances of meaning and usage that color and change the meaning of the sentence, and sometimes involve the reporter's opinion. The rule for writing news is simple: Before using a synonym for *said*, look up that synonym's definition and usage, and be prepared to support your decision.

Webster's New World College Dictionary, 4th ed., the official dictionary of The Associated Press, cautions on page xxii: "It is unwise to substitute one synonym for another automatically or unthinkingly. There are small, often subtle differences between synonyms. A person who wants to write and speak clearly and precisely must understand these differences."

Webster's explains all of this by adding, after defining some words: —*SYN.* and cites a synonym for the defined word. So, you have the definition of the word wanted; now you need its usage. You look up the cited synonym.

After the definition of the synonym is *SYN.—*, which begins the Synonymy, a list of bold-faced synonyms together with explanations for the usage of each and the differences among them.

For example: You want to use *admit*. Its definition is *to concede, to grant, to acknowledge, to confess,* and *—SYN.* cites *acknowledge, receive.* You look up *acknowledge*, which is defined as *to admit to be true, to confess.* The Synonymy lists *acknowledge, admit, own, avow, confess.* You look at *admit* and note that its usage describes "assent that has been elicited by persuasion" and "implies a conceding of a fact." If that usage of *admit* fits your story situation, if the speaker told you that persuasion was involved, you may use *admit*. Otherwise, use *said*.

The following definitions and usages of commonly used verbs of attribution are from *Webster's New World College Dictionary.*

According To—in agreement with; as stated in or reported by.

> **Caution**—This tends to cast doubt on the statement, especially if placed at the end of the sentence.

Acknowledge—admit to be true or as stated; confess.
Usage—Implies the reluctant disclosure of something that one might have kept secret. (The reporter cannot know what is in the mind of the speaker.)
Add—state further.

> **Caution**—In stories about speeches, *added* is redundant and not appropriate, since after the speaker's opening words, nothing was added, everything was all part of the speech.

Admit—concede or grant, acknowledge or confess.
Usage—Describes assent that has been elicited by persuasion and implies a conceding of a fact. (The reporter cannot know that what was admitted to was, indeed, a fact. And the reporter must ask whether persuasion was used to obtain the information.)
Advise—give advice or opinion; notify.
Usage—Recommends a course of action and implies that the giver of the advice has knowledge or experience. (The reporter cannot know what is in the mind of the speaker.)
Affirm—say positively, declare firmly, assert to be true; confirm.

Usage—Implies deep conviction in one's statement and the unlikelihood of denial by another. (The reporter cannot know what is in the mind of the speaker.)

Announce—declare publicly, formally; give notice formally; proclaim, say, tell.

Usage—Makes something of interest known publicly or officially, especially something of the nature of news.

Answer—say or write in return to a question; reply in words.

Usage—Implies saying, writing, or acting in return as required by the situation or by courtesy.

Argue—try to prove by giving reasons for or against a proposal, proposition, and the like; discuss, debate.

Usage—Implies citing reasons or evidence to support or refute an assertion, belief, proposition.

Assert—issue a firm statement with confidence.

Usage—States positively, declare, affirm, but without objective proof.

Aver—declare to be true; state positively; affirm.

Usage—Connotes implicit confidence in the truth of one's statement from one's own knowledge of the matter. (The reporter cannot know what is in the mind of the speaker.)

Avow—declare openly as a fact.

Usage—Implies an open, emphatic declaration, often as an act of affirmation.

Caution—warn; urge.

Usage—Gives advice that puts one on guard against possible danger, failure, and the like.

Claim—state as a fact or as one's belief; assert; state as a fact something that may be called into question.

Usage—What is claimed may not be a fact.

Comment—say one's opinion, usually as a criticism or explanation or interpretation.

Usage—Remarks or observes in explaining, criticizing, or interpreting something.

Concede—to admit as true or valid, as certain or proper.

Usage—What was conceded may not be true or valid.

Confess—admit a fault or a crime; acknowledge one's guilt, opinion, or view.

Usage—Applies to a formal acknowledgment of a sin, crime, and the like, but, in a weakened sense, is used interchangeably with admit in making simple declarations.

Declare—make clearly known, state or announce openly, formally, and so on; say positively or emphatically; state openly a choice, opinion, and so on.

Usage—Asserts openly or formally by an explicit or clear statement, often in the face of opposition.

Deny—refuse to accept as true.

Usage—Implies a refusal to accept as true, real, valid.

Discuss—talk or write about; took up in conversation or in a discourse.

Usage—Implies a talking about something in a deliberative fashion, with varying opinions offered constructively and usually amicably, so as to settle an issue, decide on a course of action, and so on.

Divulge—reveal; disclose.

Usage—Suggests that what has been disclosed should properly have been kept secret or private. (The reporter cannot know what is in the mind of the speaker.)

Explain—make clear, plain, or understandable; give meaning or interpretation of.

Usage—Implies making clear or intelligible something that is not known or understood.

Go On To (Say, Explain)—proceed; continue.

Usage—A wordy substitute for say. If the speaker went on to say something, the speaker said it.

Grant—acknowledge for the sake of argument; admit as true without proof; concede.

Hear—to listen to and consider.

Usage—The reporter cannot know that the person listened and considered what was said.

Imply—hint, suggest, intimate.

Usage—Suggests putting into the mind something involved, but not openly expressed, in a word, and suggests the need for inference. (The reporter cannot know what is in the mind of the speaker.)

Inform—give information.

Usage—Implies a making aware of something by giving knowledge of it.

Maintain—to defend, as by argument, to affirm, to declare in a positive way, to assert.

Mention—refer to briefly or incidentally.

Note—mention particularly; set down in writing.

Notify—make known.

Usage—Implies sending a formal notice imparting required or pertinent information.

Observe—say or mention casually, comment or remark on or upon.

Usage—Usually suggests a sense of sight.

Own—confess to something.

Usage—Denotes an informal acknowledgment of something in connection with oneself.

Point Out—show or call attention to.

Proclaim—announce orally, loudly, publicly.

Usage—Implies an official, formal announcement made with the greatest possible publicity, of something of great moment or significance.

Rebut—contradict or refute, especially in a formal manner, by argument, proof, and so on, as in a debate.

Usage—Stresses formality in refuting an argument, such as is observed in debate, court procedure, and so on.

Refute—prove to be wrong.

Usage—Implies a more thorough assembly of evidence and a more careful development of argument, hence suggests conclusiveness of proof against. (The reporter cannot know that what was said proved anything.)

Rejoin—answer.

Usage—Implies an answer, originally to a reply, now often to an objection.

Remark—say an observation or comment.

Usage—Applies to a brief, more or less casual statement of opinion, and so on, as in momentarily directing one's attention to something.

Reply—answer or respond in speech or in writing.

Usage—Refers to an answer that satisfies in detail the question asked. (The reporter cannot know that the answer satisfied in detail the question asked.)

Report—impart information on something witnessed or investigated or required. (The reporter's opinion is not part of the information reported.)

Respond—react to any stimulus spontaneously, without delay or resistance.

Usage—Implies an appropriate reaction made voluntarily or spontaneously to that which serves as a stimulus. (The reporter cannot know what is in the mind of the speaker.)

Retort—to turn an insult back upon the originator, to answer in kind or in a sharp, quick, witty way.

Usage—suggests a reply provoked by a charge or a criticism.

Reveal—make known something hidden or kept secret.

Usage—Implies a making known of something hidden or secret. (The reporter cannot know what is in the mind of the speaker.)

Say—speak, express in words.

Caution—In stories about speeches, *added* is redundant and not appropriate, since after the speaker's opening words, nothing was added, everything was all part of the speech.

Share—receive in common with another.

Note—Not appropriate as a verb of attribution.

Usage—Uses, enjoys, or possesses in common with others and generally connotes a giving or receiving a part of something.

Speak—utter words with the ordinary voice.

Usage—Connotes a formal address to an audience.

State—set forth in words, especially in a specific, definite, or formal way.

Suggest—mention as something to think over; propose as a possibility; intimate.

Usage—Implies a putting of something into the mind, either intentionally as by way of a proposal, or unintentionally, as through association of ideas.

Talk—put into spoken words.

Usage—Suggests informal, colloquial conversation.

Tell—give an account of in speech or in writing; express in words; utter.

Usage—Suggests the making known of necessary or requested information.

Urge—make an earnest presentation of arguments; advocate strongly.

Usage—Implies a strong effort to persuade someone to do something, as by entreaty, argument, or forceful recommendations.

Warn—tell of a danger, coming evil, or misfortune; put on guard; caution.

Usage—Gives advice that puts one on guard against possible danger, failure, and so on, especially when a serious danger is involved.

Appendix 2
Words: Their Definition and Usage

The writer's duty is to ensure that the reader understands what is written. Thus, the writer must understand the definitions, the nuances, and, particularly, the usages of words.

A, An, The—articles. *A* and *an* are indefinite, general; *the* is definite, pointing to something specific, something known.

Alot—not a word; **a lot**—plenty; **allot**—distribute.

All Right—two words, never *alright*.

Also—usually unnecessary, particularly following *and*.

Among—a preposition that involves more than two; see **Between**.

Another—one more just like the previous. Usually pleonastic, particularly when following *and*.

Approximations—Be frugal in the use of approximations. In general, round numbers can be assumed to be approximations.

As Far As—later in the sentence, it must be followed by *is concerned* or *goes*; **as for**—fits better than *as far as*.

Apart—not together; **a part**—included.

As Well As—means that what follows is already known to readers. Does not substitute for *and*. "The Equal Rights Amendment applies to women as well as to men." The other way around is incorrect: "The Equal Rights Amendment applies to men as well as to women."

Awhile—for a short time; object of a verb; **a while**—for a short time; object of a preposition.

Between—a preposition that takes an objective noun or pronoun: *between her and me*, not *between she and I*. In listings, it is followed by *and*, never *to* and never *or*. *Between* involves two items; *among* involves more than two.

Either takes an *or*. If you use *between* —— *or* —— , delete *between*. And, don't forget, there is nothing between *Sunday and Monday* and between *2011 and 2012*; use *from* —— *to* ——.

Biweekly—means both *every two weeks* and *twice a week*, so its use is confusing. The same is true of *bimonthly*. *Biannual* means *twice a year*; *biennial* means *every two years*.

Can Be Found—pleonastic. If something *can be found* in a certain place, it *is* in that place.

Careen—involves no forward motion; means to tip a ship onto its side to expose the bottom for cleaning.

Career—headlong flight.

Comprise—consists of everything; requires a direct object, not a prepositional phrase. *The whole comprises its parts.*

Compose—to put together; it is followed by a prepositional phrase, *of* . . . . See **Include**.

Convince—to overcome doubt and is followed by *of* or *that*; **persuade**—to influence to action or belief and is followed by an infinitive. *She was persuaded to read the book, which convinced her that she was correct.*

Continual—regularly; **continuous**—constant; *The sun rises continually and shines continuously.*

Couple—requires an *of*: *couple of*.

Crispy—long spelling of *crisp*.

Degrees—The names of academic degrees are *Bachelor of Arts, Bachelor of Science, Master of Arts, Master of Science*; no *s* or *'s* on *Bachelor* or *Master*. *Bachelor's degree, bachelor's in horticulture, master's degree, master's in agricultural development* are correct. It depends upon the preposition: The name of the degree contains an *of*. *Bachelor of Arts degree* is redundant.

Different—redundant in such usage as *They lived in three different countries, and visited three different states.*

Enormity—involves a degree of wickedness; **enormousness**—emphasizes size without opinion.

Etc.—*et* means *and*. Do not use *etc.* in a listing that begins with *such as* or *include*.

Feel—tactile word; does not substitute for *think* or *believe*. If it is used in place of *think* or *believe*, it must be followed by *that*. *John feels Mary is a fun date* implies that John is feeling Mary.

Fellow—a similar person; redundant when used with such *fellow* words: fellow *shipmate*, *fellow classmate*.

First-Come, First-Served—note the past tense *served*. The meaning is that the first to come is the first *to be served*, not the first *to serve*.

Font—for ease of reading onscreen, use a 12-point sans-serif font, such as Verdana for the PC and Geneva for the Macintosh, fonts that were designed for the screen. Although Arial is a sans-serif font, it is too small for the screen or for printing. Do not print in a sans-serif font; print in a 12-point serif font, preferably Times New Roman.

Forbid—It's *forbid to* do something, not *forbid from* doing something.

From—requires a *to*, not an en-dash: *from 2012 to 2013*, not *from 2012–2013*. Those years could be school semesters.

Here—vague; *here* is where the reader is; cite the place.

Hyphen, En Dash, Em Dash—the hyphen joins words: *long-distance runner*. The *en dash* joins numerals, scores *21–12*, votes *76–24*, dates June *12–20*. The *em dash* is a punctuation mark used to indicate a break in the thought: *His job—and it's important—is to ensure accuracy.* Note the difference in length in the three marks:

Hyphen	-
En Dash	–
Em Dash	—

Include—lists only part of the total. Do not use *etc.* at the end of the list. See **Comprise**.

Infinitive of Purpose—improper use of the infinitive, as in *she walked to town to arrive exhausted.* Arriving exhausted is not why she walked town. Recast such construction.

Insure—to contract to be paid money in case of loss; **ensure**—to make certain, to guarantee. **Assure**—to convince.

Is Located—pleonastic. If something *is located* in a certain place, it *is* in that place.

Its—possessive pronoun of third person-neuter; there is no apostrophe in any pronoun (except *'tis*, which is slang); **it's**—contraction meaning *it is* or *it has.*

Lectern—an elevated table on which to place notes while lecturing. See **Podium**.

Lay—*Lay* takes a direct object; its past tense is *laid*: he laid the book on the table.

Lie—indicates reclining; no direct object; its past tense is *lay*; he lay on the beach.

Lie—untruth. The past tense is *lied*.

Likely—to be expected. It is followed by an infinitive: *he is likely to win*; not *he likely will win*; or is followed by a *that*: *it is likely that he will win*; **probably**—designates a chance: *he probably will win* or *it is probable that he will win.*

Local—Everything is local, to some place; cite the place.

Locate—to place; redundant when used to cite a place because the present tense verb is sufficient. If it *is located* there, it *is* there. See **Situate**.

Merchant Marine—a seagoing group of seamen, not of warriors. Members are merchant *mariners*, not merchant *marines.*

Momento—not a word; the word is *memento*, from memory.

Only—opinion word. If *only* must be used, do not place it before the verb. *One of the only* is ridiculous. *One of the few* is clear.

Podium—what you stand *on*. *Pod* means *foot*. Lecturers and other speakers stand *behind* a **Lectern**.

Possessive—necessary when used with a gerund (a verbal ending in *ing*): *She objected to* his *flirting with her friend*, not *She objected to* him *flirting with her friend*. It was not him that she objected to, it was what he was doing that she objected to.

Presently—in a little while, soon. *Is presently* is ridiculous.

Redundancies

Future plans—All plans are in the future.

Past experience—All experience is in the past.

Past history—All history is in the past.

Is currently—two words meaning *is*.

Is now—two words meaning *is*.

Now currently—two words meaning *now*.

Earlier—Past tense makes it unnecessary, as in *earlier this week*.

Later—Future tense makes it unnecessary, as in *later this week*.

Someday—vague, unnecessary.

Sometime—pleonastic in such usage as *sometime next month*.

Somewhere—pleonastic in such usage as *somewhere in Texas*.

Wander aimlessly—All wandering is aimless.

Reflexive Pronouns—those ending with *self—myself, yourself, herself, himself, itself, yourselves, ourselves, themselves*—do not substitute for the objective pronouns: *me, you, her, him, it, you, them, us*. Reflexive pronouns show that the person acting and the person acted upon are the same: *I myself did the job*. The reflexive pronoun is incorrect after a preposition: *give it to Noelie and me*, not *give it to Noelie and myself*.

Reserve—the organization is the *Reserve: Army Reserve, Naval Reserve*, and the like; people in *the reserve* are *reserves* or *reservists*. You join the *Reserve* (the organization). If you join the *reserves*, you join a group of people.

Situate—redundant; if something *is situated in*, it *is in*. See **Locate**.

Species—a class or classification; it is always singular. *The United States has four kinds of highway* [not highways]: *interstate, national, state, county*. The farm produced several varieties of *cabbage* [not *cabbages*].

Subjunctive—situation contrary to fact: *If I were you.*

Such As—do not include *etc.* as part of the group, as in: *The price includes such items as meals, lodging, etc.* Make it: *The price includes such items as meals and lodging.*

That—refers to things and animals without names; **who** applies to humans and animals with names. See **Who.**

That—introduces an essential clause: *The lawnmower that is broken is in the garage*; **which** usually follows a comma and introduces a nonessential clause: *The lawnmower, which is broken, is in the garage.* See **Which.**

Then—the next step. Usually unnecessary.

The Scene—pleonastic in such usage as *fled the scene.* The scene is the only place from which anyone can flee.

The Year—redundant in *the year 2004; 2004 is* a year.

Tragic—opinion word. Requires attribution.

Try—is followed by an infinitive, a *to*, not an *and. Try to win*, not *try and win. Try and win* doubles the verb. It says that the person will try and will win. Put it in the past tense: *tried and won.*

Verbal—spoken or written. *Oral* is spoken only.

Very—opinion, unnecessary.

Whenever—each time. Does not substitute for *when*, which means *a specific time. Whenever* and *when* are not synonymous.

Which—usually follows a comma and introduces a nonessential clause: *The lawnmower, which is broken, is in the garage.* **That** introduces an essential clause: *The lawnmower that is broken is in the garage.*

While—at the same time. It does not provide the contrast that *though* and *although* provide, and it does **not** substitute for *and.* Incorrect use can be ridiculous, as this sentence from *The New York Times*, 11 January 2013, page A21: "Franklin D. Roosevelt convened his cabinet the day after the Pearl Harbor attacks [1941], while [21 years later] John F. Kennedy relied on a subset of his cabinet during the Cuban missile crisis [1963]." It's easily fixed, with a semicolon: "Franklin D. Roosevelt convened his cabinet the day after the Pearl Harbor attacks; John F. Kennedy relied on a subset of his cabinet during the Cuban missile crisis."

Who—refers **to** people; **that** refers to things and to animals without names.

Will be ——ing—progressive tense; usually not needed; simple past, present, future tense are more specific.

Grammar

Appositive—a word or phrase that means the same as another word or phrase. Appositives require two commas, one before and one after. "Dr. Eddie Davis, *interim president of Texas A&M University*, delivered the welcome address."

Attribution—State fact, attribute opinion. Do not arbitrarily put attribution at the end of the statement. Instead, put attribution where it hides, usually at the first break in the sentence:

The president said, "Read my lips; no new taxes."

"Read my lips," *the president said.* "No new taxes."

"Read my lips; no new taxes," *the president said.*

The most important parts of any sentence, paragraph, book are the beginning and the end. The middle supports both ends. The most important information in what the president said is *no* new *taxes.* In a story about a speaker, the most important information in every sentence is not the speaker, it is what the already-known speaker said. So, do not weaken the power end of such a sentence with attribution.

Defining Clause—a complete thought unit that follows an introductory phrase frequently requires a *that* for clear writing. "When he entered the room, the sheriff said he saw the body" means that the sheriff made that statement upon entering the room. "When he entered the room, the sheriff said, he saw the body" means that he made that statement later. "The sheriff pointed out the man had stolen the money" is awkward. The sheriff did not point out the man, he pointed out what the man did. Correct: "The sheriff pointed out that the man had stolen the money."

Quoting One or Two Words—quoting one or two words may change the meaning of the word(s): The sheriff said two "women" were arrested. He described the prostitute as a "good mother." If the sentence reads the same with and without the quotations marks, omit them.

Punctuation—only one space after punctuation marks.

All Periods, Commas—place *inside* all close quotation marks.

All Colons, Semicolons—place *outside* all close quotation marks.

Comma—separates items in list, and separates two thought units joined by a conjunction: *and*, *but*, and so on.

Semicolon—separates two thought units not joined by a conjunction.

Sentence Structure—Do not change the structure of sentences without valid reason. Changing to prevent boredom in readers does not work, because boring writing is boring writing regardless of the structure. Many times, repetition enhances understanding.

Subjunctive—a verb mood that indicates a condition contrary to fact or a condition of doubt. *If I were you, I would get a master's degree.*

Suspensive Hyphenation—dropping the common noun in all but the last of a series of hyphenated words. Note the space after the comma and before the *and* and the *to*. *The 11-, 12-, and 13-year-old boys were given 5- to 10-day suspensions.* There are no such words as *12-and, 5-to,* and so on.

Synonyms—There are no true synonyms; each word has additional meanings, nuances, and usages that apply in certain situations that, if used inappropriately, change the meaning of the sentence. To ensure and to enforce understanding, repeat key words. Arbitrary changing of words results in confusion.

> **Caution**—Never use any word whose definition and *usage* you have not looked up in the dictionary. Dictionaries at the collegiate and higher levels provide usage of words of similar but not interchangeable meaning. Such a listing of words follows *syn* in boldface italics after all of the definitions. If *syn* is at the bottom of a list of definitions, look up that listing and select the proper word according to the usages listed.

Epilogue

Brevity in writing is essential. Be concise. Get to the point. Delete unnecessary words. Read loud and listen to what you wrote. Rewrite as many times as needed.

Appendix 3

Keyboard Shortcuts and Why to Use Them

Here's a bonus that comes with every computer: a quick way to add accent marks to letters, add footnote numerals, an apostrophe, an ellipsis, and certain symbols.

Every PC and Macintosh computer, desktop, and laptop, has built-in keyboard shortcuts that help you speed up your typing and produce accurate copy. You should have a copy of those shortcuts near your keyboard.

Those shortcuts help you copy and paste words, sentences, and paragraphs, even whole pages; change words from lower case to upper case and c/lc and back; insert such symbols as © (copyright), ™ (trademark), and ® (registered); and, most important, to put accent marks *on* (René,) instead of *after* (Rene') letters, and such other symbols as in ñaque (junk) and cañón (canyon). You can even turn the ? upside down: ¿.

With two keys, you can put headings flush left, flush right, or centered; put words, sentences, paragraphs, or pages in **boldface** or in *italics;* insert an ellipsis (…) as a single item, instead of three separate periods; and identify chemical formulas (H_2O, H_2SO_4); with three keys, put an apostrophe in front of a letter (rock 'n' roll) or a numeral (class of '12); and with four keys, add footnote numerals ([25]Starr) and algebraic formulas ($a^2 + b^2 = c^2$).

Although computers purport to convert two hyphens (--) into an em dash (—) punctuation mark, they don't. Notice the difference in width. The em dash is the width of the capital M; the en dash is the width of the capital N, thus their names.

Appendix 4

Keyboard Shortcuts
for the Macintosh

— [em dash]—Shift Option Hyphen
– [en dash]—Option Hyphen

ALL CAPS—Command Shift A
SMALL CAPS—Command Shift K
Change Case—Command Option C

Undo Last—Command Z
Recover Last—Command Y
Boldface—Command B
Italics—Command I

<u>Underline</u>—Command U
<u>Double Underline</u>—Command Shift D
<u>Underline</u> <u>Word</u> <u>Only</u>—Command Shift W
~~Strikethrough~~—Command Shift X

Flush Left—Command L
Center—Command E
Flush Right—Command R

Single-Space—Command 1
Double-Space—Command 2
Space and One Half—Command 5

Save—Command S
Save As—Command Shift S
Print—Command P
Page Break—Command Option N

Copy Format—Command Shift C
Paste Format—Command Shift V

Quit—Command Q
New Document—Command N
Eject Memory Stick—Command E

Find—Command F
Hide Copy—Command H

Resize Font
Enlarge Font—Shift Command >
Reduce Font—Shift Command <
Enlarge Font One Point—Command]
Reduce Font One Point—Command [

Quotation Marks
" Smart (Curly) Quote (opening)—Option [
" Smart (Curly) Quote (closing)—Shift Option [
' Smart (Curly) Single Quote (opening)—Option]
' Apostrophe or Smart (Curly) Single Quote (closing)—Shift Option] Class
of '12

… [ellipsis]—Option ;

± —Shift Option +
Ø [zero]—Shift Option O
° [degree 32°]—Shift Option 8

¿ —Shift Option ?
¡ —Option 1

ã ñ õ—Option n letter
á é í ó ú—Option e letter
à è ì ò ù—Option ~ letter
â ê î ô û—Option i letter
ä ë ï ö ü ÿ—Option u letter
ç—Option c

© [copyright]—Option G
™ [trademark]—Option 2
® [registered]—Option R

Highlight one word—Click twice
Highlight one sentence—Command click once

Superscript [footnotes]—Command Shift = numeral
$a^2 + b^2 = c^2$, [23]Starr, Starr[23]
Subscript—Command = numeral H_2SO_4

Endnote—Command Option E
Footnote—Command Option F

Excel: format cells—Command 1
Excel: freeze row, column—select one cell
One row below, one column right of those needed, Window—Freeze Panes

Appendix 5

Keyboard Shortcuts for Every PC

Laptop
— [em dash]—Ctrl Fn Alt colon
- [en dash]—Ctrl Fn colon

Desktop
— [em dash]—Ctrl Alt minus key (on keypad)
- [en dash]—Ctrl minus key (on keypad)

Desktop and Laptop

Center—Ctrl E
Flush Left—Ctrl L
Flush Right—Ctrl R

ALL CAPS—Shift Ctrl A
SMALL CAPS—Shift Ctrl K

Undo Last—Ctrl Z
Redo Last—Ctrl Y
Boldface—Ctrl B
Italics—Ctrl I

Underline—Ctrl U
Double Underline—Shift Ctrl D
Underline Word Only—Shift Ctrl W

Single-Space—Ctrl 1
Double-Space—Ctrl 2
Space and One Half—Ctrl 5

Save—Ctrl S
Save As—F12
Print—Ctrl P
New Document—Ctrl N
Find—Ctrl F
Find and Change—Ctrl H

Copy—Ctrl C
Paste—Ctrl V

¼ —Ctrl Alt 6
½ —Ctrl Alt 7
Increase Font—Shift Ctrl >
Decrease Font—Shift Ctrl <

Ø [Zero]—Ctrl / Shift O
° [Degree]—Ctrl Shift space
© [Copyright]—Ctrl Alt C
™ [Trademark]—Ctrl Alt T
® [Registered]—Ctrl Alt R

Copy Format—Ctrl Shift C
Paste Format—Ctrl Shift V

Rename File or Folder—F2
Change Case—Shift F3

Paragraph Mark—Shift Ctrl 8
Page Break—Ctrl Enter

ã ñ õ—Shift Ctrl tilde letter
á é í ó ú—Ctrl ' [apostrophe] letter
à è ì ò ù—Ctrl ~` letter
â ê î ô û—Shift Ctrl ^ letter
ä ë ï ö ü ÿ—Shift Ctrl : letter
ç —Ctrl Comma c

¿ —Shift Ctrl Alt ?
¡ —Shift Ctrl Alt !

... [ellipsis]—Ctrl Alt .
' [apostrophe]—Ctrl ' ' = Class of '12

Highlight one word—Click twice
Highlight one sentence—Ctrl click once

^{12} [footnote]—Shift Ctrl = numeral ^{12}Starr, Starr^{12}, $a^2 + b^2 = c^2$
$_4$ [subscript]—Ctrl = numeral
H_2SO_4

Excel, multiple lines in one cell—
Type the information—Alt Enter Enter
Excel, format cells—Ctrl 1
Excel, freeze row, column—select one
cell one row below, one column right of those needed, Window—Freeze
Panes
Word Count—Shift Ctrl G
Track Changes On/Off—Shift Ctrl E
Move Line, Paragraph Up/Down—Shift Alt Up/Down Arrow
Macro List—Alt F8
Print Preview—Ctrl F2

Appendix 6

How to Calculate Percentage of Change

When dealing with budgets, crime, taxes, and the like, here's a quick way to calculate the percentage of increase or decrease.

Explaining percentage of change is a standard of news reporting and public relations news releases. People want to know not only how much, in numbers, something increased or decreased but also the percentage of that increase or decrease.

How much, for example, was the increase or decrease, in amount and in percentage, of taxes, tax revenue, budgets, interest, dividends, crime, insurance premiums, the price of gasoline or of potatoes or of utilities or of cell phones or of laptops or of whatever. The list of sought-for increase/decrease information is almost endless.

For example, the state comptroller's report each month on the amount of tax revenue collected notes how much more or less revenue was generated during that month compared to the previous month and to the same month a year ago. The police department provides the same information concerning crimes.

If using percentage of change, you must provide the actual before-and-after numbers, lest confusion result. For example, in each of two cities, the number of murders increased by one. In one city, the increase was from one murder to two murders, an increase of 100 percent. In the other city, the increase was from 100 murders to 101 murders, an increase of 1 percent. Reporting only the percentage increase would indicate, falsely, that the city with a 100 percent increase in murders was far more dangerous than the city with a 1 percent increase.

Calculating percentage of change is based upon elementary school arithmetic, not upon higher mathematics. Percentage of change concerns the difference between two numbers and how much of the first number added to or subtracted from the first number will produce the second number. But don't fret; calculating percentage of change is easy.

Calculation requires but four steps, and they are all simple: List, Subtract, Divide, Multiply. It only sounds complicated. Here is the formula: subtract the smaller number from larger number; divide by the older number; multiply by 100 (or move the decimal point two spaces to the right). The result is the percentage.

The Steps

The key is that the percentage of change is based upon the first number only. Calculate percentage of change this way, in this order:

1. List the numbers in rank order, the older number first.

	Older Amount	Newer Amount
Budget	$1,738,953	$2,033,864

2. Subtract the smaller from the larger.

2,033,864 minus 1,738,953 equals 294,911.

3. Divide by the first number.

294,911 divided by 1,738,953 equals 0.1695911.

4. Multiply by 100 (or move the decimal point two spaces to the right).

0.1695911 times 100 equals 16.95911 or 17 percent.

Because the second number is larger, the change is an increase of 17 percent.

If the numbers are reversed, follow the same procedure.

1. List the numbers in rank order, the older number first.

	Older Amount	Newer Amount
Budget	$2,033,864	$1,738,953

2. Subtract the smaller from the larger.

2,033,864 minus 1,738,953 equals 294,911.

3. Divide by the first number.

294,911 divided by 2,033,864 equals 0.1450003.

4. Multiply by 100 (or move the decimal point two spaces to the right).

0.1450003 times 100 equals 14.50003 or 15 percent.

Because the second number is smaller, the change is a decrease of 15 percent.

Sometimes, you can look at the two numbers and recognize the percentage of change. If the first number is two and the second number is three, the difference, one, is an increase of 50 percent because half of two is one, which, added to two equals three, the second number.

If the first number is three and the second number is two, the difference, one, is a decrease of 33 percent because one-third of the first number, which, subtracted from the first number, equals two, the second number.

Percentage Points

Percentage points differ from percentage of change and from percentages, and need only a definition to make them understandable.

A percentage point is the number that a percentage is increased or decreased.

For example, if a bank increases its interest rate from 10 percent to 15 percent, the percentage of change is an increase of 50 percent, but the new interest rate is an increase of five percentage points, from 10 percent to 15 percent.

If the bank decreases its interest rate from 15 percent to 12 percent, the percentage of change is a decrease of 20 percent, but the new interest is a decrease of three percentage points, from 15 percent to 12 percent.

Appendix 7

Writing Styles of Different News Media

Paper and the Web Similarities

- Use the inverted pyramid, with details in descending order of importance.
- Use the summary lead. In the first two sentences, explain the WHO, the DID WHAT or the SAID WHAT and TO WHOM, the Where, the When, the How, and the Why of the story.
- Get to the point quickly.
- Write tight; no story longer than one screen.
- No paragraph longer than five lines onscreen.
- Write short words and short sentences.
- Strive for conversational style: the active voice: subject, predicate, object. Tell, rather than write, your story.
- Write objectively, no opinion words.
- Use strong verbs.
- Use words correctly.
- Obey the rules of grammar, punctuation, syntax, precise word use and spelling, subject-predicate agreement, noun-pronoun agreement.
- Avoid asking questions in the story.
- Synonyms cause confusion; repeating key words reinforces understandability.
- No paragraph longer than five lines onscreen.
- Use sidebars to explain related information.

Differences

Paper

- No blank space between paragraphs.
- In longer stories, subheads are helpful but unnecessary.

The Web

- Blank space between paragraphs.
- In longer stories, use subheads to break up the screen copy and to alert readers about what is next.

Appendix 8

Terms You Should Know

All-Caps—All capital letters; sometimes referred to as *upper-case* letters.

Ascender—The part of the letter that extends *above* the x-height: b, d, f, h, k, l, t. Note that the d and the t do not ascend as high as the b, f, h, k, l.

Backshop—Where the material is published on paper.

Body Type—The font and size used in the story.

Caption—Sometimes called *cutline*; the description, in present tense, of a photograph or piece of art.

Case—The drawer—upper and lower—in which individual lead letters were kept. The upper case was for capital letters; the lower case, for small letters. Hence, *upper-case* letters and *lower-case* letters.

c/lc—Abbreviation for capital and lower-case letters.

Copy—A story; also called *piece*.

Copyeditor—A person who edits a story for accuracy and completeness and deletes undesirable words, such as redundancies, and corrects the grammar, punctuation, and the like, of stories. The verb is *copyedit*.

Deck—Smaller headline below the primary headline.

Descender—The part of the letter that extends *below* the x-height: g, j, p, q, y.

Edit—To prepare a story for publication by revising and correcting errors of fact.

Font—The family of type, also called *typeface*: Verdana, Garamond, Century Schoolbook, Times New Roman, and so on.

Graf—Paragraph of no more than five lines onscreen and no more than one inch in a column; usually one or two sentences.

Gutter—Space, at least one-eighth inch, between columns of type.

Head—Headline.

Leading (pronounced LEDD-ing)—The space between lines of type, usually one point above and one point below. Thus, *10 on 12* is 10-point type and 2 points of leading (one point above and one point below the line).

Masthead—The listing, usually on page two, of information about the publication, i.e., name, address, telephone numbers, email, Website, publisher.

Nameplate—Name of the publication, usually on page one or on the cover and on the masthead.

News hole—The space for news stories after the advertising is placed on a page.

Page One—The front page of a newspaper.

Piece—A story; also called *copy*.

Point—X-height is measured in points; 72 points per inch.

Proofread—One person reads the original copy, and another person reads printer's proofs and marks corrections to be made. It does not substitute for *copyediting*.

Pullquote—Excerpts pulled from the text for display in a larger size.

Rim—The desk where the copyeditors sit.

Sans Serif—Type that stands vertical and has no extra squiggles or feet.

Serif—A line projecting vertically or horizontally from a letter.

Slot—The chief copyeditor.

Style—The mechanical requirements of the publication, i.e., abbreviations, capitalizations, use of numbers. It does not apply to your writing style, which is personal.

Subhead—Small headline, usually 18-point, one-line, to break up long sections of text and to alert readers as to what is next.

Typeface—Same as *font*.

X-Height—The height of a lower-case x.

Paragraph Length for Reading Onscreen and on Paper

To make reading easier both on onscreen and in a two-inch-wide column on paper, the beginning sentence should be no longer than 30 to 35 words, no more than 2½ lines onscreen, and no paragraph should be longer than five lines.

In a narrow column in a newspaper or a magazine, five lines onscreen measures one inch, providing plenty of white space, which make reading easier. To facilitate reading 12-point type onscreen, stories on the Web page should provide plenty of white space by following the five-line requirement for paragraphs and by adding a blank line between paragraphs.

Appendix 9

What to Expect from Reporters from Different News Media

Television	*Radio*	*Newspaper*	*Internet*
Reaches most people, but they must be tuned in or go online	Reaches many people, but they must be tuned in	Reaches fewer people, but they must wait until published or go online	Reaches many people, but they must be online
You have some control, because audience sees/ hears you speak your own words.	You have some control, because audience hears you speak your own words.	You have little control, because reporters interpret your words.	You have some control, depending upon which medium's reporter conducts interview.
Reporter *willing* to provide questions in advance, because of time constraints.	Reporter *willing* to provide questions in advance, because of time-constraints.	Reporter *never* willing to provide questions in advance. Newspapers have no time constraints.	Television, radio *willing*, newspaper *never* willing to provide questions in advance.
Magnifies voice quality, gestures, expressions	Magnifies voice quality	Hides emotions	Does all three

Bibliography

Michael Agnes, editor in chief, *Webster's New World College Dictionary*, 4th ed. (Cleveland, OH: Wiley Publishing, 2005).

Robert Lee Brewer, *2014 Writer's Market* (Cincinnati, OH: Writer's Digest Books, 2013).

Darrell Christian, Sally Jacobsen, and David Minthorn, eds., *The Associated Press Stylebook and Briefing on Media Law* (New York: Basic Books, 2013).

Darwin Patnode, *Robert's Rules of Order: Modern Edition*, revised (Uhrichsville, OH: Barbour & Company, 1996).

Alice Sturgis, *The Standard Code of Parliamentary Procedure*, 4th ed., Revised and Updated (New York: McGraw-Hill Book Company, 2001).

Index

calculating, 277–79; as percentages, 101, 108, 114–15; roundups, 169–70; tax revenue, 101–3; tax revenue reports, 112–14; tax revenue story, writing, 114–16

technical news, 147–51; most important questions, 147; and prepublication review, 17

telephone, 10–11, 98, 121, 123, 170, 222, 250

television news, 32–33, 47, 245; broadcast news writing, 54–59; and handling the press, 179; reporters, 284

temperatures (style requirements), 64

Tenth Amendment, 8

tenure, 21, 87–88, 93, 95, 97

terms, 282–83

terrorism, 2, 48, 106

Third Amendment, 6–7

tickler files, 222

timeliness, 178, 216

time (style requirements), 65

titles, 10, 27, 99, 110, 142, 149–50, 158; audience analysis, 208–9; and CEO letter to stockholders, 126; the Fact Sheet, 191; style requirements, 66. *See also* names

tort, 131

transitions, 31, 204

trial, covering, 144–45. *See also* court reporting

trial court, three kinds of, 131–32

trial proceedings, 137–39

truthfulness. *See* honesty

Twitter, 2, 245

typeface. *See* fonts

United States: abbreviations, 66; freedoms, protection of, 5–9; future of, 3–4, 244–47; role of free press in, 1–3, 5–9, 24, 49, 244–45, 247. *See also specific topics,* e.g., government

universities, 86–87, 108; covering, 92–99; faculty as source, 21; libraries, 21; university story, writing, 98. *See*

also degree programs; education, covering; *specific topics,* e.g., research; tenure

U.S. Congress, 74–76, 78–79, 100, 103, 132, 147

U.S. Constitution, 8, 46, 48, 131, 133, 149, 245; constitutional protections, 133–34. *See also* Bill of Rights

U.S. Securities and Exchange Commission (SEC). *See* Securities and Exchange Commission

U.S. Supreme Court, 8, 66, 107, 133, 140–41

verbs: action, 37, 142, 172, 197, 202; of attribution, 73, 257–62; compound, 203

verdicts, 131–32, 137, 139

victims: keeping details private, 143; talking to, 16

video reporting, 33, 42, 50, 179, 245

vignettes, 167, 172

visual aids, 158, 220–21

Vital Speeches of the Day, 217

voice recorders, 8, 13–14, 164–65, 180, 201, 233, 243

voir dire, 138

voting, 36, 48, 247; responsibility to vote, 247; right to vote, 48, 134; votes (style requirements), 64. *See also specific topics,* e.g., groups, and covering meetings; political campaigns

The Wall Street Journal, 119

The Wall Street Journal format, 167

Web. *See* Internet

Weblogs. *See* blogs

Webmasters, 51, 53

Websites, 2, 11, 33, 50, 86, 179, 283

Webster's New World College Dictionary, 4th ed., 61, 257–58

Wells, Christine, 1

Who, What, Where, When, Why, and How, 13, 25, 29–32, 43–44, 70, 72. *See also specific topics,* e.g., meetings, covering

"who" leads, 29–30, 43–44, 70, 72,
   80–82, 99, 115–16, 128, 143
Who's Who editions, 20
wire services, 217
witnesses, in court proceedings, 7, 134,
   137–38, 144–45
witnesses and petitioners, 75–76,
   78–81
women, attire and appearance: for
   job interviews, 254; reporters, 13;
   subjects, describing, 172
word use: definition and usage, 263–
   69; editing and copyediting, 198;
   precise, 25, 36, 42, 198–99, 257,
   280
workers' compensation, 107;
   freelancing and, 174, 193–94
World Wide Web. *See* Internet

wrap-up stories, 145
writer, in chain of publishing, 60
Writer's Market, 174–75
writing: basic writing advice, 37–38;
   characteristics of good, 25, 201–2,
   269; clear, 25, 201–2; difficulty of,
   25, 192; final act in, 32; polishing,
   197; in public relations, 187–91;
   rules of thumb, general, 41–42;
   styles of different news media, 280–
   81. *See also* news writing; *specific
   topics*, e.g., feature stories
writing off the wall, 26

yes-or-no questions/answers, 13, 178,
   181, 243

zoning, 75, 111

About the Authors

Douglas Perret Starr has had a varied career. As an Associated Press newsman he covered civil rights and government issues and was part of a Pulitzer Prize–winning team. He worked as a copyeditor for three newspapers, served as a speech ghostwriter for the Florida state insurance commissioner and the lieutenant governor, and has held positions as a professor of journalism and public relations at three universities. He wrote and copyedited columns for numerous publications and professional organizations, and wrote safety manuals for the U.S. Coast Guard and the U.S. Departments of Defense and of Homeland Security. He received his B.A. in journalism from Louisiana State University and his M.A. and Ph.D. in Communication from Florida State University. He is professor emeritus at Texas A&M University and a retired USCG Commander.

Deborah Williams Dunsford, Ph.D., is a senior lecturer in Texas A&M University's Department of Agricultural Leadership, Education, and Communications. She has more than 30 years' experience in teaching, public relations, media writing, and media training. Dunsford has written for publications including *Modern Bride*; the Raleigh, N.C., *News and Observer*; and the Fayetteville, N.C., *Observer-Times*. Her professional training duties have included media and presentation skills sessions for clients and professional organizations and crisis management planning. Dunsford teaches media writing, editing, public relations, technical writing, and career planning. Her agricultural journalism bachelor's degree is from Kansas State University and her master's and Ph.D. are in English from Texas A&M University.